Tax and Family Breakdown

Related titles from Law Society Publishing:

Ancillary Relief
Andrew Newbury, Shona Alexander and Ann Corrigan

Domestic Abuse
Jane Wilson

Resolution Family Disputes Handbook
General Editor: Andrew Greensmith

Resolution Family Law Handbook (2dn edn)
General Editor: Andrew Greemsmith

Pensions and Family Breakdown (2nd edn)
David Davidson

Titles from Law Society Publishing can be ordered from all good bookshops or direct (telephone 0870 850 1422, email **lawsociety@prolog.uk.com** or visit our online shop at **www.lawsociety.org.uk/bookshop**).

TAX AND FAMILY BREAKDOWN

A Practical Guide

Jason Lane

The Law Society

All rights reserved. No part of this publication may be reproduced in any material form, whether by photocopying, scanning, downloading onto computer or otherwise without the written permission of the Law Society except in accordance with the provisions of the Copyright, Designs and Patents Act 1988. Applications should be addressed in the first instance, in writing, to Law Society Publishing. Any unauthorised or restricted act in relation to this publication may result in civil proceedings and/or criminal prosecution.

The author has asserted the right under the Copyright, Designs and Patents Act 1988 to be identified as author of this work.

While all reasonable care has been taken in the preparation of this publication, neither the publisher nor the author can accept any responsibility for any loss occasioned to any person acting or refraining from action as a result of relying upon its contents.

The views expressed in this publication should be taken as those of the author only unless it is specifically indicated that the Law Society has given its endorsement.

© The Law Society 2010

Material in the Appendices is Crown copyright and is reproduced here with the permission of the Controller of Her Majesty's Stationery Office

ISBN-13: 978-1-85328-614-8

Published in 2010 by the Law Society
113 Chancery Lane, London WC2A 1PL

Typeset by IDSUK (DataConnection Ltd)
Printed by Hobbs the Printers Ltd, Totton, Hants

The paper used for the text pages of this book is FSC certified. FSC (the Forest Stewardship Council) is an international network to promote responsible management of the world's forests.

Contents

About the author viii
Acknowledgements ix
Table of cases x
Table of statutes xiii
Table of statutory instruments xvi
Abbreviations xvii
New developments xix

Introduction: A tax perspective on financial settlements   1

1 Spouses, civil partners and cohabitees   3

    1.1 Introduction   3
    1.2 Form E   4

2 Capital gains tax   5

    2.1 General principles   6
    2.2 Hold over relief   15
    2.3 Entrepreneurs' relief   22
    2.4 The investment portfolio   28
    2.5 Land and property assets   29

3 Transfers of assets   30

    3.1 General transfers of assets: deemed market value rule   30
    3.2 Transfers of assets between connected persons   30
    3.3 Transfers of assets between couples who are married and living together   32
    3.4 Transfers of assets between couples who are married but separated   34

CONTENTS

		3.5 Transfers of assets between cohabitees or post decree absolute	42
4	**Inheritance tax and trusts**		**44**
	4.1	Inheritance tax	44
	4.2	Business property relief	55
	4.3	Agricultural property relief	58
	4.4	Gifts with reservation of benefit and pre-owned assets	60
5	**Maintenance and secured maintenance**		**64**
	5.1	Types of maintenance	64
	5.2	Maintenance payments	64
	5.3	Secured maintenance	65
	5.4	Tax credits and family breakdown	68
6	**Interests in land and property**		**71**
	6.1	The family home	71
	6.2	*Mesher* orders and transfers of property	78
	6.3	More than one property	82
	6.4	Stamp duty land tax	85
	6.5	Holiday homes or buy-to-let investment property	86
	6.6	Exchange of interests in land and property	86
7	**Stamp duty and stamp duty land tax**		**91**
	7.1	Transactions on family breakdown	91
	7.2	Exemptions	92
	7.3	Shares subject to a debt	92
	7.4	Property subject to a charge or mortgage	93
	7.5	Gifts	94
	7.6	Transfers of shares or property to a shareholder as part of a liquidation of a company	94
	7.7	Transfer of property on winding up: loan from shareholder	95
8	**Pensions, life assurance and other matters**		**96**
	8.1	Pensions	96
	8.2	Life assurance policies and investment bonds	98
	8.3	Obtaining tax relief on borrowing to fund lump sum or maintenance payments	100

	8.4	Tax considerations in unlocking assets held by family companies	101
9	**The international dimension**		**110**
	9.1	Scope of UK taxes	110
	9.2	Residence, ordinary residence and domicile	112
	9.3	Remittance basis	115
	9.4	What is a remittance?	116
	9.5	Offshore structures and anti-avoidance legislation	117
	9.6	Remittance basis in the context of divorce	122
	9.7	Commonly encountered offshore structures	125
10	**Valuation in the context of tax and family breakdown**		**128**
	10.1	Market value	128
	10.2	Capital gains tax	129
	10.3	Inheritance tax	132
	10.4	Valuation of private company shares: agreed valuation binding on both parties for tax purposes	133
	10.5	Brief overview of main valuation bases for private company shares	134
	10.6	Quasi-partnership companies: HMRC view	139
	10.7	Valuation of family companies in the context of court proceedings	140
	10.8	Undivided shares in jointly held land and property	142
	10.9	Valuation of partnership interests	143
	10.10	Contingent corporation tax	144

Appendices

1	Inheritance (Provision for Family and Dependants) Act 1975	146
2	Matrimonial Causes Act 1973, Part II	169
3	Matrimonial and Family Proceedings Act 1984, Part III	207
4	Children Act 1989, extracts	218
5	Civil Partnership Act 2004, Part 2, Chapters 3–5	231
6	Form CG34 – Post-transaction valuation checks for capital gains	237
7	Form E	240
8	Form E Notes for guidance	268

Index 272

About the author

Jason Lane, BA (Hons) CTA, is head of tax at Saffery Champness, an independent top 20 firm of chartered accountants which provides advice to individuals, owner-managed businesses, families, trusts, charities and landed estates. A member of the firm's forensic matrimonial team, he regularly reports on, and has given evidence in, family proceedings. Jason also presents seminars on essential tax issues for family practitioners.

Acknowledgements

This book has been a combined effort of various partners and tax staff within the firm. Mike Lichten, a specialist tax partner, has made a substantial contribution to chapters 4 and 9. Clare Cromwell and Peter Horsman, tax partners with expertise in family proceedings, have been invaluable sources of advice on other chapters. I am also grateful to Adam Kay and James Walker for the contributions they have made to various chapters. I would particularly like to thank Barbara Campbell-Smith for her assistance in managing the process from start to finish and dealing with the numerous amendments.

I gratefully acknowledge Central Law Training (CLT) for allowing me to use my course notes on this subject as the basis for this book. I am also grateful to the many CLT delegates who have attended my courses and the inspiration they have given to me.

Table of cases

A v. A; *sub nom.* NA v. MA [2006] EWHC 2900 (Fam); [2007] 1 FLR 1760,
    Fam Div 10.7
Administrators of the Estate of Caton v. Couch. *See* Couch (Inspector of
    Taxes) v. Administrators of the Estate of Caton
Arnander v. Revenue and Customs Commissioners [2007] RVR 208; [2006]
    STC (SCD) 800, Sp Comm 4.3.4
Aspden (Inspector of Taxes) v. Hildesley [1982] 1 WLR 264; (1981) 55
    TC 609, DC 3.4.3
Bird Precision Bellows Ltd, Re; *sub nom.* Company (No.003420 of 1981),
    Re [1986] Ch. 658; [1986] 2 WLR 158, CA (Civ Div); *affirming* [1984]
    Ch. 419, Ch D 10.6
Carson v. Carson [1983] 1 WLR 285; [1983] 1 All ER 478, CA (Civ Div) 6.2.1
Cash and Carry v. Inspector of Taxes. *See* Denekamp v. Pearce ....
Charman v. Charman [2007] EWCA Civ 503; [2007] 1 FLR 1246, CA
    (Civ Div); *affirming* [2006] EWHC 1879; [2007] 1 FLR 593, Fam Div 10.7
Couch (Inspector of Taxes) v. Administrators of the Estate of Caton; *sub
    nom.* Administrators of the Estate of Caton v. Couch (Inspector of
    Taxes); Caton's Administrators v. Couch (Inspector of Taxes) [1995]
    STC (SCD) 34, Sp Comm 10.5.2
D v. D [2007] EWHC 278 (Fam); [2007] 2 FLR 653, Fam Div 10.7
De Lasala v. De Lasala [1980] AC 546; [1979] 3 WLR 390, PC (HK) 3.4.3
Denekamp v. Pearce; *subnom.* Cash and Carry v. Inspector of Taxes (1998)
    TC 213; [1998] STC 1120, Ch D 10.5.2
Dennis (dec'd), Re; *sub nom.* Dennis v. Lloyds Bank Plc [1981] 2 All ER
    140; (1980) 124 SJ 885, Ch D 4.1.10
Dinch v. Dinch [1987] 1 WLR 252; [1987] 1 All ER 818, HL 6.2.1
Eurofinance Group Ltd, Re. *See* Parkinson v. Eurofinance Group Ltd
Farmer v. Inland Revenue Commissioners [1999] STC (SCD) 321,
    Sp Comm 4.2.2
G v. G (Financial Provision: Equal Division) [2002] EWHC 1339 (Fam);
    [2002] 2 FLR 1143, Fam Div 2.2.7, 2.2.9,
                                                                    8.2.2, 9.6.1, 10.7
Gaines-Cooper v. Revenue and Customs Commissioners [2007] STC (SCD)
    23; 9 ITL Rep. 274, Sp Comm 9.2.1
Gray v. Inland Revenue Commissioners; *sub nom.* Executors of Lady Fox v.
    Inland Revenue Commissioners; Lady Fox's Executors v. Inland Revenue

x

TABLE OF CASES

Commissioners [1994] STC 360; [1994] 38 EG 156, CA (Civ Div);
   reversing [1992] 1 EGLR 211, Lands Tr 10.9
Haines *v.* Hill. *See* Hill *v.* Haines
Harvey (Inspector of Taxes) *v.* Sivyer [1986] Ch. 119; (1987) 58 TC 569,
   Ch D 3.4.3, 4.1.8
Hazell *v.* Hazell [1972] 1 WLR 301; [1972] 1 All ER 923, CA (Civ Div) 6.1.1
Hill *v.* Haines; *sub nom.* Haines *v.* Hill [2007] EWCA Civ 1284; [2008]
   Ch. 412, CA (Civ Div); *reversing* [2007] EWHC 1012 (Ch), Ch D 2.2.7,
                                                                                                    2.2.9, 9.6.1
HMRC *v.* Trustees of the Nelson Dance Family Settlement. *See* Nelson
   Dance Family Settlement Trustees *v.* Revenue and Customs
   Commissioners
Holmes *v.* Mitchell (Inspector of Taxes) [1991] STC 25; [1991] 2 FLR 301,
   Ch D 3.4.2
Hopes *v.* Hopes [1949] P 227; [1948] 2 All ER 920, CA 3.4.2
Inland Revenue Commissioners *v.* Plummer [1977] 1 WLR 1227; [1977]
   STC 440, Ch D 4.1.7, 4.1.8
Irvine *v.* Irvine [2006] EWHC 1875 (Ch); [2006] WTLR 1417, Ch D 10.7
Lloyds TSB Bank Plc (Personal Representative of Antrobus (dec'd)) *v.*
   Inland Revenue Commissioners [2002] STC (SCD) 468; [2002]
   WTLR 1435, Sp Comm 4.3.4
Lynall *v.* Inland Revenue Commissioners; *sub nom.* Lynall (dec'd), Re [1972]
   AC 680; [1971] 3 WLR 759, HL; *reversing* [1970] Ch. 138, CA (Civ Div);
   reversing [1969] 1 Ch. 421, Ch D 10.2.4
MacArthur (dec'd) *v.* HMRC [2008] STC 1100, Sp Comm 10.5.2
Marren (Inspector of Taxes) *v.* Ingles [1980] 1 WLR 983; [1980] 3 All ER 95,
   HL; *affirming* [1979] 1 WLR 1131, CA (Civ Div); *reversing in part*
   [1979] STC 58, Ch D 3.4.6
Mesher *v.* Mesher [1980] 1 All ER 126 (Note), CA (Civ Div) 6.2.1
NA *v.* MA. *See* A *v.* A
Nelson Dance Family Settlement Trustees *v.* Revenue and Customs
   Commissioners; *sub nom.* Revenue and Customs Commissioners *v.*
   Nelson Dance Family Settlement Trustees [2009] EWHC 71 (Ch);
   [2009] STC 802, Ch D; *affirming* [2008] STC (SCD) 792, Sp Comm 4.2.1
Parkinson *v.* Eurofinance Group Ltd; *sub nom.* Eurofinance Group Ltd,
   Re [2001] BCC 551; [2001] 1 BCLC 720, Ch D 10.7
Phizackerley *v.* Revenue and Customs Commissioners [2007] STC (SCD)
   328; [2007] WTLR 745, Sp Comm 4.1.10
R *v.* Barnet LBC, *ex p.* Shah (Nilish); R *v.* Shropshire CC *ex p.* Abdullah;
   Ablack *v.* Inner London Education Authority; Shah (Jitendra) *v.*
   Barnet LBC; Shabpar *v.* Barnet LBC; Abdullah *v.* Shropshire CC;
   Akbarali *v.* Brent LBC [1983] 2 AC 309; [1983] 2 WLR 16, HL;
   reversing [1982] QB 688, CA (Civ Div); *affirming* [1981]
   2 WLR 86, QBD 9.2.2
Shinebond Ltd *v.* Carrol (Inspector of Taxes) [2006] STC (SCD) 147;
   [2006] WTLR 697, Sp Comm 10.10
Starke *v.* Inland Revenue Commissioners [1995] 1 WLR 1439; [1995]
   STC 689, CA (Civ Div); *affirming* [1994] 1 WLR 888, Ch D 4.3.4

xi

TABLE OF CASES

Strahan *v.* Wilcock [2006] EWCA Civ 13; [2006] BCC 320, CA
(Civ Div) 10.7
Todd (Inspector of Taxes) *v.* Mudd [1987] STC 141; (1986) 60 TC 237, DC ... 6.1.5
Walton *v.* Inland Revenue Commissioners [1996] STC 68; [1996] 1
EGLR 159, CA (Civ Div); *affirming* [1994] 38 EG 161, Lands Tr 10.2.4
Wanbon *v.* Wanbon [1946] All ER 366, PDAD 3.4.2
White *v.* White [2001] 1 AC 596; [2000] 2 FLR 981, HL; *affirming* [1999]
Fam. 304, CA (Civ Div) .... Intro
Xydhias *v.* Xydhias [1999] 2 All ER 386; [1999] 1 FLR 683, CA
(Civ Div) 2.2.9
Yates (Inspector of Taxes) *v.* Starkey [1951] Ch. 465; (1951) 32 TC 38,
CA; *affirming* [1951] Ch. 45, Ch D 4.1.8

Table of statutes

Children Act 1989 . . . . .4.1.5
   s.15 .App.4
   Sched.1 . . . . .App.4
      para.1(2)(d) 4.1.10
Civil Partnership Act 2004 . . . .1.1, 6.1.5
   Part 2, Ch.3–5 . . . . .App.5
   s.66 . . . . .6.1.1
Companies Act 1985
   s.459 . . . . .10.6, 10.7
Companies Act 2006
   s.994. . . . . .10.6
Corporation Tax Act 2010
   Part 22
      Ch.1 . . . . .8.4.5
   Part 23
      ss.1059–63 . . . . .8.4.5
Domicile and Matrimonial Proceedings
   Act 1973. . . . . .9.2.3
Family Law (Scotland) Act 1985 . .8.2.2
   s.8 . . . . .7.2
   s.14(1) .7.2
Finance Act 1965 . . . . .2(Intro)
Finance Act 1985
   s.83 . . . . .7.2
Finance Act 1986 . . . . .7.1
Finance Act 1988. . . . . .3.3.4
   s.60 . . . . .4.1.7, 6.1.1
   s.68 . . . . .2(Intro), 4.1.7
Finance Act 2003
   s.50 . . . . .6.4
   s.55 . . . . .6.4
   s.95 . . . . .7.4
   s.96 . . . . .7.4
   Sched.3
      para.1 . . . . .7.5
      para.3 . . . . .6.6.2

      (a) 7.4
      para.4 . . . . .7.3
   Sched.4
      para.6 . . . . .6.6.2
      para.8 . . . . .7.4
      (1B) 7.4
Finance Act 2004. . . . . .8.1.1
Finance Act 2006 . . . . .4.1.4, 4.1.5
Finance Act 2007
   Sched.26, para.4 . . . . .10.2.2
Income and Corporation Taxes
   Act 1988
      s.419 . . . . .8.4.2
      Sched.14 . . . . .8.2.3
Income Tax Act 2007
   Part 4
      Ch.6 . . . . .2.1.8
   Part 5
      s.209 . . . . .2.4
   Part 8
      Ch.3 . . . . .6.3.3
      Ch.5 . . . . .5.2.1
   Part 9
      s.466(2) 4.1.7
   Part 14
      s.809C 9.3.3
      s.809L 9.4.2
      ss.809L–809S 9.4
      s.811 . . . . .9.1.1
      s.837 . . . . .8.4.3
   Part 16
      s.1011 . . . . .3.3.4
Income Tax (Trading and Other Income)
   Act 2005
   Part 3
      Ch.6. . . . . .6.5

TABLE OF STATUTES

Part 4
    s.415 .... 8.4.2
    Ch.9 .... 8.2.2
    s.535 .... 8.2.2
Part 5
    Ch.5 .... 5.3.1, 9.5.1
    s.619 .... 9.5.1
    s.620 .... 5.3.1
        (1) 4.1.7, 4.1.8
    s.627 .... 5.3.1
    s.629 .... 5.3.1
Inheritance (Provision for Family and Dependants) Act 1975 .... App.1
Inheritance Tax Act 1984
    s.3(1) 10.3
    s.10 .... 4.1.10
        (1) 4.1.5
    s.11 .... 4.1.5, 4.1.10
    s.18 .... 4.1.5
    s.19 .... 4.1.5
    s.20 .... 4.1.5
    s.21 .... 4.1.5
    s.22 .... 4.1.5
    s.43(2) 4.1.7
    s.94 .... 4.1.1
    s.104 .... 4.2.1
    s.105 .... 4.2.1
    s.107 .... 4.2.4
    s.113B 4.2.5
    s.115(2) 2.2.4
    s.160 .... 10.3
    s.161 .... 4.1.1
    s.168 .... 10.3
    s.267 .... 9.1.3
Married Women's Property Act 1882
    s.17 .... 6.1.1
Matrimonial and Family Proceedings Act 1984
    Part III App.3
Matrimonial Causes Act 1973 .... Intro, 4.1.5, 6.1.5, 8.2.2
    Part II App.2
        s.22A 7.2
        s.23A 7.2
        s.24A 7.2
        s.24 .... 2.2.9
        s.25 .... Intro
        s.31 .... 2.1.11

Matrimonial Homes Act 1967 .... 6.1.5
Matrimonial Proceedings and Property Act 1970 .... 6.1.5
Pensions Act 1995 .... 8.1.2
Stamp Act 1891 .... 7.1
    s.57 .... 7.3, 7.6
Tax Credits Act 2002
    s.3(5) 5.4.1, 5.4.2
    s.32(3) 5.4.2
    s.37(1) 5.4.2
Taxation of Chargeable Gains Act 1992
    Part I
        s.2 .... 9.1.2
        s.3A 3.3.5
        s.10 .... 2.1.1
        s.10A 2.1.1
        s.13 .... 9.1.2, 9.5.2
    Part II
        s.16(2A) 2.1.8
        s.16ZA 2.1.8
        s.16A 2.1.8
        s.17 .... 3.1, 3.2.1, 10.2.6
        s.18 .... 3.3.1, 10.2.5
            (3) 3.2.3
            (6) 10.2.5
        s.21 .... 2(Intro)
            (1)(b) 2.1.6
        s.22 .... 2(Intro), 2.1.11, 3.4.6
        s.24 .... 2(Intro)
        s.28 .... 3.4.3
        s.37 .... 8.4.5
        s.38 .... 2.1.4
        s.44 .... 2.1.6, 2.1.7
        s.45 .... 2.1.6, 2.1.7
        s.48 .... 3.4.9
        s.51 .... 2.1.6
    Part III
        s.58 .... 3.3.1, 3.3.2, 3.3.5
        s.70 .... 6.2.2
        s.71 .... 5.3.2, 6.2.2
        s.73 .... 5.3.2
        s.86 .... 9.1.2, 9.5.2
        s.87 .... 9.1.2, 9.5.2
        Ch.II .... 2(Intro)
    Part IV
        s.115 .... 2.1.6
        s.116 .... 2.3.4
        s.117 .... 2.3.4

TABLE OF STATUTES

s.121 . . . . .2.1.6
s.135 . . . . .2.3.4
s.144 . . . . .8.4.5
s.150A 2.1.6
s.151 . . . . .2.1.6
Part V
   s.152 . . . . .6.6.3
   s.165 . . . .2.2.2, 2.2.3, 2.2.4, 2.3.7
      (1)(b) 2.2.7
   s.166 . . . . .2.2.7
   s.168 . . . . .2.2.7
      (7) 2.2.7
   Ch.III 2.3.1
   s.169Q 2.3.4
Part VI
   s.210 . . . . .2.1.6, 8.2.1
      (3) 8.2.1
   s.221(4) 8.4.4
Part VII
   ss.222–6 . . . . .6.1.5
   s.222(5) 6.3.2
      (6) 6.3.1
   s.223 . . . . .2.1.6
      (3) 6.1.5
      (4) 6.1.5

s.224(3) 6.3.3
s.225 . . . . .6.6.2
s.225B 6.1.5, 6.2.2
s.226A 6.1.5
s.247 . . . . .6.6.2
s.248 . . . . .6.6.2
s.248A 6.6.2
ss.248A–248E 2.1.5, 6.2.2
s.251 . . . . .2.1.6
s.260 . . . .2.2.2, 2.2.3, 2.2.4, 2.3.7
s.262 . . . . .2.1.7
s.263 . . . . .2.1.6, 2.1.7
s.268 . . . . .2.1.6
s.269 . . . . .2.1.6
Part VIII
   s.272. . . . . .10.2
   s.273 . . . . .10.2.4
   s.286 . . . . .3.2.2, 10.2.5
      (2) 3.2.4
Sched.7 . . . . .2.2.2
   Part II 2.2.6
     para.7 . . . . .2.3.7
Welfare Reform and Pensions
   Act 1999 . . . . .8.1.3

Table of statutory instruments

Capital Gains Tax Regulations 1967, SI 1967/149 .... 10.4
Stamp Duty (Exempt Instruments) Regulations 1987, SI 1987/516 .... 7.2
Tax and Civil Partnership Regulations 2005, SI 2005/3229 .... 1.1
Tax Credits (Claims and Notifications) (Amendment) Regulations 2006, SI 2006/2689
    reg.6 .... 5.4.2
Tax Credits (Claims and Notifications) Regulations 2002, SI 2002/2014
    reg.21(3) 5.4.2

Abbreviations

A&M	accumulation and maintenance
AEA	annual exempt amount
AIM	Alternative Investment Market
APR	agricultural property relief
BATR	business asset taper relief
BPR	business property relief
CGT	capital gains tax
CTA	Corporation Tax Act
CTT	capital transfer tax
DCF	discounted cash flow
EBIT	earnings before interest and tax
EBITDA	earnings before interest, tax, depreciation and amortisation
EEA	European Economic Area
EIS	enterprise investment scheme
ER	entrepreneurs' relief
ESC	Extra Statutory Concession
GROB	gift with reservation of benefit
HMRC	HM Revenue and Customs
ICTA	Income and Corporation Taxes Act
IHT	inheritance tax
IHTA	Inheritance Tax Act
IT	income tax
ITA	Income Tax Act
ITTOIA	Income Tax (Trading and Other Income) Act
MCA	Matrimonial Causes Act
NIC	national insurance contribution
NRB	nil rate band
P/E	price/earnings
PET	potentially exempt transfer
POAT	pre-owned asset tax
PPR	principal private residence
QCB	qualifying corporate bond
RBC	remittance basis charge

ABBREVIATIONS

SDLT	stamp duty land tax
TCA	Tax Credits Act
TCGA	Taxation of Chargeable Gains Act
ToV	transfer of value
VCT	venture capital trust
WACC	weighted average cost of capital

New developments

Following publication of the coalition Government's Finance Bill on 1 July 2010, changes are to be made to capital gains tax (CGT) and entrepreneurs' relief (**Chapter 2**).

The changes made replace the single 18 per cent rate of CGT for individuals and trustees, etc. with effect from 23 June 2010 for gains arising on or after that date.

Please see the News, Events and Publications section of **www.saffery.com** and use the 'Newsletters and other publications' drop-down search box to access the latest edition of the tax tables.

INDIVIDUALS (CHAPTER 2)

For individuals, the rate at which gains (other than gains qualifying for entrepreneurs' relief) are charged will depend on the individual's top rate of income tax for the year.

If an individual's taxable income is lower than the maximum of their basic rate band, gains up to the amount of the shortfall are charged at 18 per cent.

Any other gains of individuals are charged at 28 per cent.

ENTREPRENEURS' RELIEF (2.3)

Gains qualifying for entrepreneurs' relief will be charged at a new 10 per cent rate, instead of being reduced by four-ninths and charged at 18 per cent, and the lifetime limit on total gains eligible for relief is increased from £2 million to £5 million (having previously been increased from £1 million from 6 April 2010).

TRUSTEES AND PERSONAL REPRESENTATIVES

Gains of trustees of settlements and personal representatives of deceased persons are charged at 28 per cent.

NEW DEVELOPMENTS

GAINS ARISING IN THE TAX YEAR ENDING 5 APRIL 2011

Because different gains may be charged at different rates of CGT, there is a new rule that losses and the annual exempt amount (AEA) are deductible from gains in the order that gives the best result for the taxpayer. This will normally mean that losses and the AEA are deducted first from the gains potentially liable at the highest rate.

Because the changes to the rates of CGT take effect part of the way though the 2010/11 tax year, gains arising between 6 April 2010 and 22 June 2010 are chargeable under the old rules at 18 per cent, with gains qualifying for entrepreneurs' relief being reduced by four-ninths before being charged.

Gains arising on or after 23 June 2010 are charged under the new rules, as explained above.

CGT LOSSES

The rule for deduction of losses will apply to all gains of the 2010/11 year. This will normally involve losses and the AEA being deducted:

- firstly from gains (other than gains qualifying for entrepreneurs' relief) arising on or after 23 June 2010 that are chargeable at 28 per cent or 18 per cent;
- then from gains arising between 6 April 2010 and 22 June 2010 (including gains qualifying for entrepreneurs' relief that have been reduced by four-ninths) that are chargeable at the previous single 18 per cent rate; and
- finally from gains arising on or after 23 June 2010 that qualify for entrepreneurs' relief and are chargeable at the new 10 per cent rate.

INTRODUCTION
A tax perspective on financial settlements

The court's jurisdiction in financial relief on family breakdown is discretionary and is exercised within the guidelines set out in the Matrimonial Causes Act (MCA) 1973, s.25. The overarching principle as laid down by the House of Lords in *White* v. *White* [2000] 2 FLR 981 is one of fairness. In determining what is a fair result, the court will have regard to all the circumstances of the case in question. In balancing the needs and entitlements of the various parties involved, the exercise of the court's powers to make a financial settlement will generally involve a division and transfer of the family's assets (such as the family home) or rights to any future benefits (e.g. pension sharing) or future earnings (e.g. by way of maintenance) between the parties.

Even in less complex financial cases, the exercise of the court's powers in effecting a divison of the funds and assets available to the parties may have potential consequences in respect of:

- capital gains tax (CGT) where assets are transferred;
- inheritance tax (IHT) where assets are transferred;
- income tax where earnings, maintenance and future income are involved;
- stamp duty and stamp duty land tax (SDLT) where shares or real property are transferred.

In the more complex or 'big money' financial cases, actual or potential CGT liabilities (and other tax liabilities where appropriate) need to be brought into account since tax liabilities are a relevant consideration for the completion of Form E (see **1.2** and **Appendix 7**) in order to arrive at the net (i.e. after tax) value of assets available to the parties on any determination and fair division of the overall assets as part of a financial settlement.

Since 6 April 1990 and the advent of independent taxation, married couples have been taxed as independent individuals with their own income tax bands, allowances and reliefs. The same also applies to those who have entered into a civil partnership. Whilst there are a number of tax reliefs which apply to transfers of assets between parties to a marriage or civil partnership, these reliefs are often narrowly drawn and affected by legal separation, so careful planning is often necessary to ensure that the settlement is structured in a way that avoids or mitigates unnecessary tax costs.

Those advising on the structuring of financial settlements following legal separation therefore need to have an understanding of the potential tax implications, in addition to the ability to recognise at an early stage when it is necessary to seek more specialist tax advice. This may help to ensure protection from any potential negligence claims in circumstances where a reasonable person would assume that those advising on such matters would have a basic understanding of the tax consequences of the effects of their advice, even though the giving of specific tax advice may be excluded under the terms of client engagement.

The law is stated as at 8 April 2010.

CHAPTER 1
Spouses, civil partners and cohabitees

1.1 INTRODUCTION

Governments introduce legislation, *inter alia*, to meet social policy objectives and this includes tax legislation. Recent governments have claimed to promote marriage, although in absolute tax terms a number of the income tax benefits and allowances for married couples have gradually become eroded as compared to the position for cohabitees. Sociological evidence points to the fact that more people than ever are now choosing to cohabit outside marriage, but for unmarried couples there remains no equal legal treatment as compared to married couples.

Except in the context of tax credits, married couples and unmarried cohabitees are treated differently for tax purposes, which significantly affects how each might organise their financial affairs and how relatives and certain other persons connected with them might arrange their own. For example, on marriage not only are defined family relationships extended for tax purposes but where a married couple hold income or assets, the tax legislation might deem ownership or receipts to arise in respect of the other spouse. Equally, a married couple are protected from certain tax charges that might otherwise arise from, say, a transfer of an asset from one to the other, whereas if they are not married the transfer might be a taxable transaction. Therefore, whilst much of the tax system now looks to the taxation of people individually and regardless of family structure, significant exceptions remain to distinguish married couples from unmarried couples.

In general, married couples benefit from some very significant tax reliefs which achieve fiscal neutrality in transactions between the couple subject to greater limitations being imposed where HM Revenue and Customs (HMRC) seeks to counter what it considers to be unacceptable family tax planning relating to the mitigation of the family's tax liabilities. In contrast, cohabitees do not have the benefit of any similar tax reliefs nor are they as affected by anti-avoidance rules on family financial planning. On separation, it may also be that, in practice, property is only rarely transferred between cohabitees, and ownership follows legal title prior to separation, with financial and non-financial contributions not being recognised if they are inconsistent with legal title. This is, of course, subject to changes in legislation arising from any future government policy.

On 18 November 2004, the Civil Partnership Act 2004 created a new legal relationship that allowed same sex couples to gain formal recognition of their relationship. Those who register as civil partners are now able to access a wide range of rights and responsibilities, and this also extends to tax matters following the Tax and Civil Partnership Regulations 2005, SI 2005/3229, which apply throughout the United Kingdom with effect from 5 December 2005. The policy objective behind the Regulations was to give tax parity between civil partners and married couples. For tax purposes, the event of the formation of a civil partnership now corresponds to that of a marriage and its dissolution to that of a divorce. Therefore, civil partners now have all the same tax reliefs and benefits and the same anti-avoidance provisions relating to rearrangements of their financial affairs that apply to married couples. For the remainder of this book, unless otherwise specified, the terms spouse, marriage and derivations thereof include references to same sex civil partners who have obtained legal recognition under the 2004 Act.

1.2 FORM E

On family breakdown, spouses or civil partners (assisted by their solicitors as appropriate) may apply to the family court for a financial order to settle disputes over money or property. This is known as ancillary relief and the order may deal with the sale or transfer of property, maintenance payments, a lump sum payment and/or a pension sharing order or attachment order.

As part of the process to obtaining a financial order from the court, each party completes a financial statement (Form E), in which the party swears on oath or affirms that the contents are true, and each party's Form E is then served on the other party by way of contemporaneous exchange. In this way, both parties should be informed about each other's finances and the matters on which they agree and disagree prior to any initial hearing before the court.

Where the parties seek judicial separation without the need for the court to settle any financial dispute, perhaps through mediation or collaborative legal process, there is still a need to take into account each party's finances in arriving at an overall financial settlement (which, even if not disputed, is subject to a final court order) and a Form E or equivalent form of disclosure of financial assets and liabilities will need to be completed as part of this process.

Form E is reproduced at **Appendix 7** and is annotated and referred to in various sections of this book in order to highlight from a practical perspective the areas within Form E which on completion may raise potential tax issues in the light of any financial settlement to be made. It may be noted, for example, that the official Notes for guidance accompanying Form E (see **Appendix 8**) refer to section 2.10 of the form and the identification of any contingent CGT liabilities.

CHAPTER 2

Capital gains tax

The concept of a tax on capital gains was first introduced in the Finance Act 1965. Prior to this there was no general scheme of taxation for capital profits realised from the disposal of assets held for investment (i.e. otherwise than for revenue or trading purposes, in respect of which income tax rules would apply). Since its introduction, the capital gains tax (CGT) regime has been overhauled regularly, and there have been sweeping changes in 1985, 1997 and more recently in 2008.

All forms of property are assets for the purposes of CGT, whether situated in the United Kingdom or elsewhere, including options, debts and incorporeal property generally, currency (with the exception of sterling), and any form of property created or coming to be owned by a person without it being purchased (Taxation of Chargeable Gains Act (TCGA) 1992, s.21).

Generally, if there is a disposal (the term taking its natural meaning), or part disposal of an asset, e.g. where an interest in or right over the asset is created by the disposal, such as a lease created out of a freehold, a computation is carried out in accordance with the legislation to determine the amount of the gain accruing on the disposal. Except where the legislation provides otherwise, every gain is a chargeable gain. However, there are various assets the gains on which are not chargeable gains, i.e. they are exempt from any CGT. These assets are dealt with later in this chapter.

The meaning of the term 'disposal' is extended to include certain specific situations:

- where a capital sum is derived from an asset, notwithstanding that no asset is acquired by the person paying the capital sum, which includes compensation for damage to or destruction of an asset, capital sums in return for giving up, surrendering or not exercising rights and for the use or exploitation of assets (TCGA 1992, s.22) (this may have particular relevance to certain arrangements involving the matrimonial home in the context of deferred charges and is explained in **3.4.7**);
- occasions where assets are lost, destroyed or become worthless, whether or not any capital sum is received (TCGA 1992, s.24);

- the death of an individual (however, this is not an occasion of CGT charge although the assets are acquired by the individual's personal representatives at market value);
- where, in connection with trusts, a disposal is deemed to take place on various occasions (TCGA 1992, Part III, Chapter II).

2.1 GENERAL PRINCIPLES

> **KEY CONCEPTS**
>
> Whenever assets are sold or otherwise transferred or gifted, consideration should always be given to the potential CGT consequences. This applies as much to transfers of assets between couples or cohabitees who are separating as it does to ordinary arm's length sales of assets to third parties.
>
> Gifts or other transfers of assets at less than market value will also generally be valued at market value for CGT purposes, except in certain specific circumstances.

2.1.1 Persons liable for tax on capital gains

Individuals

Individuals are taxed separately and as an initial starting point, individuals who are resident or ordinarily resident in the United Kingdom during any part of the tax year (beginning on 6 April and ending on following 5 April) are subject to CGT in respect of chargeable gains accruing to them in that tax year. In determining the amount of CGT to be charged, chargeable gains are reduced by any allowable losses accruing on disposals of assets in that year and any allowable losses brought forward from previous years, so far as those losses have not been utilised against chargeable gains for those previous years. See **2.1.8** regarding the offset of CGT losses.

From the net amount of chargeable gains after deducting the allowable losses, an individual is then able to deduct an annual exempt amount (£10,100 for 2009/10). Any excess of net chargeable gains above the annual exempt amount is then charged to CGT.

The above tax treatment is unaffected by an individual's marital or civil partnership status.

Individuals who are not resident or ordinarily resident in the United Kingdom at the time of the disposal but who later become resident may be liable to CGT in certain specific circumstances (TCGA 1992, s.10A). These are individuals who generally have previously been longer term UK residents but who go abroad for less than five tax years, so-called 'temporary non-residents'.

Individuals who are not UK resident but who trade in the United Kingdom through a branch or agency may also be liable to CGT on assets situated in the United Kingdom which are used in or for the purposes of that trade (TCGA 1992, s.10).

An explanation of the territorial scope of CGT, as well as a guide to the impact of changes of residence on CGT exposure, is provided in **Chapter 9**.

Companies resident in the United Kingdom

UK resident companies are also required to compute chargeable gains on assets held and disposed of as investments or fixed assets; however, they are liable to corporation tax (at rates of up to 28 per cent) on, broadly, any net chargeable gains accruing after the current year or brought forward capital losses and any current year trading losses. In computing chargeable gains, companies have the benefit of an inflation allowance known as 'indexation' but do not have an annual exempt amount.

On family breakdown, couples may, individually or together, own or have a substantial beneficial interest in shares in a private family company which holds investment or property assets. The company will usually need to be valued as part of the financial separation. As part of the valuation process, the company's assets are valued and the corporation tax liabilities computed (which liabilities may only be contingent) on any inherent or unrealised chargeable gains in respect of those assets. This information will assist in the determination of the value of the shares held in the company and in any questions of liquidity and extraction of funds to finance a separation.

UK resident trusts

Trusts which are resident in the United Kingdom for CGT purposes are also subject to similar computation rules as for individuals and are also liable to CGT at the same rate as for individuals. Trust residence is covered in **Chapter 9**.

2.1.2 Rate of CGT

For disposals occurring (or treated as occurring for tax purposes) on or after 6 April 2008, the CGT rate for individuals and trustees is a flat rate of 18 per cent. This rate applies irrespective of the nature of the asset disposed of or the length of time the asset has been held. The computation of chargeable gains accruing on the disposal of certain business assets may be eligible to be reduced to a lower effective tax rate by 'entrepreneurs' relief', which is discussed in **2.3**.

In respect of disposals occurring prior to 6 April 2008, CGT was charged at the individual's marginal rate of income tax; however, in the computation of chargeable gains accruing, taper relief was available to reduce the amount brought into charge to CGT. This is no longer applicable for disposals on or after 6 April 2008, including assets held prior to that date. The detailed rules relating to the computation of chargeable gains arising prior to 6 April 2008 are beyond the scope of this book.

CGT is payable on or before 31 January following the tax year in which the gain arose.

2.1.3 CGT annual exemption

Almost all individuals are entitled to an annual exemption from CGT. This exemption is usually increased in line with inflation each year. Individuals who claim to be taxed on the 'remittance basis' in any tax year (broadly, individuals domiciled outside the United Kingdom), for tax years beginning on or after 6 April 2008, are not eligible for an annual exemption for that tax year. See **9.3** for an explanation of the remittance basis of taxation.

The CGT annual exemptions for recent years have been as follows:

- 2009/10: £10,100;
- 2008/09: £9,600;
- 2007/08: £9,200.

UK resident trusts are generally entitled to an exemption equal to half the amount for individuals.

2.1.4 CGT computation

For assets disposed of on or after 6 April 2008, and assuming no allowable capital losses, the CGT computation is as follows:

Gross sale proceeds/deemed consideration[1]	X
Less: incidental costs of disposal[2]	(X)
	X
Less:	
(a) cost of acquisition	(X)
(b) incidental costs of acquisition[2]	(X)
(c) capital expenditure to enhance asset	(X)
(d) expenditure establishing, preserving or defending title to/right over the asset	(X)
Chargeable gain	X
Less: Annual exemption (if available)	(X)
Taxable gain	X

1. See **2.1.5**.
2. Incidental costs include fees, commission or remuneration for professional services of a surveyor, valuer, accountant, agent or lawyer and the costs of transfer or conveyance (including stamp duty or SDLT plus the costs of advertising for a seller/buyer as appropriate). The reasonable costs incurred in making any valuation or apportionment in calculating the gain

and expenses reasonably incurred in ascertaining the market value of assets disposed of are also allowable (TCGA 1992, s.38).

EXAMPLE 2A

David is ordered by a court as part of divorce proceedings to sell an investment property, which he does in the tax year 2008/09. This is his only disposal in that tax year. He receives £400,000 as consideration for the property and incurs legal fees in relation to the disposal of £4,000. He originally acquired the property for £260,000 in March 2004. When he acquired the property he paid SDLT of £7,800, and incurred legal fees of £1,000. Two years ago, David extended the property and incurred capital costs of £45,000. When he extended the property, his neighbour, Lisa contested that David had built part of the extension on her land. David incurred legal costs of £3,500 defending his title to the land.

The CGT computation is as follows:

	£
Gross sale proceeds	400,000
Less: incidental costs of disposal	(4,000)
	396,000
Less:	
(a) cost of acquisition	(260,000)
(b) incidental costs of acquisition	(8,800)
(c) capital expenditure to enhance asset (and still reflected in the asset)	(45,000)
(d) expenditure establishing, preserving or defending title	(3,500)
Chargeable gain	78,700
Less: annual exemption	(9,600)
Taxable gain	69,100
Tax liability at 18%	**12,438**

2.1.5 Gifts or disposals otherwise than by way of a bargain at arm's length

Assets may be disposed of by individuals by way of gift or transferred or knowingly sold at prices which do not, or at least do not fully, reflect the market price that the asset would normally be able to fetch in other circumstances, such as a sale in the open market to an outside third party. In relation to such non-market transfers, the CGT legislation imputes market value in the computation of the gain in place of any non-market or nil consideration (in the case of gifts for no consideration). The transferee acquires the asset at that same market value, which is their CGT acquisition cost for any subsequent disposal in the future.

Cohabiting couples may not be aware that they cannot simply transfer assets between them without considering the possible CGT consequences arising from the imputation of market value to any gifts or non-market transfers.

TAX AND FAMILY BREAKDOWN

EXAMPLE 2B

Frank and Clare decide to cohabit in August 2002. Frank owns a painting which he bought in 1988 for £10,000. Frank decides to give the painting to Clare as an anniversary present in 2009. The market value of the painting in August 2009, is £50,000. As Frank and Clare are not married, Frank is treated as making a disposal to Clare and realises a gain of £40,000, which will be chargeable to CGT. If Clare comes to sell the painting, her base cost will be £50,000.

By contrast, transfers of assets between married couples and civil partners who are living together can be made without triggering a CGT charge and are tax neutral. This beneficial CGT treatment only breaks down following separation and is explored in more detail in **Chapter 3**.

2.1.6 Exempt assets

The CGT legislation provides that gains accruing on certain assets are not chargeable gains and are therefore exempt from CGT. As a corollary, any losses accruing on these assets are not allowable losses. Such assets may be transferred free of any CGT between couples irrespective of marital status, or to other family members, and where such assets appear on Form E (see **Appendix** 7) can generally be ignored for CGT purposes.

The following are exempt from CGT (noting the exceptions):

- UK sterling (TCGA 1992, s.21(1)(b));
- the family home to the extent of relief for only or main residence (TCGA 1992, s.223, see **6.1**);
- private motor cars, including vintage or antique cars (except for taxi cabs and certain single-seater sports cars) (TCGA 1992, s.263);
- foreign currency acquired for personal use when abroad (which includes amounts held for the upkeep of a home abroad) (TCGA 1992, s.269);
- medals for gallantry, unless acquired by purchase (TCGA 1992, s.268);
- betting and lottery winnings (TCGA 1992, s.51);
- gains on life assurance policies or deferred annuities unless purchased from a third party (TCGA 1992, s.210);
- gilt-edged securities, qualifying corporate bonds or options in respect thereof (TCGA 1992, s.115); most commercially marketed company debentures and loan stock will be qualifying corporate bonds;
- certain tangible movable property which has a predictable useful life not exceeding 50 years (TCGA 1992, ss.44 and 45) (racehorses, boats, antique clocks, pianos, shotguns (see IR Int 206, *HMRC Tax Bulletin* 45, February 2000) and some fine wines and spirits (see IR Int 200, *HMRC Tax Bulletin* 42, August 1999));
- winnings and damages for personal injury (TCGA 1992, s.51);

CAPITAL GAINS TAX

- certain enterprise investment scheme private company shares (TCGA 1992, s.150A);
- disposal of a debt in the hands of the original creditor (but not loan stock or similar security in a company whether secured or unsecured) (TCGA 1992, s.251);
- individual savings account investments and shares held in a personal equity plan (TCGA 1992, s.151);
- government non-marketable securities such as savings certificates and premium bonds (TCGA 1992, s.121).

2.1.7 Chattels and wasting assets

Chattels are defined in legal terms as any tangible, movable property.

An individual's personal possessions will normally be chattels and will include jewellery, household furniture, paintings, antiques, china, plate and silverware, etc. Chattels also include motor cars, motorcycles and other vehicles and personalised number plates.

However, the disposal of a private motor car suitable for passengers is not a chargeable asset and is exempt from CGT (TCGA 1992, s.263). This exemption would extend to a personalised number plate attached to the motor car on disposal.

A disposal of any other type of motor vehicle will only give rise to a chargeable gain where the vehicle has been used for business purposes and capital allowances (a form of depreciation allowable for tax purposes) were, or could have been, claimed (TCGA 1992, s.45).

Chattels also include ships and yachts, animals and livestock; however, chattels which have a predictable useful life of 50 years or less are exempt from CGT. These are known as wasting assets (TCGA 1992, ss.44 and 45). This exemption therefore will include animals and livestock, and most ships and yachts.

Chattels which have a predictable useful life of more than 50 years are subject to the following special rules (TCGA 1992, s.262), except currency of any description, which is excluded:

- where chattels were worth less than £6,000 when acquired, and are worth less than £6,000 at the date of disposal, they are exempt from CGT, so that gains are not chargeable (and equally, losses are not allowable);
- where chattels were worth less than £6,000 when acquired, but are worth more than £6,000 at the date of disposal, the gain is limited to five-thirds of the excess of the proceeds figure over £6,000;
- where chattels were worth more than £6,000 when acquired, but less than £6,000 at the date of disposal, the proceeds are deemed to be £6,000, restricting the loss;

TAX AND FAMILY BREAKDOWN

- chattels worth more than £6,000 at the date of acquisition and the date of disposal are liable to CGT in the usual way (unless they are wasting assets, and hence exempt assets as described above).

For the purposes of the above rules, where an item is part of a set or collection (e.g. a stamp collection or antique dining table and chairs), it is the value of the entire set which is relevant for the purposes of the £6,000 limit.

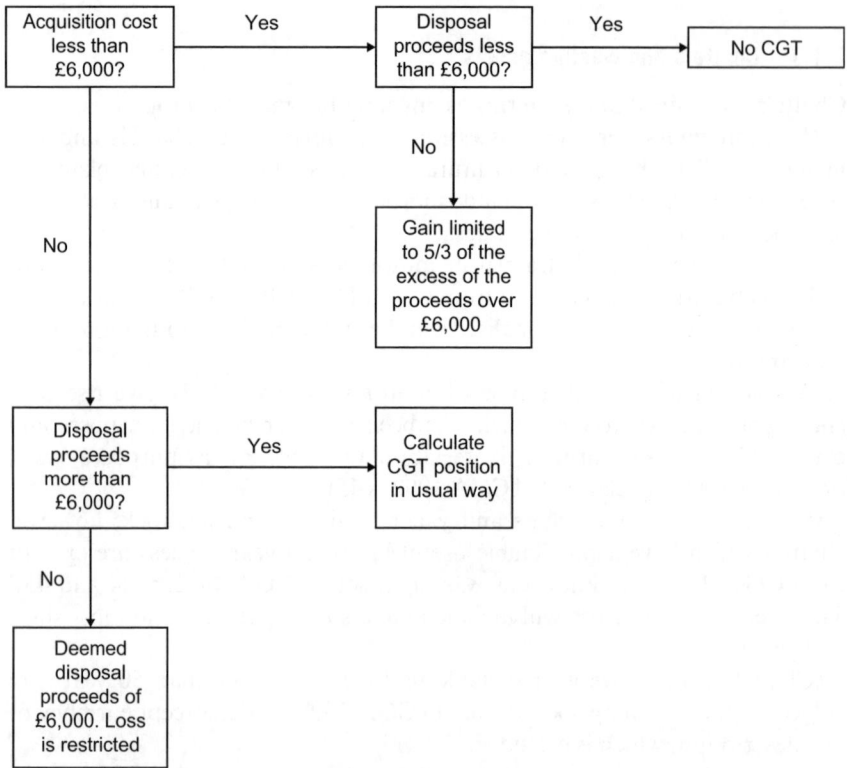

Figure 2.1 CGT rules for chattels with a predictable useful life of more than 50 years

---

EXAMPLE 2C

Mark disposes of two paintings to help fund maintenance for his ex-wife. Each was acquired for £1,000. The first painting is sold for £5,000 and the second is sold for £9,000. Mark's annual exemption for the year has already been used on other disposals.

Painting 1, acquired and sold for less than £6,000

	£
Proceeds:	5,000
Less cost:	(1,000)
Chargeable gain:	4,000

This is exempt under the rules on chattels.

Painting 2, acquired for less than £6,000 and sold for more than £6,000

	£
Proceeds:	9,000
Less cost:	(1,000)
Chargeable gain:	8,000

Gain restricted to 5/3 × (£9,000 − £6,000) = £5,000

Tax liability at 18% = £900

2.1.8 Capital losses

Capital losses on disposals of assets are computed in the same way as capital gains.

Allowable capital losses are deductible against chargeable gains accruing in the same tax year or, where the losses exceed the current year gains (or there are no current year gains), the remaining losses can be carried forward and are available to set against chargeable gains in subsequent tax years. Capital losses cannot be carried back and set against chargeable gains of earlier tax years.

Losses brought forward can be used in such a way to preserve the annual exemption, see example 2D below.

EXAMPLE 2D

Ben, who is in the process of separating from his wife, has chargeable gains of £15,000 in 2008/09 and capital losses of £20,000 in the same year. In 2008/09, £15,000 of Ben's losses will be used against his gains.

If Ben did not have losses for 2008/09 his annual exemption would have reduced his gains to £5,400 (£15,000 − £9,600); however, as current year losses have to be used before the annual exemption, Ben's annual exemption is effectively wasted.

After the offset of the losses in the current year (2008/09), Ben has £5,000 of losses to carry forward.

In 2009/10, Ben is required under a court order to transfer an asset to his wife from whom he separated during the previous tax year. He is deemed to make a gain of £12,000 as a result of the transfer. As losses brought forward of £15,000 can be used in such a way to preserve the annual exempt amount, only £1,900 will need to be offset to reduce Ben's gain to nil. Ben will then have £3,100 of losses to carry forward to be offset against gains in future years.

	£
2009/10 capital gains	12,000
Less: Annual exemption	(10,100)
	1,900
Less: Losses brought forward	(1,900)
Taxable gain	nil
Loss memorandum	
2008/09 loss	20,000
Used in 2008/09	(15,000)
Carried forward	5,000
Used in 2009/10	(1,900)
Carried forward	3,100

A loss accruing to an individual will not be an allowable loss unless, in relation to that year, the amount of the loss is notified to HMRC, normally by being included in the individual's self-assessment tax return for that year (TCGA 1992, s.16(2A)).

Furthermore, an allowable loss does not include a loss accruing to an individual where the main purpose of any arrangements for the loss to accrue was to secure a tax advantage; in other words, where tax avoidance is concerned (TCGA 1992, s.16A).

In certain very specific circumstances, capital losses on the disposal of unquoted shares in a trading company can be relieved against an individual's income rather than chargeable gains. Strict and separate criteria need to have been satisfied by the individual subscribing for shares and by the trading company concerned (Income Tax Act (ITA) 2007, Part 4, Chapter 6).

Where an individual is not domiciled in the United Kingdom and first claims the remittance basis of taxation for a tax year, losses accruing on the disposal of assets situated outside the United Kingdom in that year and all subsequent years are not allowable losses. It is possible for such an individual to make an irrevocable election under TCGA 1992, s.16ZA, such that losses on the disposal of overseas assets may be allowable; however, this is a highly complex area and specialist advice should be sought.

Generally, losses accruing to an individual during a tax year in which he is not resident or ordinarily resident in the United Kingdom for any part of the year are not allowable losses.

If an individual makes a disposal of an asset on which a loss accrues to a connected person the loss is only deductible against chargeable gains accruing on some other disposal of an asset to that same connected person. Such losses are known as 'clogged losses'. A connected person includes spouse, civil partner, brother, sister, ancestor or lineal descendant and includes certain family trusts and family companies. Cohabitees need only be concerned with their own close family members for this purpose. See **3.2** for further details.

2.1.9 Postponement or deferral of chargeable gains

In a number of situations, the CGT legislation allows chargeable gains accruing on the disposal of certain assets to be postponed or deferred depending on the circumstances. The most important of these occasions likely to be relevant to married couples and cohabitees in the context of separation are:

- hold over relief for transfers of business assets (discussed at **2.2**);
- roll over relief for disposals of, and reinvestment in, certain business assets (see **6.6.3**);
- exchange of interests in land held jointly (see **6.6.1**).

2.1.10 CGT reliefs

Married couples and cohabitees should also consider the following CGT reliefs to reduce or mitigate CGT on disposals of relevant assets and particularly in the context of separation:

- principal private residence relief (see **6.1.5**); and
- entrepreneurs' relief (see **2.3**).

2.1.11 Court orders for payments of lump sums

Under the Matrimonial Causes Act (MCA) 1973, s.31, a court can effectively replace (wholly or partly) an order for periodic payments with an order for a lump sum payment in respect of financial provision for a party to a marriage or former marriage. Such an order is a fresh exercise of its discretionary power rather than a variation of an order for periodic payments. HMRC considers that it is not a capital payment derived from an asset and TCGA 1992, s.22 does not apply (IR Int 219, *HMRC Tax Bulletin* 52, April 2001). The recipient of the lump sum payment is not liable to CGT in respect of the receipt.

2.2 HOLD OVER RELIEF

KEY CONCEPTS

This relief allows CGT to be deferred on transfers of assets in certain circumstances between, say, separated couples or cohabitees, until the asset is eventually sold.

2.2.1 Background

Advisers to couples undergoing family breakdown will be concerned with understanding the CGT implications of transferring assets, particularly those which comprise business interests, where the transfer does not amount to an actual sale in the open market, and under the computational rules explained above, there is an inherent chargeable gain on the transfer. This is not only because on separation and divorce the contingent tax on that chargeable gain will be taken into consideration in arriving at the couple's net worth (see section 2.10 of Form E (**Appendix 7**)) but where there is an actual transfer this will give rise to an immediate rather than a contingent tax liability.

It is therefore important to understand that in certain circumstances the chargeable gain that would otherwise arise on a transfer of assets such as business interests can be deferred until there is an actual sale by the making of an appropriate CGT election.

2.2.2 What is hold over relief?

Hold over relief allows gains arising on transfers of assets to be passed from the transferor to the transferee without an immediate, or where appropriate with a reduced, tax charge for the transferor, provided the transferee agrees (i.e. the gain is 'held over').

By making an election, part or all of any tax charge that would otherwise arise on a transfer is deferred until the transferee spouse (or cohabitee) disposes of the asset, i.e. usually until there is a sale in the open market. This election to claim 'hold over' relief is available for transfers of assets between married couples who have separated in a prior tax year and between cohabitees, as well as between individuals generally. The relief is available where a disposal is made otherwise than at arm's length, e.g. by way of outright (or partial) gift.

Relief is available in the following circumstances:

(a) under TCGA 1992, s.260 where the transfer is chargeable to IHT and in certain specialist IHT situations (see **Chapter 4**); or
(b) under TCGA 1992, s.165, Sched.7 where business assets are transferred.

2.2.3 Claiming relief under TCGA 1992, s.260

An election for CGT 'hold over' relief under TCGA 1992, s.260 is available, *inter alia*, for a transfer of assets of any nature which gives rise to a chargeable transfer for IHT purposes and is not a potentially exempt transfer – that is, where the transfer is immediately chargeable to IHT (see **4.1.4**).

Ignoring more specialist circumstances, this relief will generally only be relevant to individuals who, during their lifetime and on family breakdown, make gifts into a trust or settlement for the benefit of others and from which trust they, their spouse or civil partner (from whom they are not separated) and dependent minor children (including stepchildren) are excluded. This relief may be of relevance, therefore, to assets transferred into trusts to maintain a spouse or civil partner from whom the donor is separated and to similar arrangements made for a cohabitee (although separation is not relevant). Trustees of settlements can also benefit when making transfers of assets out of a trust in appropriate circumstances.

The main conditions for the relief are that:

(a) there is a disposal of an asset by an individual or the trustees of a settlement and acquisition by an individual or the trustees of a settlement;
(b) the transferee is either UK resident or UK ordinarily resident (see **9.2.1** and **9.2.2**);
(c) a claim for the relief is made by the transferor and transferee or for transfers into a settlement, by the individual transferor alone;
(d) where there is any actual consideration, the claim for hold over relief is reduced (see **2.2.5**).

The relief under TCGA 1992, s.260 takes precedence over claims for relief under TCGA 1992, s.165.

2.2.4 Claiming relief under TCGA 1992, s.165: gifts of business assets

In addition to satisfying the main conditions listed above, an election for CGT 'hold over' relief under TCGA 1992, s.165 is potentially available for transfers of assets within the classes listed below. The election is open to individuals making a disposal otherwise than as a bargain at arm's length to other persons and includes individuals or the trustees of a settlement.

The assets in question, which may be in the United Kingdom or elsewhere, are:

- unlisted shares or securities in a trading company or holding company of a trading group[1] (which includes Alternative Investment Market (AIM) listed investments);
- shares or securities listed on a recognised stock exchange in a trading company or holding company of a trading group where the transferor has at least 5 per cent of the voting rights;
- any assets or an interest in assets used in a trade, profession or vocation carried on by the transferor or by any trading company (or of a trading group) in which the transferor has at least 5 per cent of the voting rights (or in the holding company);
- agricultural property (the value of which includes 'hope' or development value, see HMRC, *Capital Gains Tax Manual* at CG66962) meaning agricultural land or pasture, including, *inter alia*, woodland and buildings used in connection with the intensive rearing of livestock or fish and

cottages, farm buildings and certain farmhouses and land occupied with them (Inheritance Tax Act (IHTA) 1984, s.115(2)); and
- where the disposal is by the trustees of a settlement, all of the above assets except listed shares, unless the trustees have at least 25 per cent of the voting rights in the company.

Note that where a claim could have been made under TCGA 1992, s.260 (see above), this takes priority over a claim under TCGA 1992, s.165.

Hold over relief cannot be claimed on transfers of shares or securities by an individual or trustees to a company.

2.2.5 Calculation of the gain held over

Hold over relief can apply where there is, broadly speaking, little or no consideration given for the relevant asset in question on the transfer, such as gifts or transfers at less than market value. The chargeable gain is computed in the normal way for the transferor, with the asset's market value substituted in place of any (or nil) consideration. The chargeable gain that arises is then reduced for the transferor ('held over') in such a way that the transferor's chargeable gain is limited to the gain that arises based only on the actual consideration they are receiving, which in the case of gifts for no consideration would be nil, i.e. no gain.

The transferee who would normally receive the asset at a base cost equal to market value for tax purposes based on the chargeable gain computed under normal rules has their base cost similarly reduced by the amount of the gain being 'held over'. So where the entire gain is held over, in effect the transferee simply inherits the transferor's original base cost and hence the transferor's original CGT position on any future disposal of the asset. If any consideration is given by the transferee which exceeds the sums allowable as a deduction in the computation, then the amount of the gain which can be deferred by hold over relief is reduced, which can mean that part of the gain will be held over, and part of the gain will arise and be chargeable to CGT immediately.

EXAMPLE 2E

James carries on a business and makes a gift of a building he uses in that business to his son, Peter. The building was originally acquired for £60,000 and is now worth £150,000. There is a mortgage on the building of £70,000 and this liability is taken on by Peter.

James's gift to Peter will be treated as a disposal of the building at its current market value and his chargeable gain will therefore be £90,000 (£150,000 less £60,000). Hold over relief will be available as it is a business asset, but the assumption of the liability for the mortgage will be treated as consideration given by Peter for the building. The value of the consideration provided is £70,000, reducing the amount available for hold over relief by the amount by which this exceeds the allowable base cost of £60,000 (£10,000). Therefore, assuming that James and Peter have jointly made the election, £10,000 of the gain is immediately taxable for James, giving rise to a tax charge at 18% of £1,800 (ignoring the annual exemption).

Peter's CGT base cost is reduced by the £80,000 hold over relief claimed, from £150,000 to £70,000 (he will be taxed in future if the building is sold for an amount in excess of £70,000).

James's CGT computation	£
Market value at date of disposal	150,000
Less: cost of acquisition	(60,000)
Capital gain	90,000
Less:	
Excess of consideration received over base cost (£70,000 less £60,000)	(10,000)
Gain available to be held over	80,000

James has a chargeable gain of £10,000, which gives rise to a CGT charge of £1,800, ignoring the annual exemption.

Peter's CGT base cost	
Market value at date of disposal	150,000
Deduct: gain held over	(80,000)
Base cost on future disposal by Peter	70,000

If the actual consideration given does not exceed the allowable deductions, no adjustment is necessary, e.g. if Peter had taken on a liability of £60,000 in Example 2E above.

Entrepreneurs' relief may also be available to reduce any gain that remains in charge to tax after hold over relief in certain circumstances (see **2.3.6**).

2.2.6 Reductions in held over gain (TCGA 1992, Sched.7, Part II)

If the asset disposed of was not used for the purposes of a trade, profession or vocation throughout the period of the transferor's ownership, the amount of the gain available to be held over is reduced. This is by reference to the fraction a/b where:

a = the number of days that the asset was so used; and
b = the whole period.

In other words, the proportion of the gain that relates to the time spent as non-business use is immediately charged to CGT as it cannot be held over.

A similar rule applies to shares or securities for transferors who are:

(a) trustees and who have held at least 25 per cent of the votes at any time in the 12 months prior to disposal; and

(b) individuals who have held at least 5 per cent of the votes in the 12 months prior to disposal.

In this case, if the company or group of companies in which the shares or securities are held has chargeable assets which are not assets used for trading purposes as at the date of disposal, the gain available to be held over is restricted. This is by the fraction a/b where:

a = the market value on the date of disposal of the company's or group's chargeable assets which are business assets; and

b = the market value on that date of all the company's or group's chargeable assets.

2.2.7 Application of hold over relief to transfers made on divorce

As noted above, if there is any consideration given for an asset, the amount of the gain that can be held over may be reduced and will affect the amount of the gain that becomes immediately chargeable. Consideration need not, of course, be in a monetary form, as Example 2E in **2.2.5** demonstrates. HMRC is of the view that transfers on separation and divorce by one party to the other amount to the surrender by the transferee of rights which they would otherwise be able to exercise to obtain alternative financial provision, the value of the surrendered rights representing actual consideration. In such cases, HMRC considers that hold over relief is not available as the effect is to reduce the held over gain to nil. However, if a gratuitous element in the transfer can be demonstrated, i.e. over and above that which the transferee might be expected to receive as a result of a contested court case, hold over relief can apply to that element. In practice, this is unlikely to be easy to establish.

In the light of comments made by Coleridge J in *G* v. *G* [2002] EWHC 1339 on the tax consequences of court orders in divorce cases, however, HMRC revised its above practice on transfers of assets in cases of separation and divorce so far as they relate to transfers under a court order. The revised practice has applied since 31 July 2002, the effect of which is that transfers of the above business assets can be free of any immediate CGT consequences, as hold over relief is now available to be claimed provided the court makes an order. This is because, if a court makes an order, HMRC considers that it reflects the exercise of a court's independent statutory judgment and is not in consequence of any party surrendering alternative rights in return for assets. *HMRC Capital Gains Tax Manual* at CG67192 sets out the practice in detail.

The correctness of HMRC's revised practice may, however, be in some doubt following the Court of Appeal decision in the case of *Haines* v. *Hill and another* [2007] EWCA Civ 1284. See **2.2.9**.

Transfers not made under a court order will continue to be treated as potentially liable to CGT as hold over relief will not be available in HMRC's view.

CAPITAL GAINS TAX

Some other general points to make on hold over relief are as follows.

- For hold over relief to apply, an election for the above treatment has to be made by both the transferor and transferee (TCGA 1992, s.165(1)(b)). There is no reason why a transferee receiving an asset should agree to join in such a claim unless the court orders them to, since in inheriting the transferor's base cost they will potentially be exposed to a larger capital gain on a future sale. If the transferee does not join in the claim, an immediate capital tax liability will arise on the transferor.
- The reductions for non-business use assets or shares transferred as mentioned in **2.2.6** which may give rise to an immediate tax charge on part of any gain arising as hold over relief are restricted.
- If the transferee is not UK resident at the time of the transfer, the relief is not available (TCGA 1992, s.166).
- If the transferee emigrates and becomes non-UK resident within six years and continues to own the asset on which hold over relief has been claimed, a CGT charge will arise on the transferee in respect of the gain held over (TCGA 1992, s.168). If the transferee fails to pay that tax, the transferor could end up paying the tax (TCGA 1992, s.168(7)).

2.2.8 Making hold over relief claims and the valuation of assets

All claims for hold over relief must be made on the claim form attached to HMRC Help Sheet 295 (HS295, see www.hmrc.gov.uk) or a copy of it. HMRC will admit a claim to hold over relief without requiring a computation of the held over gain in any case where the transferor and transferee complete the claim form. This requires a joint application by the transferor and transferee and a calculation incorporating informally estimated valuations if necessary, and a statement that both parties have satisfied themselves that the value of the asset at the date of transfer was in excess of the (transferor's) allowable expenditure. None of the information or valuations is binding on either HMRC or the claimants and if it emerges that the information given is incorrect or incomplete, computations will be carried out and CGT assessments raised as appropriate. Once made, the claim cannot be withdrawn.

With effect from 1 April 2010, the general time limit for making a claim is four years from the end of the year of assessment to which the transfer relates.

2.2.9 *Haines v. Hill and another*

Haines v. Hill and another [2007] EWCA Civ 1284 concerned the interaction of personal insolvency law and an earlier transfer of property to a wife under ancillary relief proceedings prior to the transferor husband's bankruptcy and appears to throw some doubt on the correctness of HMRC's revised practice on hold over relief outlined above. In this case, the Court of Appeal held that an order made in matrimonial ancillary relief proceedings to convey property was not a transaction made without consideration, whether following a contested hearing or a compromise agreement.

Rix LJ said that there was nothing in the concept of consideration as a whole to suggest that the compromise or release of a statutory right such as that provided by the MCA 1973, s.24 could not amount to consideration. In essence, the statutory right under s.24 has some value in the eye of the law; its value is ultimately for the family court judge to assess and fix in ancillary relief proceedings; and it is that right which is compromised and ultimately released in return for the property adjustment order of the court. As for the view expressed by Coleridge J at para.43 in *G v. G* [2002] EWHC 1339 regarding the potential consequences for the purposes of CGT (hold over relief), this could hardly be regarded as authoritative in the absence of representations from HMRC. He merely proceeded 'on the footing' that business hold over relief would be available to the husband and in doing so he appears to have drawn an unnecessary inference from the Court of Appeal judgment in *Xydhias v. Xydhias* [1999] 2 All ER 386 (that in the absence of a court order approving the same, the compromise of ancillary relief proceedings was not contractually binding).

2.3 ENTREPRENEURS' RELIEF

KEY CONCEPTS

Entrepreneurs' relief reduces the incidence of CGT on disposals or transfers by individuals and trustees of settlements of certain business assets.

In evaluating a couple's net worth on separation, entrepreneurs' relief should be taken into consideration where available.

2.3.1 Background

Entrepreneurs' relief (ER) is available to individuals (and to trustees in certain circumstances) and applies to certain CGT transactions involving relevant 'business assets' which take place on or after 6 April 2008 (TCGA 1992, Part V, Chapter III). It replaces business asset taper relief (BATR) which was withdrawn on the same date but to a far more limited extent, the former relief potentially resulting in an effective CGT rate of 10 per cent on the disposal of relevant business assets after only two years of ownership. As ER is narrower in scope than BATR, many capital gains which would have qualified for BATR will not qualify for ER.

In broad outline, ER provides a CGT exemption equal to four-ninths of the chargeable gain arising on disposals of relevant business assets held for at least one year, which at the current CGT rate of 18 per cent gives rise to an effective tax rate of 10 per cent, i.e. five-ninths of the chargeable gain remains in charge to tax at 18 per cent. There is an overall lifetime limit of £2,000,000 (this was increased from £1,000,000 with effect from 6 April 2010) on the chargeable gains against which the relief can be claimed by an individual, meaning that in effect the maximum lifetime reduction in tax is now £160,000 based on the current CGT rate of 18 per cent.

2.3.2 When is entrepreneurs' relief available?

ER is available for the following disposals of 'business assets', which may be in the United Kingdom or elsewhere:

- a disposal of all or part of a trading business[2] carried on for at least 12 months (there are rules to restrict relief on the disposal of a trading business where the business holds shares, securities or other investment assets);
- a disposal of assets used by a trading business carried on by the vendor or by the vendor in partnership for at least 12 months, where the business ceased within the past three years;
- a disposal of shares or securities held for at least 12 months in the vendor's personal company (i.e. a company in which the vendor has 5 per cent or more of the shares and can exercise at least 5 per cent of the votes). It is also necessary that either:
    (i) the company has been a trading company or holding company of a trading group, and the vendor has been an employee or officer (part or full time) throughout the year ending with the date of disposal; or
    (ii) the company has ceased to be a trading company or holding company of a trading group within the last three years and the trading and employment conditions were fulfilled in the 12 months leading up to the date of cessation;
- a disposal by the trustees of a trust can also qualify provided certain conditions are met by a beneficiary of the trust who has a relevant interest in the business asset in question, and who meets the relevant time limits and employment conditions. The beneficiary must hold an interest in possession in the trust. In trusts with multiple life tenants, there are provisions which restrict relief based on the number of life tenants. Any relief given on trustee chargeable gains reduces the individual beneficiary's lifetime limit for ER.

EXAMPLE 2F

Preeti disposes of shares in her personal trading company, realising a chargeable gain of £600,000, which qualifies for ER.

The exempt fraction of four-ninths applies to this gain, leaving five-ninths chargeable to tax, i.e. a chargeable gain of £333,333. CGT at 18% on this amount is £60,000 (ignoring the annual exemption), giving Preeti an effective tax rate of 10%.

Preeti subsequently starts another personal trading company and later disposes of these shares, realising another gain of £1,600,000, which also qualifies for ER.

Since there is a lifetime limit of £2,000,000 on ER claims, the first £1,400,000 of Preeti's gain is eligible for ER at four-ninths, a reduction in the overall gain of £622,222. The adjusted gain is therefore £977,777 (£1,600,000 less £622,222), which is taxed at 18%, i.e. £176,000 (again ignoring the annual exemption).

2.3.3 Associated disposals

Where an individual has made a disposal that qualified for ER, certain 'associated disposals' can also qualify for relief. An associated disposal is a disposal of an asset used in the business for at least 12 months ending on the earlier of the date of the sale or the cessation of the business. It is a requirement that the individual makes the associated disposal as part of a withdrawal from the business of the company or partnership, so a partial exit will not qualify for relief.

For such associated disposals, relief is reduced where:

- the asset was only used in the business for part of the period;
- only part of the asset was used in the business; or
- rent has been charged for use of the asset since 6 April 2008.

EXAMPLE 2G

Wilson disposes of shares in his personal trading company at a gain of £500,000. Three months later he disposes of the freehold building from which the company conducted its business at a gain of £250,000. The property was owned personally by Wilson and 50% of the building was used by his company while the remaining 50% was always let for investment purposes.

The gain on Wilson's shares is reduced by entrepreneurs' relief, by four-ninths to £277,778, and tax at 18% of this figure is £50,000 (an effective rate of 10%).

Entrepreneurs' relief is also available on the gain on Wilson's freehold property (since the gain derives from an associated disposal), but relief is only due in respect of the proportion of the property used in the trade: 50%, i.e. £125,000. Therefore the relief is £55,556 and the overall gain after entrepreneurs' relief is £194,444 (£250,000 less £55,556). The CGT at 18% is £35,000.

Specialist advice should be sought on associated disposals and non-business use.

2.3.4 Application of entrepreneurs' relief to company takeovers, etc.

In company acquisitions, takeovers or other company reorganisations, the consideration offered by an acquirer company for the vendor's shares in a company being sold can take the form of shares in the acquirer company or other forms of non-cash consideration. In relevant cases, no disposal may be treated as occurring at that time when CGT 'share for share exchange' relief applies and any gain is effectively deferred until the acquirer company's shares are sold (TCGA 1992, s.135).

In the vendor's hands, the shares received as consideration in the acquirer company simply inherit the base cost of the shares being disposed of in the company being sold without there being any disposal, and hence chargeable gain, for CGT purposes. In such circumstances, where shares in one company ('old' shares) are exchanged for shares in another ('new' shares), it can be the case that the old shares would have qualified for ER whereas the new shares do not, with a corresponding loss of ER relief on a future disposal of the new shares. It is therefore possible to elect to be taxed on the takeover without the 'share for share exchange' relief rules applying (TCGA 1992, s.169Q).

Where the company takeover, etc. results in shares being exchanged for loan notes or debentures which are in the form of qualifying corporate bonds (QCBs), a chargeable gain is computed at the time of the takeover, etc. but is not usually charged to tax until the loan notes are redeemed or otherwise disposed of (TCGA 1992, s.116). In computing the chargeable gain and the charge to tax, however, ER is deducted. There are specific requirements that have to be met in order that loan notes are QCBs (TCGA 1992, s.117).

EXAMPLE 2H

On 1 January 2010, Victoria sells all of her 100 shares in her personal trading company for which she originally subscribed £100, to another company in return for £400,000 worth of loan notes in the purchaser company. She has therefore realised a gain of £399,900 and as the loan notes meet the criteria for being QCBs, no tax is payable until they are redeemed. On 1 January 2012, her loan notes are redeemed at par value, causing the gain of £399,900 to become chargeable to CGT. Under ER, her chargeable gain is reduced to £222,166 (i.e. five-ninths of £399,900).

2.3.5 Spouses, civil partners and cohabitees

There are no special provisions for spouses, civil partners or cohabitees. The lifetime limit cannot be transferred and holding periods are not aggregated for the purposes of qualification for ER.

However, there may still be some planning opportunities where shares are to be sold or transferred as part of the process of separation.

Where both spouses/civil partners own shares in a trading company and one spouse is an officer/employee of the trading company and the other is not, then the 'non-employee' spouse/partner should transfer their shares to the employee spouse/partner so that ER can be claimed on all the shares.

Where both spouses are employees of the trading company, they could transfer shares between them to make the most of the ER available:

- where the couple each own less than 5 per cent of the shares but combined have more than 5 per cent, they could 'bunch' shares in the hands of one of them so that all the shares qualify for ER;
- if the couple have a joint holding of less than 10 per cent, so that they each own beneficially less than 5 per cent, they could sever the joint holding so that one of them owns more than 5 per cent of the shares and will qualify for ER;
- if one owns more than 5 per cent of the shares and the other owns less than 5 per cent, the holdings could be aggregated in the ownership of the qualifying spouse so that he or she holds more than 5 per cent, and therefore both holdings qualify for ER;
- if the couple each have more than 5 per cent but one does not satisfy the qualifying conditions, the shares could be transferred to the spouse who qualifies for ER.

The same tax planning also applies to cohabitees. However, in respect of cohabitees, and also for spouses or civil partners who are separated, any share ownership rearrangements may be immediately liable to CGT unless CGT hold over relief is, or can be, claimed. Generally, shares held in companies which qualify for ER should also qualify for hold over relief, which latter relief does not have any minimum holding or employment/office holder requirements. Couples who are not separated benefit from the no gain, no loss treatment for share transfers between them as outlined in **Chapter 3**.

It is worth noting that where an individual is employed by a qualifying trading company and has held shares in it that meet the qualifying conditions (i.e. at least 5 per cent for more than 12 months), if further shares are transferred to them, say, one month before the sale of the shares, these will also meet the test for the qualifying holding period.

2.3.6 Interaction with hold over relief

HMRC's view of the interaction of ER and hold over relief is generally that where the assets (or whole of the assets, where relevant) are gifted and the subject of a hold over relief claim, no chargeable gain will arise at that time (see *HMRC Capital Gains Tax Manual* at CG64137). Hold over relief therefore takes priority over ER and a claim would not be appropriate. However, if hold over relief is restricted because there is actual consideration, it would appear that ER can apply to reduce the gain otherwise chargeable to tax. On any subsequent disposal of the gifted assets by the transferee, any gain is calculated in the normal way. This gain may qualify for ER if the relevant conditions are satisfied in respect of the disposal by the transferee.

CAPITAL GAINS TAX

2.3.7 Hold over and entrepreneurs' relief: summary

	Hold over relief (under TCGA 1992, s.260 or s.165)	**Entrepreneurs' relief**
Who can claim relief?	Individuals and trustees	Individuals mainly; trustees in some circumstances
Nature of assets	Business assets (as defined) unless asset is transferred to a trust which excludes settlor, non-separated spouse and minor children	Only available for business assets (as defined)
Holding period for business assets	No minimum holding period	Must have held business asset for more than 12 months
Rules for unquoted shares in a trading company	No minimum holding period. Possible restriction on relief if at least 5% of votes owned in last year and company owns non-business assets (TCGA 1992, Sched.7, Part II, para.7)	Minimum 5% of shares and voting rights and must be a director/employee for holding period
Rules for shares in quoted company	Must be the transferor's personal company (i.e. own more than 5% of voting rights)	Must be the transferor's personal company (i.e. own more than 5% of voting rights)
Residence of transferee and transferor	Transferee must be UK resident. Clawback if transferee leaves UK within 6 years following end of tax year of transfer	No residence requirement. If transferor not UK resident relief may still be relevant if UK asset used in trade in UK or if caught by 'temporary non-resident' rules
Limit of availability of relief	No limit. Where there is any consideration involved, relief may be restricted	Lifetime limit of £2,000,000. Any relief given to trustees reduces limit to individual beneficiary
Claims	Claim made by both transferor and transferee, unless transferee is a trust. HMRC's view is this takes priority over ER if both are claimed (see **2.3.6**)	Available to transferor only, and claimed by transferor
How the relief is claimed	HMRC form HS295 (see **www.hmrc.gov.uk**)	On tax return for relevant year

TAX AND FAMILY BREAKDOWN

2.4 THE INVESTMENT PORTFOLIO

Individuals or couples who are separating may have earned sufficient income or capital gains to have made portfolio investments in various different asset classes. If part or all of an investment portfolio is disposed of to fund a financial settlement, or is transferred between the parties who are separating, this is likely to give rise to tax implications in respect of any actual or inherent chargeable gains (see **Chapter 3**).

The more commonly encountered investments likely to be held within such a portfolio along with the relevant tax implications for gains arising are as follows:

(i) Most quoted UK stocks and shares will be liable to CGT on a sale or transfer unless held in a tax exempt 'wrapper' such as an individual savings account.

(ii) UK Treasury gilts and most commercially marketed UK corporate bonds will be exempt from CGT.

(iii) Shares subscribed in qualifying venture capital trusts (VCTs) may be transferred without CGT consequences, although income tax relief originally given could be withdrawn if the transfer is made within the minimum period of ownership (three or five years, depending on when the shares were acquired). If earlier personal capital gains were deferred by way of subscription for VCT shares, those earlier deferred capital gains will come back into charge to CGT on the sale or transfer.

(iv) Shares subscribed in qualifying enterprise investment scheme (EIS) companies (unlisted or AIM listed trading companies meeting relevant criteria) may be sold or transferred between married couples, i.e. living together at the time of the transfer (ITA 2007, s.209), without any CGT or income tax consequences provided they have been held for at least three years and subject to the individual having also met certain other criteria. However, if earlier capital gains were deferred by subscribing for EIS shares, then those deferred capital gains will come back into charge to CGT on the sale or transfer.

(v) Units or shares held in non-reporting offshore funds (which would include offshore unit trusts, mutual funds, certain hedge funds, etc. which do not meet certain HMRC criteria) will be liable to income tax at the transferor's marginal rate of tax on any gain on sale or transfer. It should also be noted that since the gain is charged to income tax, the no gain, no loss treatment that normally applies to asset transfers between married couples or civil partners who are living together and up to the end of the year of separation does not apply. If the offshore fund has reporting fund status the gain will be subject to CGT on a sale or transfer.

CAPITAL GAINS TAX

2.5 LAND AND PROPERTY ASSETS

The tax treatment of land and property on family breakdown is covered in depth in **Chapter 6**.

CHAPTER 2 CHECKLIST

1. Consider the current residence status of the transferee on separation and, if hold over relief is to be claimed, future residence status may also be relevant (**2.1.1**).
2. Identify all assets where a transfer would give rise to CGT and consider the availability of CGT annual exemption (a client claiming the remittance basis of taxation in the United Kingdom will not have a UK annual exemption) (**2.1.3**).
3. Consider availability of any unutilised capital losses brought forward and assets which, on disposal, would give rise to an allowable loss (**2.1.8**).
4. Identify assets held which may be eligible for CGT hold over relief (**2.2**).
5. Identify assets held which may be eligible for entrepreneurs' relief and determine availability of the lifetime allowance (**2.3**).

NOTES

1. 'Holding company of a trading group' and 'trading company' mean a group of companies or company, respectively, carrying on trading activities whose activities do not include to a substantial extent any non-trading, i.e. investment type, activities. 'Substantial' in this context is interpreted by HMRC to mean more than 20 per cent and a measure of whether non-trading activities are substantial includes taking into account some or all of the following factors: turnover, income, assets, time spent by directors, company history, and any other factors appropriate to the group or company concerned.
2. A 'trading business' means anything which is a trade, profession or vocation and is conducted on a commercial basis with the view to the realisation of profits. 'Holding company of a trading group' and 'trading company' have the same definitions as for hold over relief. See **2.2.4**.

CHAPTER 3
Transfers of assets

For capital gains tax purposes (and ignoring death) there may be four key life stages which determine tax liability on transfers of assets occurring between couples who cohabit or are married or in civil partnership:

- unmarried (whether living together as cohabitees or not);
- married and living together;
- married but separated;
- divorced, following the decree absolute/dissolution.

3.1 GENERAL TRANSFERS OF ASSETS: DEEMED MARKET VALUE RULE

The basic rule found in Taxation of Chargeable Gains Act (TCGA) 1992, s.17 is that a person's acquisition or disposal of an asset is deemed to be for a consideration equal to the market value of the asset where it is acquired or disposed of otherwise than as a bargain at arm's length. This would therefore apply to gifts of assets or a transfer of an asset into a settlement by a settlor, or where one of the parties has the intention of conferring a gratuitous benefit on another party to the transaction.

Therefore, the transfer of an asset by any individual to another person will be at market value unless the transfer is a genuine sale negotiated on arm's length terms (which includes a sale which turns out to be a bad bargain). This would include transfers of assets between unmarried couples, whether living together as cohabitees or not.

3.2 TRANSFERS OF ASSETS BETWEEN CONNECTED PERSONS

> **KEY CONCEPTS**
>
> Married couples and civil partners are 'connected' for capital gains and most other tax purposes until decree absolute or dissolution. Unmarried couples are not connected.

3.2.1 Connected persons rule

A further rule applies where the person acquiring an asset and the person making the disposal are connected. Without prejudice to the general rule above, the person acquiring the asset and the person making the disposal are treated as parties to a transaction that is otherwise than a bargain at arm's length. The effect is to substitute the market value of the asset in TCGA 1992, s.17 for the consideration actually paid (if any) where connected parties are involved.

3.2.2 Who is connected?

By virtue of TCGA 1992, s.286, a connected person includes the individual's spouse or civil partner, brothers, sisters and any ancestor or lineal descendant. It also includes the spouse or civil partner of any of those persons and the individual's spouse's or civil partner's brothers, sisters, ancestors and lineal descendants. There are also further provisions relating to settlements, companies and partnerships.

Therefore, transfers of assets between spouses and civil partners and their children will always be at market value unless some other relief or exemption applies.

3.2.3 Losses on disposals between connected persons

It should also be mentioned that if on disposal to a connected person, a loss accrues to the person making the disposal, it will not be deductible against any other gains accruing except from a chargeable gain accruing to him on the disposal of an asset to the same person if made at a time when they are connected persons (TCGA 1992, s.18(3)). In other words, a loss accruing on the disposal of a chargeable asset from, say, a parent to a child can only be deducted from a chargeable gain accruing on the disposal of an asset to the same child. Such losses are known as clogged losses.

EXAMPLE 3A

James and Joanne are married. Joanne disposes of an asset to James's father, her father-in-law, and a loss of £6,000 arises. Although Joanne has other gains in the year this loss cannot be offset against them as the disposal which gave rise to the loss is a disposal to a connected person. Three years later, Joanne disposes of a further asset to her father-in-law, and the disposal of this asset gives rise to a chargeable gain. The prior loss can be offset against this gain as this is a further disposal made at a time when they are still connected persons.

If James and Joanne divorce, then only after the decree absolute will James and Joanne cease to be connected persons. Therefore, James's father will also cease to be connected with Joanne at that point.

3.2.4 Polygamous marriages

In relation to polygamous marriages, it is understood that a polygamous marriage may be recognised as valid in UK law if it is valid in the country in which the ceremony occurred and, broadly, it was contracted by persons domiciled in that country. In these circumstances, the husband will be connected with each wife under TCGA 1992, s.286(2).

3.3 TRANSFERS OF ASSETS BETWEEN COUPLES WHO ARE MARRIED AND LIVING TOGETHER

> **KEY CONCEPTS**
>
> Married couples or civil partners who are living together can transfer assets between them without a CGT charge arising up to the end of the tax year in which they separate.

3.3.1 Married and living together

In circumstances where an individual is in any year of assessment living with his spouse or civil partner and one of them disposes of an asset to another, both are treated as if the asset was acquired from the one making the disposal for a consideration of such amount as gives rise to neither a gain nor loss for the one making the disposal (TCGA 1992, s.58). This overrides the 'connected persons' rule in TCGA 1992, s.18 and described at **3.2**.

EXAMPLE 3B

Frank and Clare (see Example 2B in **2.1.5**) get married in August 2009. Frank decides to give Clare another painting, which he bought in 1999 for £15,000. At the time of the gift the painting is worth £80,000. As Frank and Clare are married and living together, this transfer is tax neutral and Clare inherits Frank's base cost of £15,000. If Clare were to sell the painting then she would be charged to CGT on the full increase in value (i.e. proceeds less £15,000).

3.3.2 No gain, no loss in polygamous marriages

In relation to polygamous marriages, a transfer between a husband and any wife with whom he is living will be within TCGA 1992, s.58 and so will be at no gain, no loss.

3.3.3 Trading stock

The no gain, no loss rule does not apply to assets which form part of the trading stock of a trade carried on by the spouse making the disposal, or if the asset is acquired as trading stock for the purposes of a trade carried on by the spouse acquiring the asset; in this case the market value rule applies and income tax or CGT may arise.

3.3.4 Who is married and living together?

For the purposes of this section, married couples or civil partners are treated as living together unless they are separated:

(a) under a court order;
(b) by deed of separation; or,
(c) as a matter of fact in such circumstances that the separation is likely to be permanent (see Income Tax Act (ITA) 2007, s.1011).

The above tax treatment applies not only to couples who are living together throughout any tax year of assessment but also to the entire tax year during which a couple cease to be living together. In other words, even if a couple cease to live together at some point early on in any tax year, asset transfers between them from then on up to the end of that tax year (5 April) will be afforded the same tax treatment.

Furthermore, as a consequence of the above definition brought in originally by Finance Act 1988 (which introduced independent taxation), there is no longer any authority for HMRC to treat a non-resident spouse as separated from a resident spouse merely because of their residence status. Similarly, a non-resident civil partner may not be treated as separated from a resident civil partner merely because of their residence status. There exists the possibility therefore of assets passing outside the UK tax net in the albeit admittedly rare circumstances of a couple living together but residing for tax purposes in different jurisdictions.

3.3.5 Tax compliance issues

Any disposal, the consideration for which is treated by virtue of TCGA 1992, s.58 (spouses and civil partners) as being such that neither a gain nor loss would accrue, is not reportable to HMRC in the personal tax return of the individual (TCGA 1992, s.3A).

If TCGA 1992, s.58 does not apply because the transfers are made after the tax year of separation, the transfers will need to be reported for the relevant tax year when the transfers are made if the amount of the chargeable gains accruing exceeds the annual exempt amount for that year or the aggregate amount or value of the consideration (i.e. market value) for the disposal of the chargeable assets by the individual exceeds four times the annual exemption for that year. These limits are there to ensure that a taxpayer is obliged to provide information to HMRC for the purposes of establishing the amount of CGT for which he is liable where more substantial amounts or values are concerned.

For 2009/10 the annual exemption is £10,100, so if the aggregate market value of all chargeable assets transferred by one spouse to the other in 2009/10 exceeds £40,400 (and this year is after the tax year of separation), then notwithstanding that the aggregate gain may be within the annual capital gains exemption, reporting of these disposals has to be made in the personal tax return of the individual making the disposal. Where the individual has not previously had to file a personal tax return because, for example, all their income is taxed at source under PAYE or at the basic rate of tax and they have had no previous chargeable gains, then they will be required to give notice to HMRC within six months from the end of that tax year (i.e. 5 October) of chargeability.

3.4 TRANSFERS OF ASSETS BETWEEN COUPLES WHO ARE MARRIED BUT SEPARATED

KEY CONCEPTS

Assets can only be transferred between the parties at no gain, no loss in the tax year of separation. After the tax year of separation, other reliefs may need to be considered to avoid an immediate tax charge.

3.4.1 Married but separated

As mentioned in **3.3**, transfers of chargeable assets between couples who are married and living together are treated for CGT as having been transferred at a consideration which does not give rise to a gain or a loss for the transferor. The consideration for the disposal is normally therefore the original acquisition cost of the asset to the transferor. As explained above, this beneficial tax treatment continues to apply throughout the tax year in which separation occurs, but not from 6 April following the date of separation.

After separation, but before the decree absolute or dissolution of the civil partnership, the parties remain connected for tax purposes since they remain spouses or civil partners in legal terms, and transfers between them are treated as taking place at market value regardless of any consideration given for the transfer in accordance with the rules at **3.2.1**.

EXAMPLE 3C

David is in the process of separating from his wife Diane. David acquired 1,000 ordinary £1 shares in a UK listed company plc in March 1992 at a cost of £20 per share. David and Diane formally separate in July 2008 which is also the date when they are treated as having separated for tax purposes.

On 5 April 2009, David transfers the shares to his wife when they are listed as being traded at £50 per share. Diane sells the shares in June 2009 to enable her to pay legal fees and to raise a deposit for a new property, and receives £50 per share net after selling costs.

Diane is treated as acquiring the 1,000 shares at a base cost for tax purposes of £20 per share, or £20,000, as the shares were transferred to her during the tax year of separation.

On Diane selling the shares, Diane receives net sale proceeds of £50,000, and therefore realises a gain of £30,000. Assuming she has already used her annual CGT exemption, she will have to pay CGT at 18% of £5,400. The tax will be due on 31 January 2011.

EXAMPLE 3D

The facts are the same as in Example 3C, except that David transfers the shares to Diane on 6 April 2009 instead. In this case, the transfer between the spouses takes place after the tax year of separation, and so the no gain, no loss rule does not apply. David is treated as making a disposal at market value (i.e. £50 per share) to Diane. David will therefore have to pay CGT of £5,400 (being £30,000 at 18%), assuming his annual CGT exemption has already been used. The tax will be due on 31 January 2011.

Meanwhile, Diane will be treated as acquiring the shares at a base cost of £50 per share, being the market value on 6 April, so if she sells the shares in June 2009, she does not realise any gain and has no tax to pay.

As these examples illustrate, the timing of transfers can alter not only who is liable for the tax but when the tax is paid since transfers made between spouses in the tax year of separation will defer tax until the 31 January next following the tax year in which the asset is sold.

To mitigate the tax payable by David in this example, if he had a chargeable asset which was standing at a loss (i.e. where the current market value is less than his allowable base cost), he might consider transferring that asset to Diane at the same time so as to crystallise a capital loss to set against the gain (see **3.2.3**).

Another option would be to consider transferring the shares into a suitably drafted trust for the benefit of his wife from whom he is now separated, which would enable a claim for CGT hold over relief to be made on the transfer to the trustees. By doing this an immediate tax charge can be avoided. CGT would only become payable when the shares are sold. The CGT would be calculated using David's original base cost, so in effect the trustees/Diane as beneficiary would be taking on David's tax liability which is deferred. Whether this is to Diane's advantage would depend on future tax rates, the price at which the shares are eventually sold, and possibly other factors. The shares could also be appointed out from the trust to Diane with hold over relief again being claimed, the tax position remaining the same. The use of a trust also brings with it inheritance tax (IHT) considerations, which may not be an issue where the value of the shares going into the trust is within the settlor's available nil rate IHT band or where other IHT reliefs and exemptions apply and the shares/sale proceeds are appointed out from the trust within a 10-year period (see **Chapter 4**). In such cases, specialist tax advice should be sought.

If one of the parties had CGT losses or the annual CGT exemption available (£10,100 in 09/10), this would also reduce the actual tax to be paid. Proper consideration should be given to identifying chargeable assets which it might be beneficial to transfer in the tax year of separation and to identify assets currently standing at a loss. In practice, this may not be practicable or possible to achieve unless the couple separate early on in the tax year and seek prompt advice.

3.4.2 Establishing the date of separation

Fundamental to the tax analysis for any chargeable asset transfer is establishing the date of separation, or at least the tax year in which separation arose.

As mentioned above, for tax purposes, couples will be treated as living together unless they are:

- separated under a court order;
- separated under a deed of separation; or
- separated in such circumstances that the separation is likely to be permanent.

This definition is seemingly straightforward but in practice there can be complications.

It is understood that HMRC accepts that a couple are separated if they are no longer living in the same house and either there is a court order or a deed of separation. HMRC will normally also accept an informal written agreement signed by both parties and a verbal agreement to separate.

The date of separation will usually be the date on which one of them leaves the home. If there is a verbal agreement, HMRC is likely to want to verify the versions of both individuals to see if they agree and, in the event of differences, try to resolve them by collating all the facts.

Where a couple are separated under a court order but continue to occupy the same house, HMRC normally continues to treat them as a couple until the earlier of the date of divorce or one of them leaving the home. This may prove useful in allowing for transfers of assets free of tax despite the legal separation. Only where the couple have set up separate households within the home would they be treated as separated for tax purposes (and from the date separate households were set up).

The relevant authority for this can be found in the 1990 High Court case of *Holmes v. Mitchell (Inspector of Taxes)* [1991] 2 FLR 301, concerning a husband who filed a petition for divorce but this was not pursued. The couple continued to occupy the same house as separate households; as the husband put it, they more or less ignored each other. The case summarises the views of Lord Denning (as he then was) in *Hopes v. Hopes* [1949] P 227 that:

> The husband who shuts himself up in one or two rooms of his house and ceases to have anything to do with his wife is living separately and apart from her effectively as if they were separated by the outer door of a flat.

Lord Denning also referred to a decision of the Divorce Division in *Wanbon v. Wanbon* [1946] All ER 366, where the parties were said to be still living in the same household, since although living at arm's length they were still sharing the same living room, eating at the same table and sitting by the same fire and thus were not living separately and apart. He commented:

> In cases where they are living under the same roof, [separation] is reached when they cease to be one household and become two households; or in other words, when they are no longer residing with one another or cohabiting with one another.

HMRC had previously stated in its *Relief Instructions Manual* at RE1000+ (which has now been withdrawn) some of the points for its inspectors to consider in deciding whether or not separate households have been set up:

- How has the accommodation been divided between them?
- What are the arrangements for using the kitchen and bathroom and other facilities which they will both need to use?
- What services do they provide for each other? For example, do they share meals? Do they do their own laundry, cleaning, cooking and shopping?
- Have they separated their financial affairs? Do they have separate bank accounts and what are the arrangements for meeting expenditure on housekeeping and accommodation?
- Is any maintenance paid and under what terms or conditions?
- Is there any contact between them? How do they organise themselves to avoid any personal contact?

In practice, HMRC is likely to want to interview both parties. If there is none of the above evidence, the decision rests on whether the couple are separated and whether the separation is likely to be permanent. This means that the couple must be living apart with an intention at that time (held by one or both parties) to obtain a divorce or to remain apart permanently.

In respect of a short or trial separation followed by reconciliation, HMRC will normally accept that a couple remained living together. If the separation exceeds a year and HMRC is unable to confirm the facts with the individual who has remained at home, the date of separation will be the date on which one of them left the other.

If there has been a permanent separation followed by a reconciliation, so that there is no longer an intention to make the separation permanent, the couple will be treated as living together from either the date they changed their minds or the date of moving back in together. Once a couple are divorced they can only be reconciled for tax purposes if they remarry.

Where a couple remain living together up to the date of their divorce, they will become separated for tax purposes from the date of the decree absolute. If a couple divorce on the grounds that they have lived apart for two or five years as appropriate, including living in the same house as part of separate households, the date of separation is two or five years before the date of the decree nisi (or decree absolute in Scotland).

TAX AND FAMILY BREAKDOWN

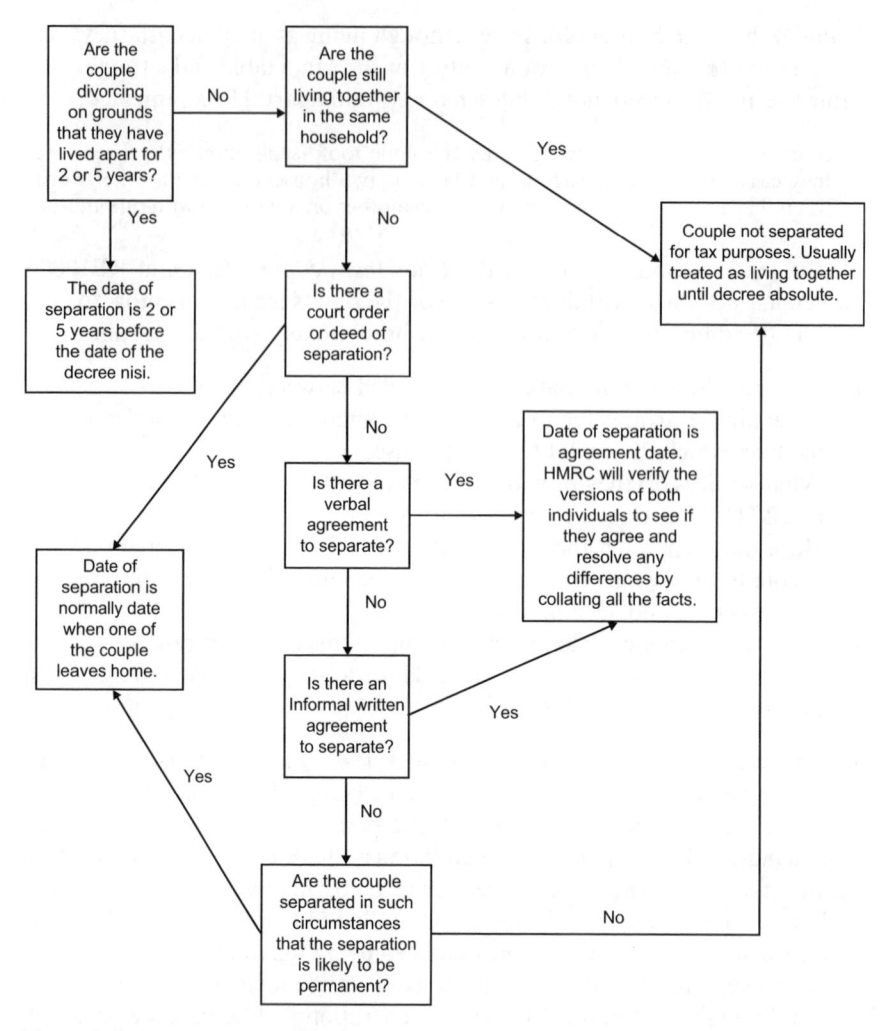

Figure 3.1 Separation flowchart

Finally, where the court has determined the date of separation for the purposes of the divorce, it is not open to couples to suggest a different date of separation for tax purposes.

3.4.3 Date of transfer

As mentioned above, transfers between married couples or civil partners during the tax year of separation do not give rise to a chargeable gain or a loss. It will be important therefore to establish the date on which a transfer takes place for CGT purposes, i.e. whether it is after the end of the tax year of separation or not.

The normal rule in TCGA 1992, s.28 is that for an asset disposed of under a contract, the time of disposal is the date the contract is made and if the contract is conditional (or if it is conditional on the exercise of an option), the time when the condition is satisfied. The completion date of a contract is not necessarily relevant for CGT purposes and for example, the time of exchange of contracts on a property purchase where completion is set for a later date (assuming exchange of contracts renders the contract unconditional) will be the relevant date.

If an asset is transferred without a formal contract, the date of disposal is the date when the asset was physically transferred.

If an asset is transferred under a court order, the disposal date will normally be the date of the order, if it is made after the decree absolute, or where it is not, the date of a consent order.

If a consent order is made before the decree absolute, there may be grounds for arguing that the disposal date is the date the parties reached agreement. HMRC will normally accept this earlier date if both parties require it but may investigate the facts further in cases where the tax at stake is material.

Where an asset is transferred by a consent order made after the date of the decree absolute or after the date the dissolution order was made final, the date of disposal is the date of the court order.

HMRC advises in its *Capital Gains Tax Manual* that this view has sometimes been disputed where the parties have approached the courts for an order to give effect to a prior agreement between them for the division of the assets of the marriage or civil partnership. It has apparently sometimes been suggested to HMRC that the agreement between the parties, which precedes the consent order, is a binding contract and so the date of any such agreement is the date of disposal of the assets. HMRC does not accept this view and cites the Privy Council decision in the non-tax case of *De Lasala* v. *De Lasala* [1980] AC 546. Lord Diplock stated that:

> Financial arrangements that are agreed upon between the parties for the purpose of receiving the approval and being made the subject of a consent order by the Court once they have been made the subject of the Court Order no longer depend upon the agreement of the parties as the source from which their legal effect is derived. Their legal effect is derived from the Court Order.

HMRC also cites support for its view in certain tax cases, for example in *Aspden* v. *Hildesley* (1981) 55 TC 609 and in *Harvey* v. *Sivyer* [1986] Ch. 119. In the latter case, Nourse J commented that it is:

> now well established that the legal effect of the provisions embodied in this kind of consent order is derived from the order itself and does not depend on any anterior agreement between the parties.

TAX AND FAMILY BREAKDOWN

The date of disposal rules are summarised in HMRC's *Capital Gains Tax Manual* (at CG22423) as follows:

Assets transferred by . . .	Date of disposal
Court order following decree or final dissolution order	Date of court order
Consent order before decree absolute or final dissolution	Accept parties' agreement or obtain documentation and advice as necessary
Other court order before the decree absolute or final dissolution order	Date of court order
Contract	Date of contract (or if conditional, the date that the condition is satisfied)
No contract	Date of transfer

3.4.4 Transfers made in the tax year of separation

The importance of the date of disposal, as explained above, is that transfers made in the tax year of separation (i.e. up to 5 April) are deemed to be made at a price which does not give rise to any gain or loss and so are free of any immediate charge to CGT.

3.4.5 Transfers made after the tax year of separation

Transfers of assets made between the end of the tax year of separation and the date of divorce (decree absolute) are deemed to be made at market value as the couple remain 'connected' for tax purposes. If the market value at the time of transfer is higher than the transferor's CGT base cost, a taxable gain may arise.

3.4.6 Asset transfers and deferred consideration

If an unconditional contract is entered into before 6 April in the tax year of separation to transfer a chargeable asset between a married couple, then for CGT to be avoided on the transfer under the no gain, no loss rule, any actual or deemed consideration payable under the contract must be 'ascertainable' even if payment is contingent on some future event and is deferred. Such might be the case in relation to the transfer of a spouse's interest in the matrimonial home in exchange for a charge over the property.

If the consideration is 'unascertainable' for tax purposes, meaning that all the events which establish the amount of the consideration occur after the date of disposal, tax will be payable if the amount of the consideration is determined and received after the tax year of separation. Tax may then be payable in the year the consideration is received.

TRANSFERS OF ASSETS

Where there is 'unascertainable' consideration, a value is placed on the right to the future consideration at the date of the contract. The valuation of that right will depend on the precise terms under which the future sum would be received, taking account of the risks and timing of such a payment. The right to unascertainable future consideration is treated as a separate asset for tax purposes (a 'chose in action'), which asset is disposed of when the actual consideration is received, which could potentially be after the tax year of separation (*Marren* v. *Ingles* [1980] 3 All ER 95; TCGA 1992, s.22).

A 'chose in action' does not benefit from any CGT reliefs, such as hold over relief or principal private residence (PPR) relief.

An example of this is at **3.4.8**.

3.4.7 Deferred charges

An example of deferred consideration is a deferred charge. Under a deferred charge, and using the matrimonial home as an example, complete ownership of the home will be vested in one spouse but the home is charged with a payment in favour of the other spouse, not to be realised until a date in the future as specified by the court order.

The future amount may be for either a fixed amount (i.e. known) or unascertainable amount (a 'chose in action').

3.4.8 Unascertainable future consideration

An example of a chose in action would occur where, for example, the house is transferred between the spouses and the consideration for the transfer is a right to a cash sum based on, say, a percentage of the future sale proceeds, which amount will, of course, not be known. For tax purposes, the right to that future cash sum needs to be valued at the date of transfer and that value is treated as consideration received for the disposal of the property when it is transferred. The right also constitutes a separate asset (chose in action) which is disposed of when the future sale proceeds are realised. The base cost of that right is the amount it was valued at when the property was transferred.

EXAMPLE 3E

Robert and Samantha own their matrimonial home, which is currently worth £500,000, in equal shares. As part of a separation under the collaborative legal process in 2009/10 (which is the tax year following the tax year of separation), Robert agrees to transfer ownership of his half share in the matrimonial home to Samantha in exchange for a deferred charge over the property which is drafted as a right to a capital sum equal to 50% of the future net sale proceeds to be realised in 10 years' time. The right to receive this future sum is considered to be worth £200,000 as at today's date and constitutes a separate asset (chose in action). This value forms the base cost for the new asset. In 10 years' of time the house is sold for £700,000 and Robert receives his 50% share of £350,000.

TAX AND FAMILY BREAKDOWN

The tax analysis is as follows: on the transfer of ownership of his half share, Robert is making a disposal for CGT purposes and is deemed to receive consideration of £200,000, being the value of the right to receive the future payment. CGT may be due on this amount, subject to a calculation of the gain arising on the disposal of his half share in the property and availability of any reliefs or exemptions. In this case PPR relief applies so no tax is due (see **Chapter 6**).

The receipt of £350,000 in 10 years' time represents a disposal of Robert's right to receive the future sum, which asset had a CGT base cost of £200,000 when it arose. In other words, a chargeable gain arises to Robert of £150,000 which is taxable at the CGT rates applying at that time. Furthermore, as the disposal is of a 'chose in action' and not the former matrimonial home, there is no possibility of PPR relief applying to the payment received (HMRC *Capital Gains Tax Manual* at CG64609).

3.4.9 Fixed deferred charge

If the charge is for a fixed (i.e. known) amount, then this amount will be taxable at the point the contract is made as the consideration for the disposal is brought into charge to tax without regard to the fact that it is contingent and without discount for the postponement of the right to receive it (TCGA 1992, s.48). Using Example 3E above, if the amount of the charge was for a fixed amount say, £250,000, Robert would be treated as disposing of his half share in the matrimonial home for £250,000. This would then fall to be taxed as consideration for disposing of his half share in the property, the gain on which is eligible to be covered by the PPR exemption. The amount when received is then free of any CGT.

3.4.10 Valuation of unascertainable consideration

It may be necessary to consider taking advice from an accountant, property valuer or other specialist valuer in appropriate cases where assets are being transferred under arrangements which give rise to unascertainable consideration at the date of disposal.

3.4.11 Inheritance tax

The date of separation has no relevance for IHT purposes.

3.5 TRANSFERS OF ASSETS BETWEEN COHABITEES OR POST DECREE ABSOLUTE

KEY CONCEPTS

Couples are no longer connected for tax purposes after the decree absolute.

3.5.1 Transfers after the decree absolute

After the decree absolute, the spouses are no longer connected for CGT purposes, and disposals between the parties are treated the same way as any other disposal between unconnected parties: market value is substituted for the price paid for the asset only if the transfer cannot be said to be a 'bargain at arm's length'. Outright gifts are not bargains at arm's length.

Where the transfer is a bargain at arm's length, the sale price for the asset will be the actual consideration received, even if it turns out to be a bad bargain. A bargain at arm's length will generally involve the parties negotiating a price and being independently advised by separate firms of accountants, lawyers or valuers, as appropriate.

A disposal under a court order can never be a bargain of any kind and will always involve the substitution of market value for assets being transferred. This means there will always be potential CGT implications to consider in these circumstances, except where the asset to be transferred is exempted or relieved from CGT, or is, say, a 'business asset' for which hold over relief applies (see **Chapter 2**).

3.5.2 Inheritance tax

After the decree absolute, transfers between former spouses are no longer exempt from inheritance tax, so tax charges could result if the transferor spouse were to die within seven years. Term assurance may therefore be considered to cover this risk unless the property in question is relevant business or agricultural property, for which IHT relief may be available (see **Chapter 4**.)

There may be scope for a limited exemption to the extent that the transfer can be shown to be for the maintenance of the former spouse/partner (see **Chapter 5**).

CHAPTER 3 CHECKLIST

1. Transfers of assets are at market value where the parties are connected; however, transfers between husbands and wives and civil partners who are living together, are at no gain, no loss (see **3.1** and **3.3**).
2. Where there is a disposal which is not a no gain, no loss transaction, consider if there are any reporting requirements in connection with the sale/transfer of an asset. Consider the due date for the payment of any tax arising, and the availability of any reliefs, exemptions and losses (see **3.3.5**).
3. The date of separation can have a significant impact on the incidence of tax due. Consider all of the relevant factors to determine the correct date of separation for tax purposes and date of transfer of the asset (see **3.4.2**).
4. Consider whether the drafting of any charge or 'deferred consideration' creates a 'chose in action' which is taxable in the future (see **3.4.6**).

CHAPTER 4

Inheritance tax and trusts

KEY CONCEPTS

Transfer of assets on family breakdown should give rise to inheritance tax (IHT) considerations only very occasionally.

When trusts (implied or express) are created as a result of family breakdown, the IHT implications will need to be explained to the parties even if there is no initial tax charge when the trust is created.

4.1 INHERITANCE TAX

Contrary to popular belief IHT is not simply a tax on the estate of a deceased person. It is in fact a tax on 'transfers of value', and prior to its transmogrification in 1984 was known as capital transfer tax, which implies this wider application. Whilst the death of an individual is the most usual occasion on which a substantial transfer of assets from the deceased to his or her family and descendants then living will occur, *inter vivos* or lifetime transfers are also within the ambit of IHT. Thus, transfers of assets on family breakdown can give rise to IHT considerations, but this arises in practice only very occasionally and usually in the case of more affluent couples with complex family arrangements. However, where trusts (implied or express) are created as a consequence of family breakdown, the immediate and future inheritance and other tax implications need to be understood and explained to the parties.

Every individual, wherever resident or domiciled, is in principle liable to IHT on transfers of UK situated assets. Generally, a tangible asset is situated where it is physically located; special rules (mostly based upon old case law) apply to determine the situs of intangible assets.

Individuals domiciled in the United Kingdom or 'deemed domiciled' (see **9.1.3**) in the United Kingdom for IHT purposes are subject to IHT on both UK and overseas assets, i.e. worldwide assets wherever they are situated. The concept of domicile is discussed in detail later (see **Chapter 9**) but very broadly an individual is domiciled in the United Kingdom if their permanent home and residence is here. This chapter assumes that individuals, their spouses, civil partners or cohabitees are domiciled in the United Kingdom.

4.1.1 Charge to inheritance tax

IHT needs to be considered whenever there is a 'transfer of value'.

A transfer of value (ToV) is a disposition which causes the transferor's estate to diminish in value. Commonly, this would be a gift of an asset but failure to exercise a right will be treated as a ToV if the value of the individual's estate is reduced and another's increased. The 'value transferred' for IHT purposes is the diminution in value to the transferor's estate and not (if different) the value of an asset transferred or the increase in the value of the estate of the transferee. In determining the value transferred, the value of any related property held by that individual's spouse or civil partner (and from whom they are not divorced) is to be brought into account (Inheritance Tax Act (IHTA) 1984, s.161).

Broadly there are three types of ToV:

(a) lifetime transfers which are potentially exempt transfers;
(b) lifetime transfers which are chargeable transfers; and
(c) transfers on death.

Though uncommon, provision is made to apportion a ToV made by certain non-commercial transactions of a close company (e.g. family owned) amongst its participators (IHTA 1984, s.94).

The value transferred by a ToV is reduced by available reliefs or exemptions (discussed below) to arrive at the 'chargeable value'.

A potentially exempt transfer (PET) is not chargeable to IHT unless the transferor dies within seven years from the date of the transfer. For a 'failed PET' which becomes chargeable, the IHT rate applicable on the death is subject to a taper relief; this progressively reduces the effective tax payable in line with the number of complete years that have elapsed between the transfer and the date of death.

A lifetime chargeable transfer is liable to IHT at the rate of 20 per cent if the chargeable value exceeds the available nil rate band (see **4.1.4**). This chargeable transfer may be subject to additional liability if the transferor dies within seven years and if the tax calculated on the death (on the same basis as for failed PETs) exceeds the tax paid on the original transfer.

An individual's chargeable estate on death (the free estate and certain settled property) is liable to IHT at the rate of 40 per cent where the chargeable value of the deceased's estate exceeds the available nil rate band (see **4.1.2**).

4.1.2 Nil rate band and the transfer of the nil rate band

Every individual is entitled to a band of chargeable transfers which will be chargeable to IHT at 0 per cent (hence, the 'nil rate band' (NRB)). It is a backward-looking exercise undertaken when a chargeable transfer is made; one compares the current NRB with the aggregate chargeable transfers made within the prior seven-year period, with any excess being available to set against the current chargeable transfer.

The NRB for the year to 5 April 2009 was £312,000. For the year ended 5 April 2010 it was increased to £325,000 and it is currently set to remain at £325,000 for tax years up to and including 2014/15.

On death, an individual's NRB remaining after set-off against chargeable lifetime transfers within the previous seven years is utilised against failed PETs (taking the earliest first) with any excess being available to set against the chargeable estate on death.

Since October 2007, the proportion of an individual's NRB unused on death can be claimed by the estate of the surviving spouse or civil partner when they subsequently die. If the NRB threshold is increased in the interval, then the benefit of the claim similarly increases. Although an individual's estate might be able to make several claims because of successive widowhoods, complex rules ensure the claim is restricted to a maximum proportion of 100 per cent of the NRB on the survivor's death.

4.1.3 Potentially exempt transfers

A ToV is a potentially exempt transfer (PET) if it is a disposition whereby the estate of another individual is increased. If the transferor survives seven years from the disposition then the PET becomes free of any IHT liability regardless of any other exemption or relief that might have applied.

4.1.4 Lifetime chargeable transfers

Generally, lifetime chargeable transfers are ToVs where the transferor's estate diminishes and the transferee is either a trust (with limited exceptions) or a company.

The Finance Act 2006 dramatically changed the IHT rules for lifetime trusts (except those for disabled persons) created on or after 22 March 2006 so that they are now taxed under the same rules as have always applied for discretionary trusts.

This means that there is an IHT liability (the 'entry charge') at 20 per cent of the chargeable value (after available NRB) on adding property to a trust and the trust itself will be subject to periodic IHT charges on such assets at up to 6 per cent on successive tenth anniversaries of its original commencement date, with further charges (the 'exit charge') when assets are distributed to or vest in beneficiaries.

The computational rules for IHT chargeable on trusts are complicated and too complex to summarise in this work. Expert advice should be sought by the uninitiated.

In circumstances of family breakdown where the financial arrangements include settlement of assets into a trust, the IHT entry charge can potentially

INHERITANCE TAX AND TRUSTS

be avoided where either or both of the exemptions for dispositions not intended to confer a gratuitous benefit or for family maintenance apply.

4.1.5 Lifetime IHT exemptions

General exemptions

Absolute transfers of assets from one spouse or civil partner to another are generally wholly exempt from IHT (IHTA 1984, s.18).

Transfers made as part of a divorce settlement will continue to be exempt from IHT, provided they are made prior to the decree absolute, even where the parties are living apart at the time of the transfer. Transfers between unmarried couples and cohabitees are not so exempted but may be treated as PETs.

It should be noted that, in the case of transfers by a UK domiciled individual to a spouse or civil partner who is domiciled outside the United Kingdom, the exemption is limited to a lifetime aggregate figure of £55,000; ToVs in excess of this limit remain to be treated as PETs. In addition, there is no limit to the transfer of assets between two non-UK domiciled spouses.

The concept of domicile is considered in **Chapter 9**. However, an individual who is not otherwise domiciled in the United Kingdom under general law is deemed to be UK domiciled for IHT purposes if they have been resident in the United Kingdom for at least 17 out of the last 20 tax years.

The following further exemptions apply to lifetime gifts only:

(i) the first £3,000 of any gifts made in a tax year (IHTA 1984, s.19);
(ii) small gifts, up to £250 in aggregate per donee per annum (IHTA 1984, s.20);
(iii) normal expenditure out of income (IHTA 1984, s.21); and
(iv) gifts up to £1,000 in consideration of marriage with higher figures of £2,500 and £5,000 dependent upon the relationship to the donee (IHTA 1984, s.22).

Dispositions not intended to confer a gratuitous benefit

IHTA 1984, s.10 provides:

(1) A disposition is not a transfer of value if it is shown that it was not intended, and was not made in a transaction intended, to confer any gratuitous benefit on any person and either –
   (a) that it was made in a transaction at arm's length between persons not connected with each other, or
   (b) that it was such as might be expected to be made in a transaction at arm's length between persons not connected with each other.

This is an important exemption relevant to transfers of property in situations of family breakdown.

A transfer of money or property pursuant to a divorce court order can fall within this exemption, as confirmed in a statement issued to that effect and made in 1975 by the Senior Registrar of the Family Division of the High Court which was agreed by HMRC ((1975) 119 SJ 596).

Transfers made after the decree absolute will therefore usually avoid IHT by virtue of this exemption. In addition, although the Registrar's statement does not specifically refer to transfers made pursuant to an agreement or voluntarily without a court order, there would seem to be no reason why such payments should not be exempt provided that they are not dissimilar to an order a court could have been expected to make in the circumstances.

In the rare cases of this exemption not applying (and certainly in the case of cohabitees), immediate exposure to IHT liability will be avoided with PETs on absolute transfers; settled transfers would need to rely upon exemptions such as business property relief (see **4.2**) and agricultural property relief (see **4.3**) and perhaps the NRB in order to avoid immediate tax liability.

In general, ToVs made in consequence of family breakdown will normally continue to qualify for IHT exemption as having no gratuitous intent even if the transfer creates settled property. Whilst a settlement created on family breakdown gives exposure to IHT periodic charges every 10 years, this may not be considered unduly onerous if there is no initial charge when the trust is created.

Family maintenance

IHTA 1984, s.11 provides that a disposition is not a ToV if it is made by one party to a marriage or civil partnership for the maintenance of the other party, or for the maintenance, education or training of the child of either party for a period not later than the year in which he attains the age of 18 or, if later, ceases full-time education or training.

Whilst 'child' includes an adopted child, payments for illegitimate children are only covered by the provision for such children of the transferor.

HMRC considers 'maintenance' to mean the supply of necessaries, such as food or clothing, so as to maintain a qualifying beneficiary in the condition of life which is appropriate to a dependant of the transferor.

See also **Chapter 5** on maintenance and secured maintenance.

Settlements created on family breakdown

A settlement can be an important and useful tool in dealing with the consequences of family breakdown where there are insufficient assets to allow for a 'clean break' so that there is a requirement for ongoing maintenance of family members, particularly children.

A trust over property may be favoured because it provides a more flexible means of balancing the conflicting needs and wishes of those involved. For example, protection may be ensured for minor children of a relationship where a legal charge over the property is not considered suitable in the circumstances.

Settlements may be formally set up by the courts under legislative provisions (e.g. the Matrimonial Causes Act 1973 or the Children Act 1989) or by agreement between the parties. But implied trusts over property can also be created under arrangements which are not so expressly labelled (or designed); unexpected tax consequences can flow where proper consideration has not been given. It is always advisable to take expert advice over arrangements where some semblance of control over assets is expected to last over a period, and particularly where there is a planned succession for benefit over assets.

Lifetime transfers to minor children generally

Prior to the Finance Act 2006, it was common practice to provide for minor children through use of accumulation and maintenance (A&M) settlements. These were required to provide an income entitlement and/or absolute entitlement to assets for one or more children on or before reaching the age of 25. ToVs to such trusts were treated as PETs and allowed income to be accumulated during the minority of the beneficiary.

One of the changes to IHT introduced in 2006 was to deny PET treatment for ToVs to A&M settlements so that there is potential exposure to a 20 per cent IHT charge. If the level of provision is likely to qualify for relief or exemption, then the limited exposure to the periodic charge every 10 years may be considered an acceptable cost to avoid the child achieving control of the assets at the age of 18.

In the absence of using a settlement, the only alternative would be to make an outright gift on bare trust; the child would then have an absolute right to the unexpended capital and accrued income at the age of 18. The transferor parent remains liable to income tax on income arising during the child's minority; however, there will not be any immediate IHT due on the transfer as this will be a PET.

Exemption on the basis of no gratuitous intent or relief for family maintenance is unlikely to be available if the assets transferred, either into a settlement or upon bare trust, are excessive in relation to a reasonable provision for the child's requirements projected through to the age where full-time education may be expected to cease.

Mesher orders

Under *Mesher* orders (covered in more detail in **Chapter 6**) each party remains beneficially entitled to their share of the former matrimonial home.

Generally, there should be no implied transfer into a settlement for IHT purposes and the value of each party's share would therefore remain in their chargeable estate for IHT purposes if they were to die before the *Mesher* order expired.

If a *Mesher* order created on or after 22 March 2006 actually constitutes a settlement for IHT purposes, potential liability needs to be considered as there will be a ToV in respect of the property share. Simply, where the ToV exceeds the available NRB (£325,000 for 2009/10) it will be necessary to establish that it is exempted from IHT by virtue of there being no intention to confer gratuitous benefit in order to avoid immediate IHT liability. The periodic 10-year anniversary charge and exit charges may still apply; each case must be looked at separately in order to quantify any potential initial and/or future tax charges.

Mesher orders implemented before 22 March 2006 which effectively created a settlement should not give rise to any IHT problems unless the transferor predeceases the other party; as previously stated, the transferor's property share would be taxed as part of their estate.

Normal expenditure out of income

IHTA 1984, s.21 provides exemption for:

> normal expenditure of the transferor ... that (taking one year with another) ... was made out of his income, and ... after allowing for all ... [such transfers] ... the transferor was left with sufficient income to maintain his usual standard of living.

This exemption will usually apply to regular maintenance payments to or for the benefit of the partner and/or children affected by the family breakdown.

4.1.6 IHT on death

On death, a person is deemed to make a transfer of value equal to the value of his free estate (i.e. the assets owned by him) and the settled estate comprised in certain settlements in which he had a qualifying interest in possession (generally all interests in possession created prior to 22 March 2006 and certain interests created in limited circumstances afterwards).

In addition, chargeable lifetime transfers and PETs made in the seven years before death are cumulated and brought into account so that additional IHT may become due upon them (see above).

As previously noted, IHT is payable at 40 per cent on the chargeable value in excess of the available NRB threshold for the fiscal year of death. Liability for the IHT due is generally as follows:

- free estate: the residuary legatee;
- settled estate: the trustees;

- PETs and chargeable lifetime transfers in the seven years prior to death: the transferee.

4.1.7 Meaning of settlement for various tax purposes

From a tax perspective, difficulty can arise when the question is asked 'Should I make use of a settlement?' because the answer may vary with whichever tax is under consideration. In consequence, differing strategies may need to be considered depending upon the particular objectives.

Inheritance tax

IHTA 1984, s.43(2) narrowly defines 'settlement'. For these purposes we can abbreviate this to: any disposition or dispositions of property, effected by instrument, by parol or by operation of law, whereby the property is for the time being:

- held in trust for persons in succession or for any person subject to a contingency;
- held by trustees with powers to accumulate income and to make payments out of that income at their discretion;
- charged or burdened (otherwise than for full consideration) with the payment of any annuity or other periodical payment for a life or other limited or terminable period.

In addition, a lease of property which is for life or lives or for a period ascertainable only by death (unless the lease was granted for full consideration in money or money's worth) is treated as a settlement of the property in question.

Capital gains tax

Taxation of Chargeable Gains Act (TCGA) 1992, s.68 defines settlement by reference to property held in it, so that settled property means 'any property held in trust other than property to which section 60 [property held as nominee or bare trustee] applies'. This is much simpler than the IHT definition but can be seen to be very similar in its objective.

Income tax

Income Tax (Trading and Other Income) Act (ITTOIA) 2005, s.620(1) provides a wide definition of settlement as including 'any disposition, trust, covenant, agreement, arrangement or transfer of assets'. That definition is used for the purposes of anti-avoidance provisions aimed at charging a settlor on the trust income.

As regards the charging of income tax on trustees of settlements, ITA 2007, s.466(2) adopts the simpler style (as used for capital gains tax, see above) of foregoing any definition of settlement as such and defining settled property as 'any property held in trust other than property [held as nominee or bare trustee]'.

Where there is no formal trust there are diverging views on whether in a particular case the 'arrangements' amount to a settlement. In this connection, Lord Wilberforce identified, in *Inland Revenue Commissioners* v. *Plummer* [1977] STC 440, that 'the courts which, inevitably, have had to face this problem, have selected the element of "bounty" as a necessary common characteristic of all the "settlements" which Parliament has in mind'. This approach is as true today as when that judgment was delivered in 1979.

4.1.8 Court orders for maintenance of children

In *Yates* v. *Starkey* (1951) 32 TC 38, CA, it was held that an order for the taxpayer to pay sums to his former wife in trust for his children constituted a settlement within the meaning of what is now ITTOIA 2005, s.620(1). Accordingly, the taxpayer was liable to tax on his payments to his children (NB in 1951, he was entitled to a deduction for making the payment!).

Many years later, in 1985, it was also held that maintenance payments made under a deed of separation by a parent directly to his children were made under a settlement (*Harvey* v. *Sivyer* (1987) 58 TC 569). Nourse J rejected the taxpayer's argument arising from *Inland Revenue Commissioners* v. *Plummer*, that payments required to be made under a court order, or a deed of separation negotiated between the parties, were made under compulsion and so lacked the element of bounty. He inferred that Lord Wilberforce thought there to be no inconsistency in his decision in *Plummer* and the earlier case of *Yates* v. *Starkey* as 'the natural relationship between a parent and a child is one of such deep affection and concern that there may always be an element of bounty by the parent, even where the provision is on the face of things made under compulsion'.

To a large degree this has become of academic interest only in understanding the difficulty of identifying a settlement for income tax purposes. Since 1988, new annual payments under deed have ceased to be either taxable in the hands of the recipient or deductible by the payer.

4.1.9 Settlements in consequence of family breakdown

Having dealt above with the IHT ramifications of making a settlement, here we look at the income tax and CGT consequences.

INHERITANCE TAX AND TRUSTS

Trusts for minor children

If an individual creates a settlement for his minor children (or is deemed to create such a settlement under a court order), then the income arising under the settlement will be treated as the income of the settlor and taxed at his marginal tax rates. He will have a right of recovery of any additional tax that he bears from the trustees.

Since 2008/09, with the standardisation of CGT to the flat rate of 18 per cent, gains realised by UK trustees of a settlement are no longer taxed upon the settlor where the beneficiaries include himself or his minor children. However, regardless of the kind of asset in question, no claim for hold over relief can be made on the transfer of chargeable assets to such a settlement.

Trusts for former spouse/civil partner

If an individual creates a settlement for his former partner (or is deemed to create such a settlement under a court order), then, provided the settlor is excluded from any benefit, the income arising under the settlement will not be treated as the income of the settlor.

The income is primarily charged upon the trustees at the basic or dividend rate (depending upon the type of income). If the trust is a discretionary trust, its income is subjected to 'the rate applicable to trusts' giving an additional charge similar to higher rates for individuals but with some relief for certain trustee expenses properly chargeable against their income.

If the trust provides for a life interest, then the net trust income is charged upon the beneficiary with credit given for the tax suffered at source and paid by the trustees. An element of relief also applies for the trustees' income expenses.

The trustees of discretionary and life interest trusts would pay CGT on realised chargeable gains above the annual exempt amount at the flat rate of 18 per cent. Settlement of certain assets may qualify for hold over relief from CGT provided the settlor cannot benefit from the settled property under any circumstance.

4.1.10 Settlements made under the Children Act 1989

What is the IHT position of a settlement made for the benefit of a child in accordance with a court order under Children Act 1989, Sched.1, para.1(2)(d)?

If the property held on trust will revert to the settlor on the termination of the trust then it could be claimed that the relief for family maintenance (IHTA 1984, s.11) covers the disposition *but only if* the trust period is specified to end on the beneficiary attaining the age of 18 or cessation of his full-time education, if later. The claim would be on the basis that the acquisition of the property via the settlement is tantamount to paying rent for the minor child's residential accommodation.

In the 2007 Special Commissioner's case of *Phizackerley* v. *Revenue and Customs Commissioners* [2007] STC (SCD) 328, the interpretation of maintenance by Browne-Wilkinson J in *Re Dennis (dec'd)* [1981] 2 All ER 140 was held to be 'wide enough to cover the transfer of a house or part interest in a house but only if it relieves the recipient from income expenditure, for example on rent'. However, if the settlement irrevocably directs the trust property to the child at the termination of the trust period, then the argument of maintenance would not succeed.

If the maintenance argument cannot succeed, that would leave only the possibility of relying upon an exemption claim that the transfer was not intended to confer a gratuitous benefit (IHTA 1984, s.10). In this case, fulfilling an obligation under a court order may be considered as not intending to confer a gratuitous benefit provided the settlor was not the applicant seeking it. Although the HMRC *Inheritance Tax Manual* refers to the exemption applying in cases of divorce, there is no specific reference to the Children Act 1989. *Dymond's Capital Taxes* (looseleaf, Sweet & Maxwell Ltd) states (at para.7.113) that 'payments in discharge of legal obligations to maintain or of any other type of legal obligation, would any way not imply a gratuitous intent'.

Generally, one would recommend an approach to HMRC to obtain comfort that the exemption would apply. HMRC (Inheritance Tax) have indicated informally to the author that an obligation under court order should meet the exemption and where necessary a written application can be made.

4.1.11 Overseas settlements

Having an overseas settlement may seem an exotic facility but it can be a pretty expensive vehicle to run and will not necessarily provide any tax breaks.

From an IHT perspective, trusts created by individuals domiciled in the United Kingdom remain subject to the IHT rules wherever the assets may be situated. Only settled property situated outside the United Kingdom escapes the scope of IHT if the settlement was made by an individual domiciled outside the United Kingdom (and not deemed domiciled in the United Kingdom), and that is the case even if the trustees are resident in the United Kingdom.

Overseas trusts may still be subject to UK withholding tax on UK source income, particularly rental, dividend and royalty income. In addition, wide-ranging and complex anti-avoidance provisions aim to tax the income and capital gains of settlors who are resident in the United Kingdom and of others who receive benefit from the settlement. More complex rules apply where non-domiciled but UK resident settlors or beneficiaries are involved.

4.1.12 Taxation summary

	Trusts set up for separated spouse or civil partner	**Trusts set up for minor unmarried children**
Income tax on trust income	Discretionary trust: at 50% Life interest trust: individual's income tax rates	Income taxed on settlor at his/her marginal rates
Capital gains within trust	18% (this is the rate for both individuals and trusts)	18% (this is the rate for both individuals and trusts)
IHT on transfer	At 20% unless: • set up on divorce and exemption applies, or • value less than nil rate band, or • BPR/APR relief applies	At 20% unless: • set up on divorce and exemption applies, or • value less than nil rate band, or • BPR/APR relief applies
CGT on transfer	At 18% unless hold over relief is claimed	At 18%, no hold over relief available

4.2 BUSINESS PROPERTY RELIEF

> **KEY CONCEPTS**
>
> Assets that qualify for business property relief may avoid an immediate liability to IHT, even where transfers to (or from) trusts are involved.

4.2.1 Overview

Where all or part of the value transferred by a ToV is attributable to the value of 'relevant business property' it may qualify for IHT business property relief (BPR), which reduces the value transferred.

It is important to note that the nature of the property gifted is not itself a condition for relief; what matters is whether the value transferred by the gift is attributable to the value of relevant business property (*HMRC* v. *Trustees of the Nelson Dance Family Settlement* [2009] EWHC 71 (Ch)).

Generally, the relevant business property must have been owned by the transferor for the two years immediately preceding the transfer; however, if it replaced other relevant business property then this condition is met if the aggregate period of ownership of both amounted to not less than two out of the five years immediately prior to the transfer.

BPR is available at one of two rates (IHTA 1984, s.104) depending on the category of relevant business property (IHTA 1984, s.105).

One hundred per cent relief applies in respect of:

- a business or interest in a business;
- unquoted (including AIM) shares in a company;
- unquoted securities of a company which alone or with other such securities and/or unquoted shares gave the transferor control immediately prior to the transfer.

The first two categories cover the shares of most family companies and assets in the majority of unincorporated businesses.

Fifty per cent relief applies in respect of:

- quoted shares in and/or securities of a company which alone or with other such shares and/or securities gave the transferor control of the company immediately prior to the transfer;
- property or equipment which immediately prior to the transfer was used for a business carried on by a company controlled by the transferor or a partnership in which he was a partner;
- property or equipment which was settled property and immediately prior to the transfer was used in a business carried on by the transferor who had a qualifying interest in possession in it.

The relief applies to chargeable lifetime transfers, transfers arising on death and failed PETs. However, in the case of lifetime gifts within seven years of the transferor's death, the property transferred must continue to be owned by the transferee and the conditions for BPR satisfied at the date of death of the transferor (or, if earlier the transferee), as well as at the date of original transfer. Subject to certain conditions, BPR continues to be available for 'replacement property' held at the relevant death, see **4.2.5**.

4.2.2 Investment businesses are not relevant business property

A business or shares and/or securities in a company are not regarded as relevant business property where the business consists wholly or mainly of dealing in shares and securities or property or holding such assets as investments. The term 'wholly or mainly' is generally interpreted to mean at least 50 per cent or more of the business; it should be noted that the question cannot necessarily be answered by applying a simple arithmetic test to any singular measure of the activities such as profits or turnover (see *Farmer* v. *Inland Revenue Commissioners* [1999] STC (SCD) 321).

4.2.3 Non-business assets

Family-owned companies or businesses, which are relevant business property, may hold assets that have not been used for the business throughout the two years prior to the ToV and which are not required for such future use. Such assets, known as 'excepted assets', must be left out of account in determining the measure of BPR in relation to the value transferred.

EXAMPLE 4A

Ashley dies, leaving (among other things) a holding of shares in XYZ Ltd to his son. XYZ Ltd is an unquoted company which carries on a publishing business. XYZ Ltd also owns a share portfolio, which is operated actively by the company such that the management of the share portfolio is agreed by HMRC to constitute a business.

XYZ Ltd's overall business therefore has two components, a publishing business and an investment business. If it can be shown that the company's overall business does not 'mainly' consist of the investment business, then BPR will apply to the total value of the XYZ Ltd shares.

EXAMPLE 4B

The facts are as above, but this time rather than owning a share portfolio in addition to its publishing business, XYZ Ltd owns a single long-term share investment which does not of itself constitute a business. In this case, XYZ Ltd's business is entirely made up of the publishing business and is therefore wholly qualifying, and some BPR is definitely available. However, the share investment is not used in the company's business, and so the value of this asset must be excluded in valuing the element of Ashley's shareholding qualifying for BPR.

4.2.4 Clawback of business property relief

As mentioned at **4.2.1**, for lifetime transfers within seven years of the transferor's death, the conditions for BPR must be satisfied not only at the time of the original transfer in respect of the gifted property but also at the time of the transferor's death (or, if earlier the death of the transferee) in respect of the property or its replacement. If this is not the case, then the additional tax on the transfer arising because of the transferor's death is computed without any BPR.

EXAMPLE 4C

Mike settles his shareholding in Wireless Ltd, an unquoted trading company, on trust for the benefit of his son. The transfer is covered by BPR and so no IHT arises immediately. The trustees dispose of the shares one year later and Mike dies just over five years after the gift when the trustees still hold the cash proceeds.

Because the settled property is now represented by cash and no qualifying replacement property was acquired within three years of the disposal, BPR no longer applies to the original chargeable transfer. Subject to the available NRB, IHT will be payable on the transfer to the trust at 40% which after 60% tapering relief (see **4.1.1**) gives an effective rate of 16.1%.

4.2.5 Replacement property (IHTA 1984, s.107)

As mentioned previously, the transferee must own the property from the time of transfer until the date of death (his death, if earlier than the transferor's death) where the transferor dies within seven years of the transfer if BPR is to continue to apply. The strictness of this rule is ameliorated if the transferee uses the 'whole of the consideration received by him for the disposal' in acquiring 'replacement property' within three years of the disposal (IHTA 1984, s.113B); both the disposal of the original property and the acquisition of the replacement property must be made in transactions at arm's length or on terms such as might be expected to pertain to such a transaction. It is not a condition that the replacement property is used in the same business but it must be relevant business property at the relevant date of death.

4.3 AGRICULTURAL PROPERTY RELIEF

KEY CONCEPTS

Assets that qualify for agricultural property relief may avoid an immediate liability to IHT, even where transfers to (or from) trusts are involved.

4.3.1 Overview

Where all or part of the value transferred by a ToV is attributable to the 'agricultural value' of 'agricultural property' it may qualify for IHT agricultural property relief (APR), which reduces the value transferred.

Agricultural value is the value of the property if it were subject to a perpetual covenant prohibiting its use otherwise than as agricultural property. Often, farmland may have value beyond its agricultural value because of hope for housing or commercial development, which value will not rank for relief.

Agricultural property includes not only farmland (situated in the United Kingdom, Channel Islands, Isle of Man or within the European Economic Area (EEA) but also such farm buildings, cottages and farmhouses (and the land occupied with them) which are of a character appropriate to that farmland. In addition, APR can apply to shares or securities which give the owner control of a company that owns agricultural property to the extent that the underlying agricultural value can be attributed to the value of the investment.

Where the property is also qualifying property for BPR purposes (see **4.2**), APR alone is given on the agricultural value element of the value transferred. Where the value transferred exceeds the agricultural value, then BPR will be available to relieve the excess.

APR is potentially available not only to owner-occupiers of farmland but also to land-owners of tenanted land.

4.3.2 Conditions to be satisfied

For APR to be available, it is necessary for the agricultural property to have been occupied by the transferor for the purposes of agriculture throughout the two years ending with the ToV, or owned by him for the previous seven years ending at that time and occupied by him and/or others for the purposes of agriculture. Occupation by a company controlled by the transferor is treated as his occupation.

Where agricultural property replaced other agricultural property, the above conditions for occupation and ownership are relaxed to two years out of the preceding five years, and seven years out of the preceding 10 years, respectively.

4.3.3 Rate of relief

The rate of relief is 100 per cent where, immediately prior to the transfer, the transferor has vacant possession of the property or the right to obtain vacant possession within the next 12 months (although this is extended by concession to 24 months). However, if neither of these positions applies because the land is tenanted under a lease which commenced after August 1995, APR at 100 per cent can still apply. In all other circumstances, the relief is at a rate of 50 per cent.

4.3.4 Farmhouses

The application of APR to farmhouses has become an increasingly difficult and litigious area. The reason behind HMRC's concerted attack probably stems from the substantial increase in the value of dwelling houses and the fact that these are the only properties where owners are entitled to any measure of relief from IHT.

Recent cases have tended to set practical parameters to filter out the number of farmhouses eligible for relief and the value of that relief.

In determining whether a farmhouse is of a 'character appropriate' to farmland, a number of factors need to be considered: its size, content and layout in relation to the land and in proportion to the requirements of the farming activities; whether it satisfies 'the elephant test' (which is that one knows a farmhouse when one sees it); whether an educated rural layman would regard the property as a house with land or as a farm; and the length of the association of the house with the land and the history of agricultural production (see *Lloyds TSB (Personal Representative of Antrobus (dec'd))* v. *Inland Revenue Commissioners* [2002] STC (SCD) 468).

Having conceded in the above case that the property was a farmhouse and of a character appropriate, HMRC then claimed before the Lands Tribunal that the value of the house exceeded its agricultural value. It was held that the

TAX AND FAMILY BREAKDOWN

agricultural value, in accordance with the argument of HMRC's expert witness, should be taken as 70 per cent of market value. The Valuation Agency now seems to employ a 30 per cent discount on market value as a rule of thumb in arriving at agricultural value.

It is now established that a farmhouse is be considered as the farmer's dwelling from which the farm is managed (see *Arnander v. Revenue and Customs Commissioners* [2006] STC (SCD) 800). This highlights the legislative requirement that the property must be occupied for agricultural purposes and the key issue is the purpose of the occupation of the premises. This also raises concerns that APR may be denied to the 'lifestyle farmer' who owns a large and valuable house with adjoining farmland likely to be contract farmed. A particular trap to be aware of is that the 'character appropriate' test can be argued to apply to land under common ownership. Where the ownership of the majority of the farmland is divorced from the farmhouse itself (perhaps due to a transfer of the farmland to children or family trust), this could lead to withdrawal of APR on the farmhouse (see *Starke v. Inland Revenue Commissioners* [1995] STC 689).

4.3.5 Clawback of agricultural property relief and replacement property

The provisions dealing with clawback of BPR on lifetime gifts (**4.2.4**) and replacement business property (**4.2.5**) apply with similar effect for APR.

4.4 GIFTS WITH RESERVATION OF BENEFIT AND PRE-OWNED ASSETS

KEY CONCEPTS

These rules should generally be of limited importance to married couples and civil partners undergoing family breakdown (unless the donee is not UK domiciled). In relation to POAT (see below), particular care is needed in cases not involving married couples or civil partners.

4.4.1 Gifts with reservation of benefit

Since lifetime gifts by an individual made more than seven years prior to his death are not brought into account with his estate for calculation of IHT on his death, it is generally good IHT planning to make outright gifts of 'surplus assets' as early as possible. However, in practice and for a variety of non-tax reasons, making such outright gifts may not be considered appropriate (e.g. to minor children) or practical (e.g. if the donor wishes to retain possession of the asset) or desirable (e.g. if the asset could be at risk of the donee's profligacy or divorce). In such cases, an individual may consider transfers of assets under arrangements where he might enjoy the gifted property in the future and/or enjoy an ongoing benefit from it immediately.

INHERITANCE TAX AND TRUSTS

Without effective anti-avoidance legislation, it would be possible to avoid an IHT charge on assets transferred out of 'legal ownership' by way of a PET more than seven years prior to death whilst continuing to enjoy the benefit of possession even until death. The classic scenario would be where a married couple sought to transfer ownership of the family home to their children, only for the children to allow them to continue living there rent free.

When PETs were introduced by the Finance Act 1986, with the replacement of capital transfer tax (CTT) by IHT, provisions were introduced along lines similar to those employed with respect to estate duty until 1975 to counter this possible tax avoidance technique.

This legislation was (and following several amendments still is) meant to ensure that where property is given away but the donor continues to use or enjoy a benefit from it without paying full consideration, the property is treated as remaining comprised within the donor's estate on death for IHT purposes. However, it does not apply in relation to the gift of assets to the extent that the ToV is exempt on a transfer to a spouse or civil partner.

Where the legislation applies, the gifted asset is defined as 'property subject to a reservation' but it is commonly referred to as a 'gift with reservation of benefit' (GROB).

If and when the donor relinquishes possession of the asset or enjoyment of any possible benefit ceases, he is treated as then having made a separate PET of the asset. Thereafter, the asset will not be included in his estate on death; however, that PET does remain potentially chargeable on the individual's death within seven years.

In divorce situations, the GROB rules are of limited importance, since if the ToV is made prior to the decree absolute then it will fall within the normal spouse exemption rules. However, care must be taken where the normal spouse exemption is limited because the donee is not UK domiciled for IHT purposes, and most certainly where a transfer takes place after the decree absolute.

4.4.2 Pre-owned assets

The purpose of the GROB legislation was relatively well understood, but contained a number of loopholes which could be exploited to a taxpayer's advantage. Despite various legislative changes following court decisions in favour of taxpayers, a plethora of avoidance schemes designed to circumvent the GROB rules continued to be widely marketed by a burgeoning tax avoidance industry.

The Finance Act 2004 introduced a completely new set of rules to penalise and/or deter individuals who have entered or contemplate entering into such GROB avoidance arrangements (with effect from 6 April 2005). Somewhat radically, this anti-avoidance legislation operates by imposing an annual income tax charge on a standardised valuation of the benefit enjoyed from the assets in question, which are euphemistically called 'pre-owned assets'; the tax charge is consequently known as 'POAT'.

The strongest criticism of the legislation was that it caught not only the marketed schemes but also the tried and tested arrangements which had been properly entered into many years beforehand with the confirmed blessing of HMRC through its own manual. Professional cries of 'retrospective legislation' were met with HMRC's riposte of 'retro-active legislation', in that it only applied to the future enjoyment of the pre-owned asset. Whatever the legal significance of this fine distinction, the practical fact remains that the legislation may catch arrangements which were put in place prior to its enactment.

The most important point to grasp concerning POAT is that it is intended to be a wide-ranging 'sticking plaster' for the GROB rules. Therefore, if the situation being contemplated is already subject to those rules (i.e. the asset will be treated as comprised in the donor's estate on death) then it is not necessary to consider the pre-owned assets legislation.

POAT is chargeable on three categories of asset, of which the first two – land (including and buildings) and chattels – will prove to be the most common. The third category covers intangible assets (such as shares and insurance products) held in settlor-interested trusts; these rules are unlikely to be often met with in practice and, as a specialist area, are not dealt with in this work.

For a POAT charge to arise on land and chattels which are not subject to the GROB provisions, the precondition is that an individual enjoys occupation or use of asset A and, after 17 March 1986 (when IHT was introduced):

- he has disposed of asset A or another asset the proceeds of which can be traced as having been used in acquiring asset A; or
- he has directly or indirectly provided the consideration used to purchase asset A; however, an outright gift of cash is excluded where it was made more than seven years before the occupation or enjoyment first commenced.

Certain disposals or provision of funds ('excluded transactions') will not invoke the POAT charge. A disposal will be excluded if it is of the whole of an individual's interest in an asset and is either an arm's length transaction to an unconnected person or under terms such as might be expected to be made at arm's length between unconnected persons.

In the context of this work, any disposition which is exempt from IHT as being for family maintenance (see **4.1.5**) and any disposal or gift (including a gift into settlement) to or for a spouse or civil partner or, where ordered by the court, a former spouse or civil partner will be excluded.

Thus, in most if not all cases involving family breakdown, transfers of assets should not give rise to POAT.

Particular care should be adopted in cases not involving married couples or civil partners. There may be unexpected effects for cohabitees in respect of the POAT charge because the 'excluded transaction' test will not operate to disapply the charge and subsequent marriage will not rectify the position.

INHERITANCE TAX AND TRUSTS

Since 2003, the GROB rules should cover any settled asset occupied or enjoyed by the settlor following termination of an interest in possession of and during the lifetime of a former spouse or civil partner. By definition, POAT could not then apply.

Where POAT is applicable, the charge on property is generally based upon the annual market rental for a landlord's repairing and insuring lease. For chattels, it is based upon notional interest at the official rate (as is applied for income tax on beneficial employee loans) on a notional loan equivalent to the value of the assets enjoyed.

In both scenarios, the POAT charge is discounted where the individual did not effectively provide the whole of the asset and will also be reduced by any amount which the individual is legally obliged to pay for the occupation or enjoyment.

EXAMPLE 4D

Mike and Susie's marriage ends in divorce in 2002. As part of the divorce settlement the court orders that Mike transfers the family's holiday home in France into an interest in possession trust for his former spouse, with the proviso that if she marries again her interest in possession will cease. The holiday home is gifted into trust in December 2002 (there may be other tax considerations in relation to this transaction). In July 2009, Susie remarries and her interest in possession ceases such that Mike and the children become entitled to an interest in possession in the property. Because Susie's interest was not terminated by her death, Mike is subject to a POAT charge once her interest ends. If the trust had been created after 20 June 2003, Mike would be liable under the GROB rules instead of POAT, meaning that the value of the property will be included in his estate on his death unless he ceased to occupy it more than seven years beforehand.

CHAPTER 4 CHECKLIST

1. Check if the donee spouse/civil partner is non-UK domiciled for IHT purposes (**4.1.5**).
2. Obtain advice on whether a trust will be created as a consequence of the family breakdown (**4.1.9**).
3. Confirm which of the lifetime IHT exemptions may be relevant (**4.1.5**).
4. Check if BPR/APR is available to reduce the ToV (**4.2** and **4.3**).
5. Exercise caution in relation to unmarried couples as regards POAT (**4.4.2**).

CHAPTER 5

Maintenance and secured maintenance

5.1 TYPES OF MAINTENANCE

There are essentially two types of maintenance that can be awarded under a court order:

- maintenance payments which may be secured against non-income producing assets, such as land;
- a secured maintenance order which requires one spouse to transfer income producing assets on trust to trustees, the income from which trust is used to pay maintenance to the other spouse. Once the order has ceased, the trust ceases and the assets revert to the transferor spouse. If the transferee spouse is owed money in respect of unpaid maintenance, he/she must look to the trustees to recover this. The transferor spouse has no personal obligation to pay maintenance.

It is understood that these orders are rarely made, but when made give rise to potential capital gains tax (CGT) implications. In certain cases, however, and where the CGT implications are not material, there may be income tax advantages for the transferor.

5.2 MAINTENANCE PAYMENTS

> **KEY CONCEPTS**
>
> There are generally no income tax or CGT implications of making maintenance payments. Where conditions are met, there are no inheritance tax implications either.

5.2.1 Income tax

Maintenance payments under agreements or court orders made in EU Member States since 15 March 1988 are generally outside the UK tax system. This was extended to European Economic Area (EEA) member states from 1 January 2004. Payments are made without deduction of tax and the recipient is not taxed on the receipt of the payment. In other words there is no relief for the payer where payments are made out of taxed income or gains.

The exception is where one of the parties to the marriage or civil partnership was born before 6 April 1935, in which case relief is given to the payer as an income tax reduction limited to the minimum married couple's allowance (£2,670 for 2009/10) at the rate of 10 per cent (Income Tax Act (ITA) 2007, Part 8, Chapter 5). From 5 December 2005, the relief given to the payer was extended to payments made by one parent of a child to the other parent for the maintenance of the child by the other parent, or by one person to another (even if not a spouse or civil partner) for the maintenance of a 'relevant child' of theirs, being a child, other than a foster child, who has been treated as a child of their family. The date of birth requirement for one of the parties remains unchanged.

The parties must not be 'living together' at the time the payment is made and the recipient of the payments must not have remarried or entered into a new civil partnership.

5.2.2 Capital gains tax

There are no CGT implications for ordinary maintenance payments.

5.2.3 Inheritance tax

As discussed in **Chapter 4**, Inheritance Tax Act (IHTA) 1984, s.11(1) provides that:

> A disposition is not a transfer of value if it is made by one party to a marriage or civil partnership in favour of the other party or of a child of either party and is:
> (a) for the maintenance of the other party, or
> (b) for the maintenance, education or training of the child for a period ending not later than the year in which he attains the age of eighteen or, after attaining that age, ceases to undergo full-time education or training.

Therefore, all payments under ordinary maintenance agreements (which are likely to include transfers of property such as the family home, provided that the transfer was to maintain the spouse) should be covered by this exemption. Where a transfer only partly satisfies the provisions, some exemption may still be available. However, all cases will need careful consideration of the facts in order to ascertain what exemptions may be available.

5.3 SECURED MAINTENANCE

KEY CONCEPTS

Although rare, where secured maintenance is used as part of the divorce settlement, there are income tax, CGT and IHT issues to consider. Consideration should be given to the nature of the asset(s) subject to the secured maintenance to mitigate liabilities where possible.

5.3.1 Income tax

For income tax purposes, there is a general anti-avoidance rule found in Income Tax (Trading and Other Income) Act (ITTOIA) 2005, Part 5, Chapter 5, such that where a settlor creates a settlement but, *inter alia*, retains an interest in it (apart from certain exceptional circumstances including death or bankruptcy), any income arising within the settlement is taxable on the settlor. The definition of 'settlement' is widely drawn and includes any disposition, trust, covenant, agreement, arrangement or transfer of assets made directly or indirectly. 'Settlor' in relation to the settlement means any person by whom the settlement was made (ITTOIA 2005, s.620). In particular, it includes any person who has provided, or has undertaken to provide, funds directly or indirectly for the purpose of the settlement, or has made a reciprocal arrangement with another person for that other person to make or enter into the settlement.

A settlor retains an interest if:

(a) the settlor or the settlor's spouse or civil partner:
    (i) can receive the property, or income from that property; or
    (ii) can or may receive income from any other property directly or indirectly representing proceeds of, or income from, that property; or
(b) income or proceeds from that property will or can become payable to, or applicable for the benefit of, the settlor or the settlor's spouse or civil partner.

For this purpose, a spouse or civil partner does not include a spouse or civil partner from whom the settlor is separated under a court order or by deed of separation or where the separation is likely to be permanent. In addition it does not include a person to whom the settlor is not married or in civil partnership but whom he may later marry or become a civil partner to.

If the disposition or arrangement is an outright and unconditional gift of property which cannot benefit the donor in any circumstances, and the property carries the right to the whole of any income arising from the gift and is not wholly or substantially a right to income, the above rules do not apply.

Given the wide definition of settlement, a secured maintenance order is a trust or a settlement for this purpose. It is not an outright gift, since as the spouse providing the assets is entitled to the return of the trust assets when the obligation to pay maintenance terminates, the transferor spouse is deemed to have retained an interest in the settlement. Therefore, the trust income is potentially taxed on the transferor spouse.

However, ITTOIA 2005, s.627 provides an exclusion from a charge to income tax on the transferor where a settlement is made by one party to a marriage or civil partnership to provide for the other party to the marriage or civil partnership in relation to income arising after the marriage or civil partnership has been dissolved or annulled, provided that the income is payable to, or is applicable for the benefit of, the other party.

In addition, the exclusion extends to income which arises under such a settlement while the parties are separated under a court order or under a separation agreement or where the separation is likely to be permanent.

The income that is distributed to the other spouse as maintenance is charged to income tax on the recipient at their marginal income tax rates. This can potentially be more advantageous than for ordinary maintenance in circumstances where the recipient is taxed at lower marginal income tax rates on the income than the payer.

Any income received by the trust that is not distributed for maintenance purposes is taxable on the transferor spouse since the exclusion only applies to income that is payable or applicable for the benefit of the other party.

If the secured maintenance order is for the benefit of a minor child (which means a person under the age of 18) who is unmarried and not in a civil partnership, it is also likely to create a settlement for tax purposes (following the same definition); however, all trust income will remain the taxable income of the transferor spouse and will not be taxable on the minor child. This follows the general rules for child maintenance found in ITTOIA 2005, s.629.

5.3.2 Capital gains tax

Secured maintenance orders can cause CGT complications. The transfer of income producing assets appears to create a settlement and the transfer of the assets into a trust constitutes a chargeable transfer for CGT purposes regardless of the fact that the transferor retains an interest in the trust capital.

The transferor and the trustees are connected persons for CGT and so the transfer is deemed to take place at market value (see **2.1.5**). Therefore, the transferor has a potential charge to CGT on the market value of any chargeable assets transferred less the transferor's allowable base cost.

On a disposal of any of the trust's chargeable assets, further charges to CGT will arise to the trustees in the normal way to be taxed at the rate of 18 per cent under current law.

When the obligation to pay maintenance ceases, the assets will revert to the transferor spouse with a further potential charge to CGT, as there will be a deemed disposal and reacquisition of the trust's chargeable assets at that time. There can be no claim to hold over any gain (as discussed at **2.2**) as the settlor has an interest in the trust. Again, any chargeable gains will be taxed on the trustees at the rate of 18 per cent under current law.

If the death of the 'maintained' spouse is the reason for the reversion of the trust assets and the transferor is still alive, the transferor will normally reacquire the assets at a value that realises neither a gain nor a loss (TCGA 1992, s.73).

If the transferor dies, then the person entitled to the assets under the deceased's will acquires them at their market value on the termination of the secured maintenance trust (TCGA 1992, s.71).

5.3.3 Inheritance tax

A secured maintenance order would appear, in normal circumstances, to create a settlement; however, on divorce it may be posssible to argue that the transferor has received full consideration for a transfer as the transferee will give up the rights to further claims.

Following the 22 March 2006 changes made to the IHT regime for trusts, a secured maintenance order is potentially subject to the new rules on *inter vivos* trusts, and although the initial transfer should be exempt if it is made for maintenance of the spouse, the trust will still be subject to a potential 10-year charge at 6 per cent and to exit charges. See **Chapter 4**.

In addition, if the transferor spouse dies before the trust has terminated, the value of the trust assets may have to be included in their estate under the 'gifts with reservation of benefit' rules (see **4.4.1**).

5.3.4 Maintenance and secured maintenance: summary

	Maintenance	**Secured maintenance**
Income tax	Income tax exempt in hands of recipient spouse but no tax relief for payer either	Income taxed on recipient spouse if distributed, otherwise taxed on transferor spouse
CGT	No CGT implications as no transfer of assets	Creates a settlement for CGT purposes; potential CGT issues for transferor spouse
IHT	Should be covered by relevant IHT exemption	Potential for IHT charges to apply

5.4 TAX CREDITS AND FAMILY BREAKDOWN

KEY CONCEPTS

Couples in receipt of tax credits will have to inform HMRC of their change of circumstees very promptly following separation. They will also need to continue to supply HMRC with both parties' details in order that tax credit entitlement can be calculated.

5.4.1 Introduction

A married or civil partnership couple living together, and also cohabitees and same sex couples living together, may be in receipt of tax credits. Currently, these comprise the working tax credit for families in work but with low earnings, and the child tax credit for families with children. Both tax credits are means related, and the income which has to be taken into account is the aggregate income of the couple (the 'tax credit limit'). However, this requirement only applies to a married or civil partnership couple who are living together (Tax Credits Act (TCA) 2002, s.3(5)), with an equivalent rule for cohabitees living together as 'husband and wife' and same sex couples in an analogous situation.

Tax credits are awarded in respect of income tax years, and the relevant income is normally the income of the preceding tax year (later adjusted to current year income if current year income is lower than preceding year income, or it exceeds it by more than £25,000, when only the excess over £25,000 is taken into account).

5.4.2 Permanent separation

When a couple permanently separate following relationship or marriage breakdown, the consequence is that the previous tax credit unit and award terminates, and each cohabitee or spouse becomes an independent unit (TCA 2002, s.3(5)). Not later than one month after the permanent separation occurs, there is a mandatory obligation to notify HMRC of the termination, but the legislation extends the time limit to one month after the person became aware of the change if that is a later date (see Tax Credits (Claims and Notifications) Regulations 2002, SI 2002/2014, reg.21(3) as amended by SI 2006/2689, reg.6). In the case of a joint claim, a notice of termination of the tax credit unit is effective if it is given by either spouse or cohabitee.

A notification may be given orally or in writing to an appropriate officer, but in practice HMRC's preference appears to be for notification by phone to the tax credits helpline. The maximum penalty for failure to give a compulsory notice of change of circumstances is £300 (TCA 2002, s.32(3)), plus the recovery of any overpaid credits, with interest if there has been fraud or neglect (TCA 2002, s.37(1)).

5.4.3 Tax year of separation

In the year of permanent separation the tax credit award has to be split. For the part of the year in which the couple were living together, the award will be a joint award based on the circumstances of the couple and on the aggregate annual preceding year income of the couple, later adjusted to current year income if appropriate. The award itself will be time-apportioned to cover only that part of the tax year the couple were living together. For the remainder of the year, each cohabitee or spouse must make a new application as a single person, provided they each satisfy the qualifying conditions, but the amount of any new tax credits will still be based on that person's taxable income of the preceding year.

Following the end of the tax year in which a couple separate, both persons may expect to receive a notice requiring confirmation of their income and circumstances for the year of separation. This notice will require details of their joint income for the whole of the year of separation, not just for that part of it when they were living together. In practice, it may prove difficult for either cohabitee or spouse to provide joint income on a single return, but as each person will be required to make a return, HMRC should be able to aggregate their separate returns of income to determine the joint income. If for the part of the year after separation, either person has claimed tax credits as an individual, a separate confirmation of circumstances and income will be required for the new award. The income required will also be for the whole of the tax year of separation, and this may therefore result in the same information having to be provided twice to HMRC. An example provided by HMRC in the notes accompanying the 2008/09 tax credits renewal pack illustrates the point.

EXAMPLE 5A

Mr and Mrs Smith claimed tax credits as a couple for 2008/09. On 21 August 2008, they separated. On 5 September 2008, Mrs Smith made a new claim for tax credits as a single claimant. The claim was backdated to 22 August 2008. Mr Smith was no longer eligible for tax credits.

Mr Smith will receive a renewal pack for the joint claim for the period from 6 April 2008 to 21 August 2008. Mrs Smith will also receive a renewal pack for the joint claim for the period from 6 April 2008 to 21 August 2008. She will also receive a pack as a single claimant, for the period from 22 August 2008 to 5 April 2009.

In relation to claims for child tax credit following permanent separation and divorce, etc., the usual test to be applied is that the child is 'normally living with' the claimant(s). Where there are competing claims, the test is who has the main responsibility for the child. This is subject to a joint election as to who has the main responsibility, but in the absence of such an election HMRC will decide on the information available.

CHAPTER 5 CHECKLIST

1. If maintenance payments are to be part of the divorce settlement, consider if there are any tax implications of implementing these (**5.3.4**).
2. Where secured maintenance is to be agreed, consider what assets are used. Is there a possibility of transferring assets which have a low inherent CGT liability (or are standing at a loss) or assets that are business assets for CGT or IHT purposes in order to take advantage of any reliefs available (entrepreneurs' relief (**2.3**), BPR (**4.2**), etc.)? (**5.3.2**)
3. Consider the implications of the separation on tax credits. HMRC should be advised of the change in circumstances within one month (**5.4**).

CHAPTER 6

Interests in land and property

6.1 THE FAMILY HOME

> **KEY CONCEPTS**
>
> Transfers of the family home between separating couples will normally be wholly relieved from capital gains tax (CGT) in most cases. Where more than one residence is owned, CGT complications may arise, although with suitable planning it is possible to mitigate such tax liabilities.

In many cases, the family home will be the single largest financial asset of a couple who are married or in civil partnership or cohabiting. In a family breakdown situation, however, there may be insufficient equity in the property to warrant an immediate sale simply to facilitate the realisation of a capital sum to enable a clean break to be made. In addition, the welfare and interests of any children who are under the age of 18 or in full-time education who are resident in the property may also render an immediate sale not possible. There are various actions which are available to the courts to deal with such situations in the context of family breakdown.

The courts can exercise their jurisdiction in the following ways:

- by recognising an existing equitable interest of the spouse or civil partner who does not have legal title to the dwelling house;
- by ordering the spouse or civil partner owning the home (or an interest in it) to transfer it to the other spouse or civil partner;
- by ordering the spouse or civil partner owning the home (or an interest in it) to hold it on trust for the other spouse or civil partner for a limited period;
- by ordering the spouse or civil partner owning the home to sell it and to pay the other spouse or civil partner a capital sum out of the proceeds of sale;
- by both determining that one spouse or civil partner had an equitable interest in the home and ordering the other spouse or civil partner to transfer some or all of their interest to the first spouse or civil partner, or to pay the first spouse or civil partner a capital sum out of their share of the sale proceeds.

The family home is *prima facie* a chargeable asset for CGT purposes and any disposal or transfer of the family home at a price (or market value where appropriate) which exceeds its original acquisition cost plus any enhancement expenditure will give rise to a chargeable gain unless this is can be covered by any available reliefs or exemptions.

6.1.1 Establishing ownership for CGT purposes

For CGT purposes, the key issue in a family breakdown situation is to establish beneficial ownership of the family home rather than who holds legal title. It may be that one party has an equitable interest in the property by virtue of contributions made, or rights of occupation, such that the other party, whilst having legal ownership, owns the property under a constructive trust of land. In *Hazell v. Hazell* [1972] 1 All ER 923, it was held that if a wife contributes directly or indirectly in money or money's worth towards the initial cost, or towards mortgage instalments, she acquires an interest in equity in the matrimonial home proportional to those contributions. Similarly, a husband who contributes directly or indirectly also acquires in equity an interest in the matrimonial home proportional to those contributions, even though the wife alone is registered as the legal owner.

The Taxation of Chargeable Gains Act (TCGA) 1992, s.60, in relation to property held by a person as a nominee for another person or as trustee for another person absolutely entitled as against the trustee (i.e. as bare trustee), applies as if the property were vested in, and the acts of the nominee or trustee in relation to the property were the acts of, the person or persons for whom he is a nominee or trustee. Therefore any acquisitions from or disposals to the nominee/bare trustee by that person or persons are disregarded accordingly.

The Married Women's Property Act 1882, s.17, enables the court to recognise an existing equitable interest of the wife in the home. Civil Partnership Act 2004, s.66, similarly enables the court to recognise an existing equitable interest of a civil partner in the home. If the court recognises an existing equitable entitlement or its existence is established by agreement between the parties (or their solicitors), it is understood that HMRC will accept the existence of an equitable interest of up to one-half in the home from the outset without investigation, unless 'exceptionally there is obvious evidence to contradict it' (HMRC *Capital Gains Tax Manual* at CG65310).

6.1.2 Ownership as joints tenants or tenants in common

If the home is held by the couple legally and beneficially as joint tenants, it may be noted that divorce or separation has no effect on survivorship if one of the joint tenants dies with the property passing to the survivor. This may not be a desirable state of affairs for either joint tenant. Pending transfers in

INTERESTS IN LAND AND PROPERTY

the course of separation, couples may therefore wish to sever the joint tenancy so the home is held as tenants in common. The beneficial interests can then be disposed of in accordance with their wills in the event of the demise of either party during the divorce proceedings.

Cohabitees, by contrast, may be advised to own properties as tenants in common or in their sole names.

6.1.3 Practical effects of beneficial ownership

The practical effect of determining who has equitable or beneficial ownership of the family home where it is in a proportion such as 50:50, is to divide the sale proceeds, cost of acquisition and all other relevant expenses in proportion to the equitable interests irrespective of who actually bore the expenditure on the property.

Thus, it would not matter who provided the initial capital for its acquisition or funded the repayments of any mortgage or who incurred the expenditure on any capital improvements. Therefore, once the beneficial ownership has been determined and in what proportion, all relevant expenses are split in that proportion, so there is, in simple terms, only one CGT calculation, with any net gain (or loss) being split in the same proportion.

EXAMPLE 6A

Mark and Ben bought a home together as tenants in common following their entry into a civil partnership in June 2006. The property cost £300,000, inclusive of costs and SDLT, and was bought with a joint mortgage of £200,000 and a £100,000 cash deposit, 70% of which was contributed by Mark from funds recently inherited and 30% was contributed by Ben. Ben agrees, however, to fund the full costs of the mortgage as Mark is on a low wage. To reflect the fact that Mark has made a larger initial contribution to the cost of the property, but giving some allowance for Ben funding the mortgage costs, it is decided between them that Mark is to own 60% of the equitable interest in the family home and Ben 40%.

Ben and Mark's civil partnership ends in 2009 at a time when the outstanding mortgage is £100,000. The property is immediately sold for net proceeds of £400,000; so a capital gain arises of £100,000 (i.e. sale proceeds less base cost of £300,000); £60,000 of this gain is assessable on Mark and £40,000 on Ben in accordance with their tenancy in common.

Having paid off the outstanding mortgage from the net sale proceeds, Mark and Ben receive actual cash proceeds in the amounts of £180,000 and £120,000, respectively. On the face of it and in economic terms, however, Mark only put in £70,000 which has returned him a gain or profit of £110,000, whereas Ben, by contrast, has put in £130,000 (deposit plus repayment of the mortgage) yet has received only £120,000, so has lost £10,000. Some form of cash equalisation between the former couple may take place in practice but this would not affect the CGT calculation unless HMRC recognised Ben as having a greater equitable ownership in the property by virtue of his contributions towards the repayment of the mortgage.

Ben and Mark are unlikely to have a taxable gain in the above example, due to the availability of principal private residence (PPR) relief. See **6.1.5**.

6.1.4 Division of assets

When it has been established who beneficially owns the property, on a division of assets as part of family breakdown, the individual who is making a transfer of their beneficial ownership is the one who is deemed to be making the disposal for CGT purposes.

6.1.5 Principal private residence (PPR) relief

Purpose of the relief

PPR relief is given under TCGA 1992, ss.222–226.

The stated purpose of the relief according to HMRC is to enable a person to replace their existing home with another home of similar value by ensuring that the proceeds of sale of the old home are not diminished by a charge to CGT. In most cases, the gain arising on the disposal of a person's home is relieved from CGT.

The relief is not available in circumstances where taxpayers seek to exempt disposals of more than one residence by routing a disposal through a discretionary trust (TCGA 1992, s.226A).

What qualifies as a principal private residence?

PPR relief is available where a gain arises from the disposal of an interest in:

- a dwelling house; or
- part of a dwelling house

which has at some time been its owner's only or main residence.

The relief extends to the surrounding garden or grounds of that residence up to a permitted area of 0.5 of a hectare, which includes the dwelling house. Only in very exceptional circumstances (such as a very large dwelling house) will the permitted area be greater and in those cases specialist advice should be taken.

The relief is non-territorial in scope and so a residence which is outside the United Kingdom may also qualify for relief if the relevant conditions are met.

Where there is more than one property, careful consideration may need to be given to which property is the PPR for relief purposes; this is covered in detail in **6.3**.

Last 36 months of ownership

If a dwelling house has been used as its owner's only or main residence at some time in his or her period of ownership, then generally the final period of ownership will always qualify for PPR relief even if the owner is not in occupation during that period. For disposals on or after 10 December 2003, this period will almost always be 36 months.

The purpose of the final period exemption according to HMRC is to help an owner-occupier who puts his or her house up for sale but cannot find a buyer. The downturn in the housing market prompted an increase in the period to 36 months for disposals after 19 March 1991; however, the Treasury has retained a power to vary this period to 24 months for disposals after a specified date by an order in Parliament. A further order can then restore the final period to 36 months. The intention is to allow flexibility to deal with fluctuations in the housing market. So far, the period has not been varied from 36 months.

Although the final period exemption is intended to apply where there are difficulties finding a buyer, it currently applies 'in any event'. In other words, the exemption is available for the final period if the dwelling house has been its owner's only or main residence at some point, regardless of the use of the dwelling house in that final period.

In the straightforward example, where an individual acquires a property, moves into it immediately as their only home (their PPR) and remains there until it is sold, there is no CGT on any gain arising on the disposal of the property. Furthermore, even if the individual moves out of the original property, acquiring and occupying another property as their main residence with the original property not being sold until three years after moving out, the final period exemption of 36 months would provide relief from tax on any gain arising on the property during this period. The relief also applies to transfers between the parties to a family breakdown within three years of the owning spouse ceasing to occupy the property.

Further relief for non-occupation

Where an individual has let out the property as residential accommodation in their period of ownership, if there is a gain arising by reason of the letting then further relief is available in relation to the gain in the let period (TCGA 1992, s.223(4)). The amount of further relief available is the higher of:

(a) the PPR relief available on the property;
(b) the gain arising in the let period; and
(c) £40,000.

Taking on a single lodger (or providing a furnished room under HMRC's 'rent a room' scheme) would not normally affect PPR relief and would be ignored.

It may also be the case that where a person has been unable to occupy their main residence as a main residence, due to employment or the situation of his place of work, PPR relief may also be claimed for the period of absence. This is generally limited to an absence of up to four years and requires that the taxpayer occupies the property as their main residence both before and after the absence (TCGA 1992, s.223(3)).

Occupation by a non-owning spouse

In a situation where the family home is legally and beneficially owned by only one of the parties and that party has moved out, the continued occupation by the non-owning spouse (or civil partner) does not provide continuing relief for the purposes of the owning spouse's eventual disposal. If the owning spouse has not occupied the property for more than three years, CGT could arise on the disposal since the final period exemption will have been exceeded.

In the application of the relief and the final three-year exemption period, PPR represents a relatively generous relief, since the calculation is made on a proportionate basis.

EXAMPLE 6B

Guy legally and beneficially owns the matrimonial home which he bought on 1 July 1990. He and his wife Andrea lived in the property for 15 years prior to his moving out on 1 July 2005 following their separation, at which point Guy moved into a new residence. As part of the divorce proceedings, it is agreed that Guy will transfer the property to Andrea, the date of transfer being agreed as 30 June 2009 for tax purposes.

Guy's CGT base cost is £125,000 and on the date of transfer the property has a market value of £600,000. The capital gain arising on the transfer is therefore £475,000 and this cannot be covered by the spouse exemption as the transfer is being made after the tax year of separation. However, PPR relief is available as the property was Guy's main residence prior to 1 July 2005.

As PPR relief applies on a proportionate basis, it is necessary to consider the length of time Guy has owned the property, which is a total of 19 years (1 July 1990 to 30 June 2009). Of that period, he actually lived in the property for 15 years and to this period can also be added the final period exemption for the last three years. In other words, the period for which PPR relief applies is 18 out of the 19 years of ownership. PPR relief will therefore be applied to exempt 18/19ths of the gain of £475,000, or £450,000, leaving the balance of the gain of £25,000 chargeable to CGT. Assuming Guy has available his annual CGT exemption of £10,100 (for 2009/10), the taxable gain reduces to £14,900, on which he will pay tax at 18%, a liability of £2,682.

As can be seen from this example, where the family home has been owned for a number of years, the combined effect of the denominator in the fraction (period of ownership) and final period exemption of three years can be to significantly reduce the taxable gain.

If Guy had bought the property on 1 July 2004 and moved out on 1 July 2005, with all other facts remaining the same, the PPR relief available would be a total of four years and the period of ownership five years, thereby exempting £380,000 of the gain (four-fifths), leaving £95,000 chargeable to tax. Without the final period exemption of three years, the taxable gain would have been very much higher.

Transfer as part of a financial settlement

Where a couple are separating and there is a property transfer in circumstances similar to that described in Example 6B above, HMRC recognises that it may be considered inequitable that tax should be paid simply because it has taken more than three years after the owner spouse has moved out for the property to be transferred as part of a financial settlement.

INTERESTS IN LAND AND PROPERTY

By virtue of TCGA 1992, s.225B (formerly HMRC Extra Statutory Concession D6), if an individual ceases to occupy the family home whilst the other spouse or civil partner continues to reside in it (as their only or main residence), and then later the individual disposes of it to the occupying spouse or civil partner as part of a financial settlement, the home may continue to be regarded as the main residence of the transferring partner if a claim is made. In other words, the final period exemption is extended by this concession beyond the three years. In Example 6B, this would mean that the PPR relief could be extended to the full period of ownership, thereby exempting the whole of any gain from tax. The relief only applies if the disposal is made pursuant to a separation agreement or court order in connection with divorce, etc.

The legislation does not apply, however, if the transferring partner has elected that some other house should be treated as their main residence for this period. In practice, as the last three years of ownership are treated as exempt, this extended relief is generally only of relevance where the former home is likely to be retained significantly beyond that period and where, absent a relief, the CGT is likely to be substantial. In most cases, however, the proportionate nature of the calculation of the relief will mean that there is likely to be little benefit to claiming the extended relief and the transferring partner will normally want to elect that their new home should be treated as their main residence.

HMRC view

In relation to the application of PPR relief to cases of divorce, etc., the following extract also appears in HMRC *Capital Gains Tax Manual* at CG65330:

> In endorsing the agreed terms for a settlement on divorce or permanent separation, the Courts have regard to:
>
> - the Matrimonial Homes Act 1967
> - the Matrimonial Proceedings & Property Act 1970
> - the Matrimonial Causes Act 1973
> - the Civil Partnership Act 2004.
>
> Furthermore, in considering the financial provision to be made for a spouse or a civil partner, the Courts have wide discretionary powers to set aside or adjust the respective legal or equitable interests in the matrimonial or civil partnership home.
>
> Any decision on relief where the matter is in doubt must begin with an examination of the order made by the Court together with any relevant items of correspondence between the parties' solicitors establishing the basis on which the transfer of the home was determined. Because of the Courts' wide discretion, and because the parties do not always act with the tax consequences of their actions in the forefront of their minds, it can be difficult to determine the effect of the order made by the Court. If you have any difficulty which cannot be resolved by these instructions Capital Gains Technical Group will advise.

Joint but unrelated owner-occupiers

There is some uncertainty as to whether joint owners of a property who are not husband and wife (or civil partners) are entitled to full PPR relief. Helpfully, HMRC takes the view that in general they will be entitled to relief, and therefore in relation to cohabiting couples who are separating, this will normally be the case. This is on the basis that HMRC considers each to have an undivided share in all of the property (see *Todd* v. *Mudd* (1986) 60 TC 237 for a case involving tenants in common).

In other exceptional cases, a property in joint ownership may be divided into separate and identifiable homes each exclusively occupied, for which PPR relief is not available, although reference to Extra Statutory Concession (ESC) D26 (as legislated for in TCGA 1992, ss.248A–248E from 1 April 2010, see **6.6.2** and IR Int 22, *HMRC Tax Bulletin* 3, May 1992) should be made if there is an exchange of joint interests.

Other matters

In situations where, during the period of ownership, the family home has been wholly or partly let, or part of the home has been used for business purposes, or there have been periods of absence by the owner due to work or employment, and in certain other situations, the relief may be restricted and specialist tax advice should be sought. A full factual history of the use and occupation of the property during the entire period of ownership (which does not include any period before 31 March 1982) will be required in order to determine eligibility for, and the amount of, the relief.

On divorce/dissolution, it should also be noted that hold over relief (see **2.2**) could be relevant where a farmhouse is being transferred which, although a main residence, is also a business asset.

6.2 *MESHER* ORDERS AND TRANSFERS OF PROPERTY

KEY CONCEPTS

Mesher orders are now less commonly ordered by a court where a couple is separated. However, *Mesher* orders can have more favourable CGT implications than certain deferred charges placed on the family home. Depending on the drafting of the court order, there may also be IHT issues to consider in some more complex cases.

6.2.1 *Mesher* orders: general

Where a marriage breaks down, in order to ensure that there are adequate housing arrangements for any minor children, a *Mesher* order may be used. A *Mesher* order, named after the case in which the principle was first set out (*Mesher* v. *Mesher and Hall*, a 1973 case reported at [1980] 1 All ER 126), requires that the interest in the property of the non-occupying individual is transferred into trust.

The terms of the trust allow the beneficiaries – the individual and children residing at the property – to occupy on appropriate terms and when the property is sold the sale proceeds are divided between the former couple in agreed terms.

A *Mesher* order is therefore typically an order by the court that a spouse holding an interest in the matrimonial home should hold it on trust for a limited period, for example, until:

- remarriage of the other spouse; or
- death of the other spouse; or
- the 18th birthday of the youngest child of the marriage, or if later on the cessation of his or her full-time education.

The other spouse is then entitled to occupy the home for the duration of the trust period.

A disadvantage of a *Mesher* order is that the sale of the property is forced when the child reaches a specified age, even if the share of the sale proceeds is not sufficient to buy the occupying spouse another property. There is no statutory power for a *Mesher* order to be varied once it has been made (see *Dinch* v. *Dinch* [1987] 1 All ER 818 and *Carson* v. *Carson* [1983] 1 All ER 478).

6.2.2 *Mesher* orders: capital gains tax

By virtue of TCGA 1992, s.70, a transfer into settlement whether revocable or irrevocable is a disposal of the entire property into the trust, notwithstanding that the transferor has some interest as a beneficiary under the settlement and is a trustee or the sole trustee of the settlement. HMRC accepts that a *Mesher* order creates a settlement and deems that the interest in the property of the non-occupying individual owning the property is transferred into trust, thus constituting a disposal for CGT purposes of the whole of the property at its current market value when the *Mesher* order is made.

In most cases, PPR relief will be available under the normal rules to avoid any taxable gain arising, i.e. full relief would apply where the disposal took place within three years of the person ceasing to occupy the property as a PPR.

For a home owned as joint tenants, the resident spouse will continue to be covered by PPR as PPR relief is also extended to private residences occupied under the terms of a settlement (TCGA 1992, s.225) where the property is the only or main residence of a person entitled to occupy it under the terms of the settlement. In this case, joint notice must be given by the trustees and the person entitled to occupy the property of the claim to PPR relief applying to any gain on the property arising to the trustees. PPR relief will therefore be available for the period of the *Mesher* order for so long as the occupying spouse continues to live in the property as their only or main residence.

When the trust ceases, for CGT purposes there is a disposal by the trustees of the whole interest in the house at its then market value to the owner(s). This is because, when the stipulated period ends, the spouse holding the interest in the property which is subject to the trust will generally become absolutely entitled to it and there will be a deemed disposal by him or her as trustee under TCGA 1992, s.71(1) for a consideration equal to market value. The trustees may have a capital gain if the market value at that time is greater than the market value when the trust was originally created (i.e. the date of *Mesher* order). However, because the house has been occupied by the beneficiaries (resident spouse and children) as their main residence, the whole gain arising during the *Mesher* period will usually by covered by PPR for the reasons outlined in the paragraph above. Furthermore, since the owner(s) acquires the property at its then market value, any gain arising in the period after the *Mesher* order has expired is generally likely to be small, on the basis that the property would be sold shortly after the *Mesher* order had expired.

It should also be noted that not only does the disposal by the trustees of the family home normally benefit from the PPR relief, but in the meantime the non-occupying individual can claim the benefit of PPR relief on his or her new home without affecting the relief available to the trustees. This is in contrast to the position of a non-occupying spouse claiming the benefit of (the former) ESC D6 (now TCGA 1992, s.225B, see under 'Transfer as part of a financial settlement' at **6.1.5**) on a transfer to the occupying spouse after three years, where they cannot also claim PPR on any new home acquired during the period.

HMRC has confirmed that the above CGT treatment applies whether there is a court order or whether the parties make a binding agreement without a court order (HMRC *Capital Gains Tax Manual* at CG65365). The party in occupation and the trustees of the settlement must sign a joint notice electing that the property is to be treated as his or her only or main residence for this purpose.

EXAMPLE 6C

Mr Jones bought a house in June 1990 for £70,000 and occupied it with his wife until May 1994, when they separated. In February 1996, when the house was worth £95,000, a court ordered that the house should be transferred to the spouses' joint names in equal shares, with a sale not to take place until their youngest child reached the age of 18.

In October 2008 the youngest child attained the age of 18, at which point the house had a market value of £270,000. The house was sold in February 2008 for £300,000.

Mr Jones had also bought a new house for himself whilst Mrs Jones remained in the matrimonial home.

On creation of the *Mesher* order in February 1996, Mr Jones is treated as disposing of the house to himself and his wife as trustees on trust for sale for the benefit of them in equal shares. Any gain arising from the property in the period between purchase and the *Mesher* order will be covered by PPR relief as long as Mr Jones occupied the property. There is therefore no CGT to pay on the creation of the *Mesher* order.

When the *Mesher* order terminates in October 2008, the house is disposed of by the spouses as trustees at its market value and thereafter the spouses are deemed to hold it as bare trustees for themselves as beneficial owners. The trustees have a capital gain on this disposal of £175,000 (£270,000–£95,000); however, as Mrs Jones has occupied the property throughout the period of ownership of the trustees as her main residence, PPR relief will apply to the whole of the gain.

When the house is actually sold in February 2009, Mrs Jones can claim PPR relief on her share of the £30,000 gain accruing since October 2008 but Mr Jones will have a chargeable gain of £15,000. He will not be entitled to any PPR relief, and the last 36 months concession will not apply to him. On the basis that Mr Jones has his annual exemption available (2008/09 £9,600) he will have to pay CGT at 18% on £5,400, tax of £972.

If, in Example 6C above, Mr Jones had legally and beneficially owned the property and the court had instructed that the property be sold and part of the net sale proceeds be paid to Mrs Jones, Mrs Jones would not be chargeable to CGT on the sum she would receive out of the sale proceeds. This is because it would represent financial provision for her ordered by the court and is not a sum received in consideration for the disposal of an asset (HMRC *Capital Gains Tax Manual* at CG65377).

6.2.3 *Mesher* orders: inheritance tax

Under a *Mesher* order, each spouse remains beneficially entitled to his or her share of the former matrimonial home and there is no settlement for IHT purposes, unlike for CGT purposes. The value of the spouses' shares will therefore form a part of the deceased spouse's estate for IHT purposes if they were to die before the *Mesher* order expired.

Even where a *Mesher* order results in a sufficient succession of interest for there to be a settlement for IHT, orders implemented before 22 March 2006 should generally not give rise to any IHT issues unless the spouse who created the settlement predeceases the other spouse. In this case, the value of the deceased spouse's reversionary interest would be precluded from being excluded property (and therefore outside the scope of IHT) and would therefore be taxed as part of their estate.

Where a *Mesher* order is created after 22 March 2006 and is a settlement for IHT purposes, there are potential IHT issues which will need to be considered. If the value of the property which is subject to the *Mesher* order exceeds the nil rate band (£325,000 for 2009/10) then it will be important to establish that the initial transfer is exempted by virtue of it being a gift which is not intended to confer gratuitous benefit. The 10-year and exit charges may still apply, and again, each case will need to be looked at individually on its own facts in order to quantify any potential tax charges.

6.2.4 Transfer of property subject to a deferred charge

An alternative to a *Mesher* order is the transfer of the home to the resident spouse but with the imposition of a charge on its sale proceeds at a specified future date (deferred charge). HMRC views this as a disposal by the absentee spouse of an interest in the property in exchange for a different asset in the form of a charge, as explained at **3.4.7** and **3.4.8**.

6.2.5 Sales occurring between former spouses or civil partners after divorce or dissolution

Where a husband and wife are divorced or where a civil partnership is dissolved, HMRC normally accepts that a subsequent sale (as opposed to a court order) of an interest in the property by one former spouse or civil partner to the other is a transaction at arm's length. If, exceptionally, the sale price appears to HMRC to differ substantially from the expected market value, HMRC considers this may be indicative of a bargain not at arm's length, but recognises that the open market value in these circumstances would have to take account of the rights of occupation of the spouse or civil partner residing in the house. In cases of doubt, HMRC may consult the Valuation Office Agency (HMRC *Capital Gains Tax Manual* at CG65364).

6.2.6 Summary assuming main residence occupied by transferee spouse

	Inheritance tax	Capital gains tax
Mesher order (see **6.2**)	Possible trust depending on facts	Creates a trust which should be tax neutral for the duration of order
Deferred charges (see **3.4.8** and **3.4.9**):		
Unascertainable consideration	n/a	CGT when charge matures on sale depending on value of right to receive further consideration
Ascertainable (i.e. fixed charge)	n/a	CGT on fixed amount but available to be covered by PPR relief

6.3 MORE THAN ONE PROPERTY

> **KEY CONCEPTS**
>
> Owning more than one property as a residence creates potential tax issues but also gives rise to opportunities to mitigate tax with appropriate planning, which may be relevant to couples on separation and divorce. The issue of the availability of, and steps undertaken to effect, such planning require suitable specialist advice.

6.3.1 Nomination of the PPR

With marriages generally now occurring later in life, and with subsequent marriages, it is not uncommon to find parties entering marriage owning their own property. More affluent couples may also acquire a second property during the course of their relationship or marriage, perhaps as a holiday home (either in the United Kingdom or abroad) or city *pied-à-terre*, or due to the increasing popularity of buy-to-let residential investment property.

For PPR relief, a married couple living together (or civil partners living together) may only have one PPR at any one time (TCGA 1992, s.222(6)).

The general rule as to which of two or more properties is actually the main or principal residence will be determined on the facts of the case. HMRC will look at where the couple normally reside, where they are registered to vote, which address is used for official correspondence, etc.

For example, where a couple's main family home is in Gloucestershire, but one spouse uses a small flat in London to stay in during the working week, it may be considered that the Gloucestershire home would more naturally be treated as the PPR.

This is one area, therefore, where cohabitees may benefit from a more favourable tax treatment than married couples or civil partners: if they each continue to own a property, and use both properties as residences, they can obtain PPR relief on the disposal of both properties. Couples who are about to get married or become civil partners who each own a property which has been occupied as a main residence and so will lose the benefit of the relief on one of them from the date of marriage may wish to consider whether to 'rebase' that particular property to its current market value immediately before the marriage without any CGT. The possibilities include transferring the property by way of a gift, to a trust or to the other party to the marriage or civil partnership. In this way, the loss of PPR relief in the future on that property will be mitigated since it is only the gain made from the date of the transfer rather than the date of ownership that will be subject to tax.

Married couples and civil partners living together with more than one residence have the right to nominate which residence should be treated as their principal residence for tax purposes, rather than allowing HMRC to make its own determination subsequently based on the facts. Both must give notice as to the same property to HMRC unless both properties are owned in the sole name of one of the couple, in which case only that individual need give notice as the other is not affected by the election. There is no prescribed form for notifying HMRC and a nomination letter signed by both parties and sent to the inspector at the tax office dealing with the couple's tax affairs will suffice. Formal acknowledgment to the letter should, however, be requested and obtained from HMRC and kept on file in case of any later HMRC enquiry.

There are strict time limits for making the nomination as it must be submitted to HMRC within two years of the need to nominate arising.

The need to nominate would generally arise:

- on the occasion of the marriage or entering into civil partnership of two individuals each of whom previously owned their own property or where the properties are owned jointly;
- on the acquisition of a second or any subsequent properties or on the occasion where a second property which has been acquired but was let, subsequently becomes a residence of the couple;
- on the disposal of a property, if the couple still own two or more properties after that disposal.

The ability to nominate which of one or more residences is to be treated as an only or main residence for PPR relief purposes gives rise to potential tax mitigation opportunities arising out of the final period exemption. This is acknowledged by HMRC and is outlined in Example 6D below (HMRC *Capital Gains Tax Manual* at CG64510). It may take effect up to two years before the nomination.

6.3.2 Final period of exemption: planning point

Once a nomination has been made, if both parties agree, it is possible to vary that nomination at any time by giving a further notice to HMRC that the second residence will be the PPR and from what date. Having given notice in respect of that second residence, it is then possible to vary the nomination again back to the originally nominated property (TCGA 1992, s.222(5)). In this way, it is possible to secure the deemed 'last three years' relief in respect of the property which has not generally been the PPR for the loss of PPR relief on the property originally nominated, potentially only for a limited period.

EXAMPLE 6D

Paul and Ella were married in 1998 and acquired a flat in London where they lived until 1 April 2004. They then moved to a large detached house in Hampshire which cost £450,000.

Paul and Ella kept the London flat so Paul could stay there during the week, and they jointly nominated it as their PPR. They expected to sell the London property in due course and they considered it would be likely to have the higher gain on disposal.

Divorce proceedings commenced in 2008, and it is determined that the Hampshire house will have to be sold to fund the settlement.

The Hampshire home is now estimated to be worth £1 million, therefore a significant gain of £550,000 will arise. Paul will keep the London flat.

The transfer of Ella's share in the London flat to Paul would not give rise to any CGT as the gain will be fully exempted by PPR relief provided the transfer takes place before the deemed occupation period of three years has elapsed. However, without further planning, the disposal of the Hampshire home would result in a total tax bill of £99,000 (£550,000 at 18% ignoring annual exemptions), leaving only £901,000 available to fund the settlement.

Paul and Ella could, however, write to their tax offices and vary their nomination, nominating the Hampshire property as their main residence from 1 January 2008.

Since the Hampshire property will be treated as the PPR, periods of actual occupation and the deemed three years of ownership will be relieved on a proportionate basis. If Paul and Ella

separated on 1 April 2008, both moving out, and sold the property on 31 December 2008, then:
- the ownership period would be four years nine months (4.75 years);
- the deemed period of occupation would be the last three years, 1 January 2006 to 31 December 2008;
- the actual period of occupation as the PPR would be 1 January 2008 to 31 March 2008 (which overlaps the above);
- PPR relief would exempt 3÷4.75 of the gain;
- the taxable gain would be £202,632;
- the total tax liability would be £36,474 ignoring annual exemptions;
- there would after tax be £963,526 to fund the settlement.

6.3.3 Restrictions on nominations as the PPR

It is only possible to nominate one of two properties if it is actually the residence of the person concerned. This would not therefore be available if one of the properties had always been let out as an investment property.

Furthermore, a property acquired wholly or partly for the purpose of realising a gain from the disposal of it is not eligible for PPR relief; or, if partly eligible, relief is not available for the part of any gain relating to expenditure incurred for that purpose (TCGA 1992, s.224(3)). In certain circumstances, all or part of the gain could be liable to income tax rather than CGT if the property was acquired with a view (or if intentions later changed) to developing and selling it. Part or all of the gain would be taxed either as trading income, or under Income Tax Act (ITA) 2007, Part 8, Chapter 3, which prevents the avoidance of income tax by persons who have a sole or main object of realising a gain from disposing of or developing land, and taxes the transaction at the person's marginal income tax rates instead of the 18 per cent CGT rate.

6.4 STAMP DUTY LAND TAX

Under normal circumstances, if there is a land transaction involving the sale or transfer of an interest in a property for chargeable consideration by an individual, that transaction will be liable to stamp duty land tax, applying the relevant SDLT thresholds (Finance Act 2003, ss.50 and 55). A transfer of the matrimonial or civil partnership home or any other real estate as part of a financial settlement on divorce or dissolution is also, *prima facie*, a transfer on which SDLT would be payable.

However, if there is a transfer of the matrimonial home or any other real property between the parties to a divorce, there is a specific exemption from SDLT. This is explained in more detail in **Chapter 7**.

It is important to note that the exemption only applies to transfers made between the parties to the divorce or dissolution, so if, for example, a property is owned by a family trust and is to be transferred, this exemption would not apply. Whilst cohabitees also do not have the benefit of this exemption, it would seem that a transfer on separation would rarely occur between them in practice (see R. Tennant, J. Taylor and J. Lewis, *Separating from Cohabitation: Making Arrangements for Finances and Parenting*, DCA Research Series 7/06 (Department of Constitutional Affairs, October 2006)).

6.5 HOLIDAY HOMES OR BUY-TO-LET INVESTMENT PROPERTY

As described earlier, a married couple or civil partners living together can nominate a second (or further) property which is used as a main residence as their PPR for CGT purposes, in which case some or all of the gain on that nominated property may be relieved from tax on disposal.

In some cases, second homes are not occupied as a main residence but are holiday homes which may also be commercially let as holiday accommodation. In such cases, no nomination is possible as a PPR (unless the property subsequently becomes a residence).

Entrepreneurs' relief (ER) may be available to reduce the tax charge on disposal if the property is situated in the EU and fulfils the conditions to be classified for tax purposes as a furnished holiday let (i.e. the commercial letting of holiday accommodation for at least 70 days a year (not being in the same occupation for more than 31 days) and available as such for at least 140 days; if the property is also in the same occupation for periods of more than 31 days these periods cannot exceed 155 days in total (Income Tax (Trading and Other Income) Act (ITTOIA) 2005, Part 3, Chapter 6). Further, if the property qualifies as a furnished holiday let, then hold over relief (see **2.2**) may also be available if such a property is transferred between the parties.

Normal buy-to-let investment properties are taxed under general CGT principles, also explained in **Chapter 2**.

6.6 EXCHANGE OF INTERESTS IN LAND AND PROPERTY

KEY CONCEPTS

Where jointly owned property is being transferred between the parties, there may be scope to reduce the CGT arising by way of a further statutory relief and concession.

6.6.1 Exchange of non-business interests in land and property

There may be circumstances in the family context where a dwelling house is the only or main residence of a family member other than its owner. This

INTERESTS IN LAND AND PROPERTY

would result in a failure to qualify for relief if the dwelling house were to be sold. In general, relief is only due if the dwelling house has been the only or main residence of its owner.

It sometimes occurs, however, that properties will be exchanged, particularly in the context of joint beneficial owners of land, so that each becomes the sole owner of one of the properties in question as part of rationalising such interests, whether on separation or in other circumstances.

6.6.2 Roll over relief on disposal of joint interest in land (ESC D26, TCGA 1992, s.248A)

ESC D26, published on 19 December 1984, provided relief on exchanges of land by joint owners.

The concession has now been superseded by TCGA 1992, ss.248A–248E (as HMRC has identified some Extra Statutory Concessions which appear to exceed the scope of its administrative powers under the Taxes Acts), which legislative provision is intended to have equivalent effect. Reference should be made to the legislation in relation to any disposals made on or after 6 April 2010.

The relief applies in two very specific circumstances:

- where the land received does not include a dwelling house which is, or within six years becomes, used as an only or main residence to which PPR relief will apply (so as to ensure that an otherwise chargeable gain rolled over is not then made permanently exempt);
- where joint owners exchange interests in their respective residences (which would qualify for PPR relief immediately afterwards).

Where two or more individuals jointly owning their respective residences become sole owners by exchanging the appropriate interest, full PPR relief may be given in respect of the gain accruing up to the date of exchange, provided that:

- each of the individuals satisfies the conditions for total exemption under the PPR rules in respect of the interest in the property which they occupy; and
- each undertakes to accept that for CGT purposes they will be deemed to acquire the other's interest in the property transferred to them at the original base cost and the original date upon which that joint interest was acquired.

For the purpose of the relief, a married couple (which it is assumed means 'living together') are treated as if they were a single individual. So an exchange of interests which results in a married couple alone being the joint owners of a residence may attract relief. Civil partners are also treated in the same way.

TAX AND FAMILY BREAKDOWN

EXAMPLE 6E

In January 2003, Mr Kay and Miss Walker cohabited and jointly bought Summer Cottage for £100,000. They lived there together until May 2005 when they jointly bought Autumn Cottage for £150,000. Thereafter Miss Walker lived at Autumn Cottage while Mr Kay remained at Summer Cottage for reasons of work. By November 2009, the relationship has broken down and they decide to separate. Miss Walker exchanges her interest in Summer Cottage for Mr Kay's interest in Autumn Cottage, so that she is sole owner of Autumn Cottage and he is sole owner of Summer Cottage. Because Autumn Cottage is more valuable than Summer Cottage, she pays him £30,000 as part of the transfer arrangement.

If each of them disposed of their respective cottages immediately after the transfer – that is, if Miss Walker were to sell Autumn Cottage and Mr Kay were to sell Summer Cottage – the gains on each disposal would attract full PPR relief. So, if:

- Miss Walker undertakes to accept for CGT purposes that she acquired Autumn Cottage for £150,000 in May 2005, and
- Mr Kay undertakes to accept for CGT purposes that he acquired Summer Cottage for £100,000 in January 2009

any gains arising on the transfer of either interest are treated as fully relieved. The equalisation payment is ignored and forms no part of the base cost.

Land that is not a dwelling house

In respect of land which is not a dwelling house, the relief operates on similar lines to TCGA 1992, ss.247 and 248 (which provide relief for gains arising to land-owners whose land is compulsorily purchased but who reinvest the consideration received in acquiring other land) and may be claimed to alleviate the charges to CGT that would otherwise arise. The effect of the relief is that, where the values of the interests to be exchanged are identical, no CGT should arise. If, as may commonly be the case, this is not the position for the spouses, there will be an immediate charge to CGT for the spouse who receives the 'excess' value on exchange as only the amount of any gain which is greater than the excess can be deferred. This can be complicated and is best illustrated by way of an example.

EXAMPLE 6F

In January 2000, Helena and Simon bought a plot of land (Plot A) for £60,000 which they owned as joint tenants. In February 2002, they bought a further plot of land (Plot B) for £100,000, again held as joint tenants. In April 2010, following the breakdown of their marriage in May 2009, it was agreed that Simon would have absolute ownership of Plot A and that Helena would receive Plot B. At that time, a half share in Plot A was valued at £120,000 and a half share in Plot B was valued at £200,000.

The transfers are deemed to take place at market value. This is the case if the exchange happens between separation and divorce and if the transfer takes place after divorce but as part of the overall divorce settlement.

On this basis, Simon is deemed to receive £200,000 for his half share in Plot B and Helena is deemed to receive £120,000 for her half share in Plot A.

Equally, Simon is deemed to have paid £120,000 for his share in Plot B and Helena is deemed to have paid £200,000 for her share in Plot A.

	Plot A	Plot B
Date of acquisition	January 2000	February 2002
Base cost	£60,000	£100,000
Full value at date of exchange	£240,000	£400,000
Eventual owner	Simon	Helena

As there is a difference in the values being exchanged, a liability to CGT may still arise.

Simon's gain on the disposal of his half share of Plot B is computed as follows:

	£
Value of transfer	200,000
Less acquisition cost	(50,000)
Gain	150,000
Less roll over relief under ESC D26	(70,000)
Chargeable gain taxed at 18%	80,000

Only £70,000 of Simon's chargeable gain of £150,000 is deferrable. This is because the consideration of £200,000 that he is deemed to have received for his share of Plot B exceeds by £80,000 the £120,000 that he is deemed to have paid for Helena's half share in Plot A.

Simon's dates and costs of acquisition of Plot A moving forward will be:

	£
Half share in January 2000	30,000
Half share in April 2010	120,000
Less roll over relief	(70,000)
Base cost	80,000

Helena's gain on the disposal of her half share of Plot A is computed as follows:

	£
Value of transfer	120,000
Less acquisition cost	(30,000)
Gain	90,000
Less roll over relief under ESC D26	(90,000)
Chargeable gain taxed at 18%	nil

Helena's dates and costs of acquisition of Plot B moving forward will be:

	£
Half share in February 2002	50,000
Half share in April 2010	200,000
Less roll over relief	(90,000)
Base cost	160,000

If roll over relief is not claimed, then Helena would have a taxable gain of £90,000 but an unreduced base cost of £200,000 on the eventual disposal of Plot A.

It should be noted that the benefit of the relief must be claimed.

There may also be SDLT to consider on the exchange of interests in land where the values exceed the lower SDLT threshold. These so-called exchanges covered by the relief are partitions for SDLT purposes (Finance Act 2003, Sched.4, para.6) which means that the interest held by the purchaser immediately before the partition does not count as chargeable consideration. Therefore, in applying SDLT and the various thresholds, it is the value of the interest being transferred that is subject to SDLT. However, in practice, where the provisions of Finance Act 2003, Sched.3, para.3 apply (transactions in connection with divorce, etc., see **Chapter 7**) the transaction is exempt from charge.

6.6.3 Exchange of interests in land and property used in a trade

Similar principles apply where a couple carry on a trading business from two jointly owned properties and after relationship or marriage breakdown, each individual is to carry on a separate business from one of the properties if given outright ownership of that property.

In this case, relief is provided in TCGA 1992, s.152, known as 'replacement of business assets' roll over relief. The relief is of general application to individuals, members of a partnership, companies, trustees and others carrying on trading activities where old assets used in the trade are sold and replaced with new assets out of the sale proceeds.

HMRC has confirmed that this relief can apply to asset disposals between husband and wife (and civil partners) and generally where assets are exchanged, subject to meeting all other relevant conditions. If the interests in the properties are not of equal value, roll over relief is restricted to the amount of the deemed 'reinvestment' in the asset being acquired, and the 'excess', as in example 6F, is taxed accordingly.

Specific advice should be taken, as the conditions for the relief to apply are complex and involve a mixture of HMRC statements of practice, concessions and interpretations.

CHAPTER 6 CHECKLIST

1. Establish who has an equitable interest in the family home and in what proportion and the tax effect of likely transfers of such interests on separation and divorce (**6.1.1**).
2. Consider the availability of PPR relief and whether specialist tax advice needs to be taken, particularly where the property has not always been occupied as a main residence or if more than one property is involved (**6.1.5**).
3. Consider the use of *Mesher* orders as an alternative to certain deferred charges over the family home if there may be substantial tax at stake (**6.2.1**).
4. If there is to be a *Mesher* order, consider also if it creates a settlement for IHT purposes, and if in doubt seek specialist advice (**6.2.3**).
5. Identify any jointly owned property which may be the subject of an exchange of interests in land and seek specialist advice (**6.6.2**).

CHAPTER 7

Stamp duty and stamp duty land tax

> **KEY CONCEPTS**
>
> A transfer of assets between married couples or civil partners who are separating should not give rise to stamp duty or stamp duty land tax (SDLT), except on rare occasions. Cohabitees, however, may have a stamp duty or SDLT liability, particularly where shares or property are transferred for consideration which includes the assumption by the transferee of a debt or mortgage.

7.1 TRANSACTIONS ON FAMILY BREAKDOWN

SDLT replaced stamp duty upon land transactions with effect from 1 December 2003 subject to certain complex transitional rules which are unlikely now to be of relevance to most practitioners.

SDLT applies at rates of up to 4 per cent to transactions relating to an estate, interest, right or power in or over land in the United Kingdom or the benefit of an obligation, restriction or condition affecting the value of any such estate, interest, right or power.

SDLT does not apply, however, to mortgages and certain other property financing transactions, nor does it generally apply to a licence to occupy or use land or to a tenancy at will.

Stamp duty remains applicable to transactions relating to shares and marketable securities (Stamp Act 1891) where stamp duty reserve tax also applies (Finance Act 1986), and to transfers in writing of partnership interests where the partnership owns stock or marketable securities, to the extent that the consideration or deemed consideration for the transfer is apportioned to shares or marketable securities. The ad valorem rate in these cases remains 0.5 per cent, subject to certain reliefs and exemptions. There is also now a de minimis threshold of £1,000 at or below which figure no stamp duty is payable on transfers of shares and most marketable securities where that fact is certified.

7.2 EXEMPTIONS

Finance Act 2003, Sched.3, para.3 provides that land transactions are exempt from SDLT if made between the parties to a marriage or civil partnership and as a result of:

- a court order made on grant of a divorce, nullity or judicial separation;
- a court order made in connection with a dissolution, annulment or judicial separation at any time after the granting of such a decree;
- a court order made under Matrimonial Causes Act (MCA) 1973, ss.22A, 23A or 24A;
- an incidental court order made under Family Law (Scotland) Act 1985, s.8(2) by virtue of s.14(1);
- an agreement between the spouses or civil partners made in contemplation of or in connection with the dissolution or annulment of their marriage or civil partnership, judicial separation or separation order.

The exemption applies not only to acquisitions of land but also to new leases which give effect to the court order or agreement. Furthermore, there is no basic obligation to report a transaction, such as a sale of residential property, falling within the above exemption.

Finance Act 1985, s.83, provides a similar exemption from stamp duty for transfers of shares in connection with divorce, dissolution of civil partnership, etc. (Category H of Stamp Duty (Exempt Instruments) Regulations 1987, SI 1987/516).

It is important to note that, in both cases, the exemptions only apply to transfers between spouses or civil partners and do not extend to:

- unmarried couples;
- a child of the marriage;
- a company share buy-back.

Furthermore, the exemptions do not apply to a separation agreement between the parties where no divorce, judicial separation or court order is in contemplation.

In circumstances where there is a transfer of property in contemplation of a dissolution, etc. but this event does not occur (because the couple either are subsequently reconciled or become content to maintain the status quo), the exemption applies so long as there was a genuine contemplation of dissolution, etc., at the time of the transfer of the property.

Where the transaction is exempt from SDLT under the above provisions, there is no statutory obligation to report the transaction to HMRC.

7.3 SHARES SUBJECT TO A DEBT

Circumstances may arise where shares are mortgaged and they are held in the name of one of the parties, or in their joint names, and the shares are to be transferred into the sole name of the other. The critical question is whether the transaction to which the conveyance gives effect is or is not a sale. If it is, Stamp Act 1891, s.57, applies and the conveyance of the shares will be chargeable to ad valorem duty at 0.5 per cent on the amount of the debt assumed. If it is not a sale, no stamp duty will be payable.

If shares are transferred subject to a debt and the transferee covenants to pay the debt or indemnify the transferor against his personal liability to the lender, such a covenant constitutes valuable consideration and establishes the transaction as a sale. If the transferor covenants to pay the debt and the transferee does not assume any liability for it, no chargeable consideration has been given and there is no sale. The transfer would then be a voluntary disposition, i.e. an unencumbered gift which will be exempt from stamp duty. It should be noted that implied covenants by the transferee are also treated by HMRC as transactions by way of sale unless there is contrary evidence that it was the intention of the parties at the time that the transferor should be liable for the whole of the mortgage debt. HMRC considers that an implied covenant may arise where shares which are in joint names subject to a debt are transferred to one of the joint holders, even where both parties were jointly liable on the mortgage.

If only part of any debt is assumed by an express or implied covenant, only the amount of that part is treated as chargeable consideration. The foregoing does not affect any statutory exemption, so for married couples or civil partners, transfers of shares from one party to the other in connection with divorce, dissolution, etc. will not give rise to any stamp duty. Cohabitees, by contrast, will need to consider the foregoing in appropriate cases and reference should be made to HMRC Statement of Practice 6/90 for more information.

7.4 PROPERTY SUBJECT TO A CHARGE OR MORTGAGE

Finance Act 2003, Sched.4, para.8 contains provisions which deal, *inter alia*, with property which is conveyed subject to a debt. The chargeable consideration is the actual consideration plus the mortgage liability (principal and accrued interest) or the market value of the property if this is lower than the liability (Finance Act 2003, Sched.4, para.8(2)).

In family matters, the assumption of liabilities is likely to occur in many situations, for example, where a property subject to a charge is transferred out of joint names into the name of one of the owners (or vice versa). In this case, however, only a part of the mortgage is brought into charge (Finance Act 2003, Sched.4, para.8(1B)). This is the proportion of the property to which the incoming party becomes entitled, or to which the outgoing party was entitled, and where appropriate, the lower rates of tax apply.

Another practical issue is that it is unlikely that in domestic circumstances the parties will have sought professional advice at the inception of a transaction, and the details may only emerge later on separation when there are obligations on professional advisers to comply with money laundering legislation and the professional adviser may face penalties for assisting the preparation of an incorrect land transaction return (Finance Act 2003, ss.95 and 96).

The above is subject to the exemption that applies for transfers on divorce, so in practice the transfer of a property subject to a mortgage between separated spouses will not give rise to any SDLT or reporting requirements. Cohabitees, however, do not have the luxury of any such exemption.

7.5 GIFTS

Straightforward gifts of property between individuals where there is no chargeable consideration are exempt from SDLT (Finance Act 2003, Sched.3 para.1). A gift of land subject to a mortgage or in satisfaction of a debt is, however, generally chargeable as discussed above.

As regards any other SDLT exemptions and reliefs which may be applicable to the land or property transaction in question, reference should be made to an appropriate property tax specialist.

7.6 TRANSFERS OF SHARES OR PROPERTY TO A SHAREHOLDER AS PART OF A LIQUIDATION OF A COMPANY

Dividends *in specie* consisting of shares are exempt from stamp duty provided the dividend is not declared as a final cash dividend. If it is a final cash dividend, the transfer will attract stamp duty under Stamp Act 1891, s.57, as being a transfer in satisfaction of the debt constituted by the declaration of the dividend. In these cases to avoid a charge it will be necessary to consider the use of:

- an interim dividend; or
- a dividend of a fixed amount to be satisfied by the transfer of the shares.

Distributions by companies of land or property *in specie* or on liquidation are exempt from SDLT because there is no chargeable consideration for SDLT purposes. However, where the property is subject to a charge and liability to the mortgage is being assumed a charge to tax may arise, as similarly noted in **7.4**.

Such transactions may also operate to cause a clawback of some previously obtained SDLT exemption for intra-group property transfers or company reorganisations and specialist advice should be sought in more complex company situations.

The above may potentially be relevant in the context of unlocking an asset held by a company for the purposes of making a financial settlement on divorce, dissolution, etc.

7.7 TRANSFER OF PROPERTY ON WINDING UP: LOAN FROM SHAREHOLDER

HMRC has confirmed, in *SDLT Technical News*, August 2007, that it will not seek to argue that a dividend *in specie* should bear SDLT in a situation where an individual owns the shares of a company and has lent money to the company to buy a property, the loan being secured by a mortgage on the property. If the company is later wound up and property is distributed to the shareholder as beneficial owner of the equity in the property (the loan not being released), there is no assumption of liability nor any form of consideration given by the shareholder such that SDLT will arise.

CHAPTER 7 CHECKLIST

1. Stamp duty and SDLT should not be overlooked, but will very rarely result in a charge for married couples or civil partners due to the various exemptions **(7.2)**.
2. If there is a sale or transfer of shares or land for consideration, cohabitees may have a stamp duty or SDLT liability **(7.4)**.
3. Consideration includes the assumption by the transferee of any liability, including a mortgage, and care should be exercised in relation to advising cohabitees **(7.4)**.

CHAPTER 8
Pension, life assurance and other matters

> **KEY CONCEPTS**
>
> This chapter deals briefly with pensions, life assurance policies, tax relief on borrowings and the tax consequences of the more common methods likely to be encountered of realising cash or assets from family owned companies.

8.1 PENSIONS

8.1.1 General background to registered pensions

In December 2002, the government produced proposals for simplifying the taxation of pensions. The proposals aimed to abolish a multiplicity of rules and regulations, with the institution of a unified regime for registered pension schemes from 6 April 2006 based on a lifetime allowance for the amount of pension savings that can benefit from tax relief. The new regime, originally established by the Finance Act 2004, currently consists of, *inter alia*:

- a single lifetime allowance on the amount of pension savings that can benefit from tax relief;
- an annual allowance on the increase in value of an individual's pension fund;
- the levy of certain tax charges where funds are in excess of the lifetime allowance or annual allowance;
- a tax free lump sum of up to 25 per cent of the pension fund;
- more flexible retirement age, the minimum retirement age being 55 from 6 April 2010.

For 2009/10, the lifetime allowance was set at £1,750,000 and the annual allowance was set at £245,000. For 2010/11, the lifetime allowance is set £1,850,000 and the annual allowance is set at £255,000.

For more detailed information on the new regime, the rules applying to pension rights arising prior to 6 April 2006, and subsequent legislative changes, reference should be made to the relevant HMRC *Manuals* and updated online material, and to specialist pension providers.

PENSION, LIFE ASSURANCE AND OTHER MATTERS

For couples who are separating, there are essentially two ways in which a relevant pension might be dealt with by the courts.

8.1.2 Attachment orders: Pensions Act 1995

An attachment order allows the courts to order the payment of maintenance from a pension receivable by one of the spouses or civil partners. When the member of the pension scheme becomes entitled to receive payment, the scheme trustees pay the amount specified in the order directly to the ex-spouse:

- the pension remains the income of the scheme member;
- he or she is chargeable to income tax on the whole amount; and
- no deduction is available for the amount paid under the attachment order.

The pension received by the non-scheme member ex-spouse is tax free in his or her hands. An attachment order may also be referred to as an earmarking order.

8.1.3 Pension sharing: Welfare Reform and Pensions Act 1999

The law changed in 2000 to allow the pension rights of an employee to be shared with the ex-spouse as an alternative to an attachment or earmarking order. Under the new provisions, some or all of the employee's benefit rights are passed over to the ex-spouse. This allows the ex-spouse to receive benefits in his or her own name.

The pension sharing provisions can be applied in divorce proceedings that commence on or after 1 December 2000. Pension rights can be shared under approved or non-approved pension arrangements, including buy-out contracts, personal pension schemes and retirement annuity contracts. The court will make an order stating how much of an employee's pension benefits must be shared with the ex-spouse, although in some cases, in particular in court orders under Scottish law, it is understood that the pension sharing will be set out in a legally recognised 'qualifying agreement' between the divorcing couple.

Under these provisions, the ex-spouse will be entitled to receive a pension, which will be taxable in his or her hands.

In terms of the actual mechanics, where a pension sharing order is received the pension scheme member's benefit rights are valued to arrive at a cash equivalent. The cash equivalent is then reduced by the amount stated in the pension sharing order. This is known as the pension debit.

The cash equivalent of the reduction in the member's benefit rights is then allocated to the ex-spouse or former civil partner to provide benefit rights in his or her own name. These new benefit rights are known as a pension credit.

The pension credit can be retained in the same scheme as that to which the original member belongs, or more commonly is transferred into another pension scheme for the ex-spouse or civil partner, such as a personal pension scheme, possibly newly created for this purpose. If the person receiving the pension credit is already a member of an existing scheme, the receipt does not count for the purpose of the member's annual allowance nor have any bearing on the member's capacity to make contributions to the scheme.

If the member's pension is already in payment at the time the pension sharing order is made, the member's ongoing pension would be reduced to take account of the effect of the pension debit.

There is nothing to prevent a member making up any shortfall which arises from the pension debit caused by the implementation of a pension sharing order other than the normal restrictions on tax relief on contributions.

For the purposes of the recipient's lifetime allowance, a pension credit might count towards it depending on when the pension sharing order took place and whether or not the pension credit derives from benefit rights that were in payment at the time of the order. The recipient must also notify HMRC in certain circumstances, and specialist advice should be taken based on the facts of each case.

In cases of family breakdown, advice on pension transfers should be sought from relevant pension, legal and actuarial specialists.

8.2 LIFE ASSURANCE POLICIES AND INVESTMENT BONDS

8.2.1 Capital gains tax

A gain accruing from any policy of insurance or contract for a deferred annuity on the life of any person in the hands of the person who originally paid the premium or premiums is not a chargeable gain for CGT purposes (Taxation of Chargeable Gains Act (TCGA) 1992, s.210). This covers receipts of sums assured, transfers of investments to the policy owner and policy surrenders.

If the rights or any interest as a co-owner in the rights under the policy have been acquired by any person for actual consideration (as opposed to any deemed consideration arising under the TCGA 1992), any gain on subsequent disposal is a chargeable gain for CGT purposes (TCGA 1992, s.210(3)).

Actual consideration does not include amounts paid by way of premium under the insurance policy or amounts paid under the contract for a deferred annuity. A disposal made by one spouse or civil partner to the other, or any approved post-marriage or post-civil partnership disposal by one spouse or partner to the other, will not be treated as actual consideration for the transfer.

An approved post-marriage or post-civil partnership disposal is one which is made in consequence of the marriage or civil partnership's dissolution or annulment, is made with the approval of a court (or other person or body) having the appropriate legal jurisdiction, and where the right (or interest) disposed of was held by the person making the disposal immediately before the marriage or civil partnership was dissolved or annulled.

8.2.2 Income tax

Life insurance, and also purchased annuities and capital redemption policies (including 'investment bonds'), can give rise to 'chargeable events' which give rise to 'chargeable event gains' which are liable to higher rate tax as income of an individual (Income Tax (Trading and Other Income) Act (ITTOIA) 2005, Part 4, Chapter 9).

Gains arise if the owner of a relevant policy receives value or a capital sum in excess of allowable deductions and gains calculated on any earlier events under the policy. Chargeable event gains will most clearly arise when a policy is sold to an unconnected third party for cash consideration, or is surrendered for a capital sum. However, there may also be circumstances where the policy or rights under it are assigned for money or money's worth even though there is no actual cash consideration, for example, on separation and divorce.

Following the judicial observations of Coleridge J in *G* v. *G* [2002] EWHC 1339 regarding CGT hold over relief, the advice from HMRC (see IR Int 257, *HMRC Tax Bulletin* 68, December 2003) is currently that where there is recourse to the courts and a court makes an order for ancillary relief under the Matrimonial Causes Act (MCA) 1973 or for financial provision under the Family Law (Scotland) Act 1985 or formally ratifies an agreement reached by the parties that deals with or includes the transfer of a life insurance policy, the spouse to whom the rights under the policy are transferred does not give money's worth in the form of surrendered rights for their transfer. A court order made in these circumstances reflects the exercise by the court of its independent statutory authority in HMRC's view.

Accordingly, transferring ownership of rights conferred by a life insurance policy, purchased life annuity or capital redemption contract under a court order is not for money or money's worth and no taxable gain should arise in these circumstances.

Arrangements which are not made part of a court order or are for money or money's worth may continue to give rise to a taxable gain, which gain will need to be reported to HMRC by the transferor via the usual self-assessment process. The gain will normally be calculated as the difference between the current value of the policy less any amounts paid in as premiums under the policy to be taxed at the individual's higher rate of tax; however, there are special rules giving relief for such gains by way of 'top-slicing relief'. The gain which is charged is averaged over the years of investment and it is only then added to the individual's other income for the year to determine whether higher rate tax is payable. Any higher rate tax so calculated is then multiplied by the number of years the investment has been held (ITTOIA 2005, s.535).

8.2.3 Life assurance premium relief

Income and Corporation Taxes Act (ICTA) 1988, Sched.14, provides for life assurance premium relief to continue after divorce in respect of premiums paid by one party on the life of the other if they were married when the policy was taken out but were divorced after 5 April 1979. By Extra Statutory Concession A31 this treatment is extended to premiums paid by a divorced person on a policy which was taken out prior to the marriage. A Treasury order is due to give legislative effect to this concession to ensure that premiums paid after the date of marriage or civil partnership continue to be given life assurance premium relief. Although the relief only applies to certain life insurance policies or deferred annuity contracts issued before 13 March 1984, a significant number of such policies and contracts remain in force. The relief is currently set at the rate of 12.5 per cent on premiums up to £1,500 or one-sixth of the payer's total income.

8.3 OBTAINING TAX RELIEF ON BORROWING TO FUND LUMP SUM OR MAINTENANCE PAYMENTS

8.3.1 Sole traders/partnerships: withdrawal of capital

HMRC accepts and allows tax relief for interest where a business takes out an additional borrowing (secured or unsecured) which funds are then used to allow a sole trader or partner to withdraw part of their profits and/or capital invested in the business to be applied for personal or non-business purposes, provided that the owner or partner's capital account does not become overdrawn (HMRC *Business Income Manual* at BIM45700). The loan will, of course, be a liability of the business.

An individual involved in family breakdown who is working as a sole trader or partner can therefore replace all or any capital personally invested in a business with bank or other forms of interest bearing borrowing, use those borrowed funds to pay maintenance or a capital sum, and still obtain tax relief for the interest cost as if those funds had been used in the business. This is fair and equitable given that an interest bearing loan is in reality replacing the business's working capital requirement, albeit in a different form.

The following example is based on those in HMRC's *Manuals* and is by way of guidance only.

EXAMPLE 8A

Nathan is required to pay maintenance to his ex-wife Brenda of £2,000 a month. Nathan's bank manager agrees to increase the business overdraft facility by £100,000. Nathan increases the level of cash drawings from the business by £2,000 a month, so he is withdrawing part of his capital as well as the profits being earned by the business. His capital account does not become overdrawn. The interest payable on the increased overdraft is an allowable deduction for business purposes. Proprietors of businesses are entitled to withdraw their capital from the business, even though substitute funding then has to be provided by interest bearing loans. This is on the basis that the purpose of the additional borrowing is to provide working capital for the business. There will, however, be an interest restriction if the proprietor's capital account becomes overdrawn.

The same principle described above can also apply to borrowings taken out against the equity in a property investment business, e.g. a buy-to-let property or portfolio.

EXAMPLE 8B

Peter owns a house in London, which he bought 10 years ago for £125,000 and which now has a market value of £750,000. He has a mortgage of £80,000 on the property. As part of the dissolution of his civil partnership he is required by the court to make a lump sum payment of £100,000 to his former civil partner Alberto. He wishes to downsize to a smaller flat but keep the house in order to rent it out and provide him with an income. The opening balance sheet of his rental business shows:

	£
Property at market value	750,000
Mortgage	(80,000)
	670,000
Capital account	670,000

He renegotiates the mortgage on the house, converting it into a buy-to-let mortgage and secures an additional borrowing of £400,000. He withdraws £400,000 and pays £100,000 to Alberto to satisfy the court order and applies £300,000 towards the acquisition of a small flat. The balance sheet at the end of Year 1 shows:

	£
Property at market value	750,000
Mortgage	(480,000)
	270,000
Capital account	670,000
Withdrawal	(400,000)
	270,000

Although he has withdrawn capital from the business, the interest on the mortgage loan is allowable in full against the rent on the property because it is funding the transfer of the property to the business at its open market value at the time the business started. The capital account is not overdrawn.

8.4 TAX CONSIDERATIONS IN UNLOCKING ASSETS HELD BY FAMILY COMPANIES

8.4.1 Introduction

In some family situations, one or both of the couple may own, or have a significant and substantial interest in, shares in a family owned company which might be trading, or own investments, or both. The parties to a divorce and, where appropriate, the court will often be concerned with understanding the company's ability to realise any cash or assets ('liquidity') to fund maintenance or a lump sum for either party. As part of that process, it will usually be necessary to determine the likely income tax, corporation tax or CGT consequences and net after tax sums available.

TAX AND FAMILY BREAKDOWN

Family owned companies will more often than not be 'close companies' for tax purposes, which in this context means, broadly, companies controlled by five or fewer shareholders (aggregating the interests of shareholders who are associated with each, i.e. close family and certain other relationships), or by shareholders who are directors. There are a number of specific tax rules surrounding such close companies which are aimed at preventing families exploiting opportunities to arrange the company's affairs in such a way as to mitigate overall taxation within the family context, be it income tax, CGT or inheritance tax.

8.4.2 Taxation of sums received from a family company

Spouses or civil partners who are separated or divorced, and cohabitees, are taxed on amounts received personally as salary and benefits under the PAYE code, and to income tax under self assessment on dividends or other distributions in respect of any shares owned in the company.

Furthermore, if a family company which is a close company makes loans or advances to shareholders, it is likely (or liable) to be assessed to corporation tax (ICTA 1988, s.419) at the rate of 25 per cent in respect of any amount of the loan or advance which remains outstanding nine months after the end of the company's accounting period. Any corporation tax paid is repayable to the company to the extent that the loan or advance is subsequently repaid, released or written off. If the company releases or writes off the whole or part of the debt in respect of the loan or advance, income tax will be charged under ITTOIA 2005, s.415. The person liable for any tax charged is the person to whom the loan or advance was made. The tax charge is on the gross amount of the debt released or written off in the tax year and is grossed up by the dividend ordinary rate for that year, which is currently 10 per cent.

If the company incurs any expenses in the provision of living or other accommodation, entertainment, domestic or other services, or of other benefits and facilities, to a family shareholder, that too is treated as a distribution to the extent that the expense is not reimbursed by the shareholder.

Whereas salary will be taxed at rates of up to 40 per cent (or 50 per cent where relevant) under PAYE and attracts national insurance contributions (NICs), dividends or other distributions are taxed at the dividend ordinary rate of 32.5 per cent (or 42.5 per cent where relevant) for a higher rate taxpayer and carry a notional tax credit of 10 per cent, so that the effective tax rate is 25 per cent (36.6 per cent where relevant) of the net cash dividend received.

8.4.3 Jointly held shares

For jointly held shares in most small family companies, a husband and wife or civil partners living together are taxed on dividend income on their actual underlying beneficial entitlements; i.e. if the shares are in joint names but owned beneficially in the proportion 70:30, any dividend income will be split between them in that same proportion. Following separation, and also for cohabitees, the income is split jointly, i.e. 50:50, unless an election is made for each of the parties to be taxed on their actual underlying beneficial entitlement.

This contrasts with the general position for property held jointly and beneficially by spouses or civil partners who are living together, where the income is split equally for income tax purposes unless the husband and wife formally make a declaration to be taxed on income corresponding to their unequal underlying beneficial entitlements (Income Tax Act 2007, s.837). HMRC states that the declaration ceases to operate on permanent separation or divorce, albeit the legislation makes clear that it continues until there is a change in beneficial ownership of the income or of the property itself (see HMRC *Independent Taxation Manual* at IN137).

The jointly held asset rule for spouses and civil partners living together does not apply to income from any partnerships or from commercial letting of unfurnished holiday accommodation (as defined for tax purposes). In other words and, just as for cohabitees, their income is taxed according to their actual beneficial entitlements.

For CGT purposes, any gain on the disposal of a jointly held asset would be in proportion to their actual beneficial interests notwithstanding any different income tax treatment. The same applies for spouses and civil partners as for cohabitees.

8.4.4 Tax on extraction of funds from family owned companies

The following tax implications arise from spouses/civil partners who are director shareholders withdrawing funds from a company to pay maintenance or make a lump sum settlement.

Withdrawal of a director's loan to company

There will be no tax on amounts which represent capital repayments of a director's loan account. Interest on any increased overdraft facility taken out by the company to make the repayments should be corporation tax deductible for the company where the overdraft is simply replacing working capital previously provided to the company by the director.

Bonus or increased remuneration

The payment of a bonus or increased remuneration will be liable to income tax at the director's marginal income tax rate of up to 50 per cent, plus employee's/employer's NICs.

It is arguable whether the payment of a bonus or additional remuneration should be corporation tax deductible for the company unless it can be shown that the amount was wholly and exclusively for the purposes of the trade. In practice, a company which is owned and controlled by, say, its sole director will commonly have levels of remuneration which are determined by the personal circumstances of that director rather than being set at a level which corresponds to what would be paid on an arm's length basis. HMRC does not appear to take the corporation tax point in practice.

Dividend: cash or in specie distribution of an asset

The payment of a dividend (whether in cash or of an asset) will be taxable at 32.5 per cent in the hands of a higher rate taxpayer or 42.5 per cent where the new 50 per cent tax rate applies. The effective tax rate is 25 per cent (36.6 per cent for a 50 per cent taxpayer) of the net cash dividend, since the net dividend is grossed up by a notional 10 per cent tax credit which can be credited against the tax due at 32.5 per cent (or 42.5 per cent as appropriate).

If the company declares a dividend which is to be satisfied by the transfer of a chargeable asset rather than cash, which asset is standing at a gain, corporation tax may be payable depending on the ability of the company to shelter the gain through any available tax reliefs or losses. The asset is deemed to be disposed of at market value for this purpose and received at market value by the shareholder, who will pay income tax on that value as above. Note that if the asset is shares or land and property, any implications arising under stamp duty or stamp duty land tax will need to be considered.

Share repurchase by the company

A spouse or civil partner from whom a proportion of his shares are repurchased by the company and who continues to retain at least a 30 per cent interest in the company (or a lesser interest which has not been 'substantially reduced' from what his interest was before (TCGA 1992, s.221(4)) will be taxed on amounts received for the shares so purchased as dividend income (see above), excluding amounts representing repayments of share capital originally subscribed.

A potentially more favourable tax treatment which accesses lower CGT rates of 18 per cent (or 10 per cent where entrepreneurs' relief (ER) applies) can sometimes be achieved on a share buy-back where the company is a trading company and the spouse's interest is being substantially reduced as a result of the repurchase (see below). Tax advice should be taken in specific cases.

Beneficial loan followed by a dividend

On the basis that the company is unlisted, it is understood that a loan to a director, whilst voidable by the shareholders under company law, is not unlawful.

It is possible, therefore, for a family company to make a loan to a director which is left outstanding for a period to be repaid by a dividend declared at a future date which provides an opportunity to defer paying significant personal taxes. In family companies, it is not uncommon to see quite large directors' loan accounts outstanding which are subsequently cleared by a later payment of remuneration or dividend. The benefit of taking out loans can be seen in terms of cash flow rather than an outright tax saving and can defer the payment of significant tax liabilities for up to three years, depending on the precise circumstances.

EXAMPLE 8C

A court orders Mr Green to pay a lump sum of £675,000 to be raised from his company, which has cash balances of £2m, in excess of the £1.2m cash working capital requirements for the business, as at 31 December 2007.

The manner in which this could be achieved together with the tax costs associated with it are as follows.

Mr Green borrows £675,000 from the company on 31 July 2008. The company is left with cash of £1.325m for working capital based on the 31 December 2007 cash balances.

On 30 September 2009, a dividend of £900,000 is declared to repay the loan to Mr Green of £675,000. The balance of £225,000 remains undrawn and is retained in the company as a loan from Mr Green to provide working capital to the business if required. That is, cash in the company will remain at £1.325m as increased by any additional cash from trading profits in the period.

On 31 January 2011, Mr Green pays tax at his marginal income tax rate of 32.5% on the grossed up dividend, amounting to tax of £225,000 computed as follows:

	£
Dividend	900,000
Tax credit (1/9th)	100,000
Gross dividend	1,000,000
Tax thereon at 32.5%	325,000
Less tax credit	(100,000)
Tax payable	225,000

The company's retained cash up to 31 January 2011 will therefore be £1.325m and on 1 February 2011 it would be £1.325m less the repayment of Mr Green's loan of £225,000 to enable him to pay the tax, i.e. the company has net cash of £1m. However, to these figures must be added three years and one month's net cash generated from trading (1 January 2008 to 31 January 2011) which should ensure that working capital requirements continue to be met.

TAX IMPLICATIONS OF THE LOAN

Assuming the loan to Mr Green is interest free and since Mr Green is a director of the company, he will be deemed to receive a taxable benefit equal to the interest foregone which is pegged at the HMRC official rate. Based on 6.25%, as the tax on the benefit will be 40%, the effective rate of 'interest' is only 2.5%.

Therefore the tax on the benefit of a loan which is outstanding for 14 months (31 July 2008 to 30 September 2009) is:

14/12 months @ 6.25% p.a. × £675,000 = £49,218 @ 40% tax = £19,687

The tax due of £19,687 will be paid in two instalments, £11,250 on 31 January 2010 and £8,437 on 31 January 2011. This is because the loan spans two tax years (and ignores any tax implications arising out of how these liabilities are to be funded).

The company will also be required to pay Class 1A NICs on the benefit of £49,218 at 12.8% (£6,300). This will be £3,600 by 19 July 2009 and £2,700 on 19 July 2010.

TAX IMPLICATIONS OF PAYING DIVIDEND ON 30 SEPTEMBER 2009

Provided that Mr Green repays the loan within nine months of the end of the company's accounting year (in this case the year end date is 31 December 2008 and so the loan should be repaid no later than 30 September 2009), a corporation tax charge on the company is avoided (see **8.4.2**).

Repayment of the loan can be achieved by declaring a dividend of £900,000, of which £675,000 is used to 'repay' the loan. The tax on the dividend of £225,000 as stated above is not due until 31 January 2011.

8.4.5 Tax considerations on acquiring a separated spouse's or civil partner's shares in a company

The potential tax liability on acquiring a spouse's or civil partner's interest in a company will, of course, be relevant to any transfer between spouses following the tax year of separation. The tax effect of some potential methods of realising an interest in a company held by a spouse are described below.

Transfer or sale of shares

The sale of shares or transfer to a spouse or civil partner will result in a capital gain (or loss) depending on the difference between the cost (or deemed cost) of the shares and net sale proceeds (market value in the case of a transfer to a spouse). Hold over relief and ER may also be in point.

Use of options as part of a deferred or structured share purchase

Options may be used to defer the sale and purchase of shares between a separated couple until such time as funds are available to make the purchase possible or to improve the tax position where, for example, the minimum holding period for ER has not yet been met but there is a desire for certainty that the shares will be able to be sold after that period has elapsed. The use of 'put' and 'call' cross-options (with corresponding but not simultaneous exercise periods) may also be considered as a means of postponing a disposal but providing some certainty to both parties involved that a disposal will occur on some future event.

The grant of an option will normally be at market value and the grant of an option is a separate asset (namely the option itself) for CGT purposes with no base cost (TCGA 1992, s.144). CGT may therefore be payable when the option is granted.

However, when the option is exercised, the option and the disposal of shares are treated as a single transaction, being the disposal of the underlying asset, i.e. the shares under the option at that time. Tax will normally be due on 31 January following the end of the tax year in which the option is exercised.

The original option consideration (or market value) will be taxed as consideration for the shares which, if full ER applies, will result in the effective tax rate being at 10 per cent. The exercise of the option will also give rise to a repayment of tax if tax has been paid on the earlier grant of the option.

Share repurchase by the company

Subject to company law requirements and the company having sufficient distributable profits, the company could arrange for a spouse's shares to be purchased by the company either for cash or by way of a distribution of an asset.

A share buy-back would normally be treated as an income distribution for tax purposes to the extent that the amount distributed exceeds the original capital subscribed for the shares, and would therefore normally be taxed at an effective rate of 25 per cent for a higher rate taxpayer (and 36.6 per cent for a 50 per cent rate taxpayer) as explained above.

There would also be a capital gain since the shares are being disposed of to the company; however, to the extent that an amount of the proceeds received has already been charged to income tax, no gain arises (TCGA 1992, s.37). In practice, a CGT loss usually arises equal to the original purchase cost of the shares in circumstances where the shares were originally purchased at a price greater than the original amount subscribed for the shares.

An asset (as opposed to cash) can also be distributed by the company, although in this case there may be a gain arising on the asset in the company based on the asset's current market value on which corporation tax would potentially be payable, in addition to the 25 per cent effective tax charge on the recipient shareholder.

If the company is a trading company, the share buy-back can be treated as a capital gain and is therefore taxable at 18 per cent, with the possibility that ER could be claimed, which may provide an effective tax rate of 10 per cent. This assumes certain conditions are fulfilled and is provided that the spouses are no longer living together (even if not yet divorced). The main conditions for this beneficial tax treatment to apply are that the share buy-back must be for the benefit of the company's trade (which may well be the case where spouses who are both shareholders have separated); the spouse must have owned the shares for at least five years (including any period when owned by a transferor spouse provided they were then living with each other) and be resident and ordinarily resident in the United Kingdom. Immediately following the share buy-back, the departing spouse's interest in the company must be 'substantially reduced'. This means that the spouse's interest in the company as a proportion of the reduced share capital after the buy-back must be reduced to below 75 per cent of the corresponding fraction before the buy-back, and to below 75 per cent of any combined interest in the company, including shares held by the couple's minor children. The departing spouse, together with his or her 'associates', i.e. any spouse whom he or she lives with or minor children, also must not own 30 per cent or more of the company (Corporation Tax Act (CTA) 2010, ss.1059–63).

EXAMPLE 8D

Henry and Henrietta have each owned 45 shares in the family trading company for over five years, and their children Humphrey (age 17) and Helen (age 15) each own five shares. There are 100 issued shares in total. Henry and Henrietta legally separated in 2005. If the company were to buy back all of Henry's shares then his holding, together with that of his associates, would be 55% before the buy-back (being his 45 shares plus the five shares owned by each of Humphrey and Helen) and 18% after the buy-back (being the 10 shares owned by Humphrey and Helen, out of the reduced total share capital of 55).

This satisfies the substantial reduction condition and Henry should benefit from the applicable CGT rate subject to obtaining tax clearance from HMRC.

Formation of new company to acquire one of the spouse's shares

If a company does not currently have sufficient distributable reserves to effect a share buy-back but is profitable, a bank may be prepared to lend on the security of the company's assets and forecast future cash flows.

The non-exiting spouse could then form a new company which takes out the loan which is used to acquire the entire issued share capital of the original company. The loan is used to pay cash for the exiting spouse's shares and the non-exiting spouse exchanges their shares in the original company for shares in the new company. The loan from the bank is subsequently repaid out of future profits of the original company which is now, of course, a wholly owned subsidiary.

Provided HMRC grants tax clearance that the transaction is being carried out for bona fide commercial reasons, the spouse who has received cash should be liable to CGT on the disposal, rather than being charged to income tax. The non-exiting spouse will not be deemed to have made any disposal for tax purposes so the transaction is tax neutral as far as he or she is concerned.

Splitting up a company currently owned by both spouses

If a company owned by both spouses has two or more businesses, or separate investment and trading activities which each spouse has a continuing interest in owning, consideration might be given to separating out the two businesses. Normally this involves forming two new companies to which the businesses are separately transferred on liquidation of the existing company (known as a liquidation demerger). Each spouse would end up with a 100 per cent interest in the company holding the business in which they are interested. Provided tax clearances are obtained from HMRC, this would avoid any tax charges until such time as the shares in the respective companies are sold. This can be useful where, for example, one spouse wishes to continue a family farming business, part of which includes a separate furnished holiday letting business. This might then provide both spouses with continuing income/assets without the need for a third party disposal.

Where the company only has investment activities, the liquidation demerger route will not be tax effective and both corporate and personal tax considerations will be an important factor in any overall fair division of the assets. Specific advice will need to be taken.

Transfer of trade between companies

Where a trade is transferred between companies in common ownership, CTA 2010, Part 22, Chapter 1 permits the continuation of trading losses and capital allowances on the transfer. The companies must be at least 75 per cent owned by the same person or persons. In this case, ownership by spouses, civil partners and certain other 'relatives' counts as the same ownership. This beneficial tax treatment applies even if the couple are separated but not yet divorced, thereby allowing trading businesses (comprising the business's assets and liabilities) to be transferred prior to divorce whilst preserving trading losses and capital allowances, subject to meeting the relevant conditions. This applies even where the two companies are, or will come to be, owned separately by the spouses or civil partners immediately following decree absolute or dissolution. There may, depending on the circumstances, be other tax charges arising out of the transfer of the trade between the companies and specialist tax advice should always be sought on any company reconstructions.

As unmarried or unregistered couples are not considered 'relatives' for the purpose of the common ownership test, the relief is unlikely to be available in most circumstances.

CHAPTER 8 CHECKLIST

1. Identify those situations where specialist pensions advice will be required (**8.1**).
2. Consider if life insurance policies are liable to income tax on transfer and if a court order is required (**8.2**).
3. HMRC tax clearance may be required in appropriate cases of family company purchase of own shares and company reconstructions (**8.4.5**).

CHAPTER 9

The international dimension

> **KEY CONCEPTS**
>
> The scope of an individual's liability to UK taxes is dependent upon their tax status under three headings – residence, ordinary residence and domicile.

9.1 SCOPE OF UK TAXES

The scope of an individual's liability to UK income tax (IT), capital gains tax (CGT) and inheritance tax (IHT) is dependent upon his or her tax status under one or more of three important categories: residence, ordinary residence and domicile. These statuses are dealt with at **9.2**.

9.1.1 Territorial scope of income tax

A UK resident individual is *prima facie* chargeable to IT on his worldwide income, whilst a non-UK resident individual is only chargeable to IT on UK source income. For certain types of UK source income, a non-UK resident's IT liability is limited to tax deducted at source or tax credits in respect of that income (Income Taxes Act (ITA) 2007, s.811).

A non-domiciled but UK resident individual may claim that his income from non-UK sources for a tax year will only be taxed when remitted to the United Kingdom. See **9.3** which deals with this 'remittance basis' in more detail.

An individual is normally regarded as UK resident or ordinarily resident for the whole of a tax year when they are so resident for any part of it. However, where an individual takes up long-term residence in the United Kingdom or leaves for permanent residence abroad, an Extra Statutory Concession (ESC A11) can operate to divide the year into two parts either side of the arrival/departure date. This is referred to as 'split year' treatment. The scope of the individual's exposure to IT is established separately for each part by reference to his residence status in that part year. However, the concession will not be available where it is being relied upon for tax avoidance.

9.1.2 Territorial scope of capital gains tax

CGT is chargeable on gains realised by a UK resident or ordinarily resident individual (Taxation of Chargeable Gains Act (TGCA) 1992, s.2) and, on gains apportioned upon or attributed to him:

- as a participator in a non-UK resident company (TCGA 1992, s.13);
- as a UK domiciled settlor in respect of disposals made by non-UK resident trustees (TCGA 1992, s.86); or,
- as a beneficiary in receipt of a 'capital payment' from a non-UK resident settlement (TCGA 1992, s.87).

In addition, gains realised on disposals of UK assets employed in a trade carried on through a UK branch or agency are chargeable to CGT wherever the owner is based.

Rules were enacted in 1998 to counter avoidance of CGT by individuals leaving the United Kingdom for at least a complete tax year and realising capital gains whilst absent and outside the scope of CGT. These provisions impose a charge on an individual who leaves the United Kingdom and returns after completing less than five full tax years abroad, if he had been UK resident or ordinarily resident in four out of the seven years immediately preceding his departure. In such cases, gains (or losses) realised whilst abroad on assets which he owned at the time of departure (and other amounts, as above, which would have been chargeable upon the individual if he had been resident in the United Kingdom during the intervening non-UK resident period) are treated as accruing to him in the year of his return.

ESC D2 operates for CGT in a similar (but not identical) fashion to ESC A11, to enable a tax year to be split for new long-term residents and emigrants and only charging gains respectively realised after arrival or before departure.

The concession is not available for the arriving individual who has been UK resident or ordinarily resident at any time during the five tax years preceding the year of arrival, or for the departing individual who was UK resident or ordinarily resident for the whole of at least four out of the seven tax years immediately preceding the year of departure.

The trustees of a UK resident settlement are chargeable to CGT on the net capital gains of the settlement. If the trust ceases to be UK resident, the trustees will be deemed to dispose of and to reacquire all of the trust assets at their market value on the date of the migration with the resulting net gains chargeable to CGT.

Since 6 April 2008, significant changes have been made to the way in which the gains of non-UK resident settlements and close companies are taxable on non-UK domiciled beneficiaries. Prior thereto, such attributed gains could be ignored where the beneficiaries were not UK domiciled as they were specifically excluded from being charged. See **9.5** which deals with this in more detail.

TAX AND FAMILY BREAKDOWN

9.1.3 Territorial scope of inheritance tax

The scope of IHT over an individual's estate may be limited by reference to his domicile status.

For the purposes of IHT, an individual who is not UK domiciled will however be deemed to be UK domiciled at any time when he has been resident in the United Kingdom in at least 17 of the last 20 tax years (including the year of transfer), or if he was domiciled in the United Kingdom within three years immediately preceding that time (Inheritance Tax Act (IHTA) 1984, s.267).

Individuals domiciled, or deemed domiciled, in the United Kingdom are subject to IHT on their worldwide estates whilst others are subject to IHT only on the part of their estates (net of any related liabilities) situated in the United Kingdom.

9.1.4 Foreign tax

Having considered the scope of UK taxes, it is important to remember that tax may also be payable in overseas territories.

When assets are situated outside the United Kingdom, it is important to obtain local tax advice on the implications of making transfers in connection with matrimonial proceedings. Local equivalents to CGT and gift/inheritance taxes will need to be considered, often at a national and municipal level; there may be registration/transfer taxes in respect of real property.

Double tax treaties may provide protection from being taxed twice on the same income/gains with relief limited to a withholding tax at a rate specified under that treaty. This generally means that the individual will only suffer tax at the higher of the UK and the local tax rates.

However, if there is no relevant treaty, in most cases a UK resident can obtain relief in the United Kingdom for the foreign tax suffered, up to the amount of the UK tax suffered on the income/gains.

9.2 RESIDENCE, ORDINARY RESIDENCE AND DOMICILE

9.2.1 UK residence

A continuing source of frustration for taxpayers and their advisers is the fact that 'residence' is not defined within tax legislation; accordingly, the word should take its ordinary meaning. Whilst there have been a number of cases on what it means to be resident in the United Kingdom, these were each decided on the particular facts, which are sometimes contradictory, and so it is not possible to distil a set of hard and fast rules to apply generally.

HMRC's published guidance on residence (IR20) was applied in relation to determining a taxpayer's affairs for the years to 5 April 2009. This guidance was both relatively easy to understand and normally adopted as if it was statute. However, following the high profile case of *Gaines-Cooper* v. *HMRC* [2007] STC (SCD) 23, HMRC has withdrawn from the position of absolute reliance on the wording of IR20, claiming that it is not to be bound by it, even though it has been in effective circulation for 70 years.

A replacement document, HMRC 6, issued on 31 March 2009, is considered to be vague and unhelpful when compared to IR20, and is presented on the premise that HMRC can ignore it if it so chooses.

Nevertheless, the universal test remains effective for most individuals, who will be resident in the United Kingdom if physically present in the United Kingdom for more than 182 days (counting days where the individual is present at midnight) in a tax year.

Where that physical presence test is not satisfied, an individual should be regarded as UK resident if he is present in the United Kingdom on average for more than 90 days per tax year measured over the most recent four years, or, if he first arrived in the United Kingdom less than four years beforehand, from the date of arrival.

Even where an individual averages less than 90 days per year (and is present for less than 183 days in any one year) he may still be regarded as resident in the United Kingdom; this is a particular issue for an individual who was previously resident in the United Kingdom and has sought to cease residence without sufficiently severing his ties with the United Kingdom. In such a case, the individual is treated as never having left the United Kingdom, notwithstanding his or her extended presence abroad.

In all cases, the intentions of the taxpayer should be of overriding importance, assuming, however, that these have been documented in some fashion and, preferably, can be objectively supported by contemporary evidence.

HMRC may agree that residence and/or ordinary residence in the United Kingdom can begin or end part way through a year of assessment for IT and/or CGT purposes if the criteria in ESCs A11 and/or D2 are satisfied (see **9.1.1** and **9.1.2**).

9.2.2 Ordinarily resident in the United Kingdom

As for residence, ordinary residence is not defined in the tax legislation.

The guidance in HMRC 6 (at para.3.2 'What does ordinary residence mean?'), states that ordinary residence in the United Kingdom requires a person to have 'come to the United Kingdom voluntarily'; for his presence to have 'a settled purpose'; and for his presence to form part of 'the regular and habitual' mode of his life for the time being. This is based upon the decision in a case relating to an applicant for a local education authority student grant that required him to be 'ordinarily resident' to qualify (*R* v. *Barnet LBC, ex p. Shah* [1983] 2 AC 309 at 343).

9.2.3 Domicile

Domicile is a legal concept aimed at connecting an individual with a jurisdiction for a variety of non-tax reasons. However, it has been adopted for UK tax purposes to provide a limiting role on the scope of IT, CGT and IHT.

Every individual has only one form of domicile at any one time. But, whilst it has some form of structure with different categories it has no formal definition.

An individual acquires a 'domicile of origin' at birth. This will be his father's domicile if born legitimately and his father is alive, otherwise it is his mother's domicile. A domicile of origin can only be changed for another as a result of adoption.

The domicile of origin may be supplanted by the individual (aged over 16) acquiring a 'domicile of choice'. A domicile of choice takes precedence over the domicile of origin and, so long as the individual retains his domicile of choice, it will be his domicile for UK tax purposes. Generally, it may be considered that the prime requirements for an individual to acquire a domicile of choice in a jurisdiction are acquisition of a main residence there and fixing an intention to reside there permanently or indefinitely. The domicile of choice will be lost when the individual no longer satisfies those criteria.

A child (under age 16) may have his domicile of origin supplanted if the relevant parent's domicile changes, or if the parents separate and the child lives with the mother who has a different domicile from that of the father, whereupon the child will acquire that domicile as a 'domicile of dependency'. When the child reaches age 16, his domicile of dependency will be retained as a domicile of choice.

If any domicile of choice is abandoned, without acquisition of an alternative domicile of choice, then the domicile of origin revives.

A woman who married before 1974 took her husband's domicile as a domicile of dependency but under the Domicile and Matrimonial Proceedings Act 1973 this was amended to a domicile of choice with effect from 1 January 1974. This domicile of choice could be abandoned or lost as described above, with the domicile of origin reviving. Women marrying after 1973 no longer automatically acquire a domicile of choice on marriage and their domicile will depend upon their individual circumstances.

Strictly speaking, a domicile is held in a 'jurisdiction' so that an individual would be domiciled in Scotland rather than the United Kingdom. The same principle applies to the states of the USA and Australia or the cantons of Switzerland. However, for simplicity, any reference to UK domicile means a domicile in any of England, Scotland, Northern Ireland or Wales.

9.3 REMITTANCE BASIS

9.3.1 Remittance basis of taxation

An individual who is not UK domiciled under general law (i.e. ignoring any deemed domicile status for IHT purposes) for an entire tax year is entitled to make a claim to be taxed on the remittance basis. Under this basis, the individual's non-UK source income and capital gains realised on non-UK situated assets are taxed only when the funds are remitted to the United Kingdom. All UK source income and capital gains arising on UK situated assets continue to be assessed on an arising basis.

Although a rare circumstance, a UK domiciled individual who is resident but not ordinarily resident in the United Kingdom is entitled to claim for his overseas income (but not capital gains) to be taxed on the remittance basis. However, this section is principally aimed at non-UK domiciled individuals.

The remittance basis acts as a deferral of potential liability. This deferral mechanism may become permanent if the funds are spent overseas, never remitted, or remitted once the individual has lost his UK residence/ordinary residence status and is no longer within the scope of UK income tax and CGT (see **9.1**).

Significant changes have been introduced to the remittance basis for non-UK domiciled individuals with effect from 6 April 2008. However, despite complex legislation and case law on the subject of whether funds have been remitted to the United Kingdom (see **9.4**), the position broadly remains that it is possible for a non-UK domiciled individual to defer (and possibly ultimately avoid) tax on his foreign income and capital gains.

9.3.2 Claims and associated costs

It is important to note that a non-UK domiciled individual must consider whether the remittance basis would be advantageous for him for each tax year. If it is beneficial, then he must actually make the claim, unless:

- he only has unremitted foreign income and gains in that year of less than £2,000; or
- he has been UK resident for less than seven of the last nine years and, in the tax year in question, he has no UK income or gains and remits no foreign income or gains,

when the remittance basis applies without any need for him to make a claim.

If an individual does claim the remittance basis then he is not entitled to the personal allowance for income tax or the annual exempt amount for CGT. In addition, if the individual has been resident in the United Kingdom for at least seven out of the previous nine tax years, he will be required to pay the remittance basis charge (RBC) for the year (for 2008/09 and 2009/10 it is £30,000).

Further difficulties can arise with respect to the remittance basis claim and the RBC because of the complex rules relating to 'nominated income and gains'.

9.3.3 Nominated income and gains

When the RBC was first announced in October 2007, concerns were expressed that individuals would not be able to obtain credit for it against taxation liability in another jurisdiction. This was because the charge was not perceived as levied upon any particular foreign income and gains.

To address these concerns, HMRC introduced the concept of 'nominated income and gains' (ITA 2007, s.809C) in an attempt to provide a linkage between the RBC and specified income and/or gains. This is principally aimed at assisting US citizens who are long-term residents in the United Kingdom; doubt still remains (at the time of writing) over the Inland Revenue Service (USA) attitude to claim for tax credit relief for the RBC.

An individual who claims the remittance basis must nominate some or all of his offshore income and/or gains of the year. The items nominated must not exceed an amount which, if remitted in that year, would have given an increased tax liability equal to the RBC amount.

Far from making life easier for the long-term resident claiming the remittance basis, the legislation surrounding the nominated income and gains concept provides a plethora of complex rules designed to lessen the possibility of HMRC giving credit for the RBC paid until UK tax is ultimately borne on remittance of all other offshore income/gains. For example, if the individual actually remits any of his nominated income/gains whilst other amounts remain unremitted, the remittance will be deemed out of the other amounts and in an order designed to maximise the tax liability.

The issues surrounding nominated income and gains make the complex subject of the remittance basis even more complicated. Therefore, specialist advice should be sought in this regard.

9.4 WHAT IS A REMITTANCE?

It would be a simple matter to arrange for an individual's foreign income/gains to be brought to the United Kingdom by another person and to claim that the individual had made no remittance. Accordingly, wide-ranging provisions are included within the legislation (ITA 2007, Part 14, Chapter A1, ss.809L–809S) to lay down rules to ensure a tax charge upon the individual whose income/gains are remitted not only by him but also by a person closely associated with him. In this context, remittance need not be identified as being for the benefit of the taxpayer himself.

9.4.1 Relevant person

The legislation employs the term 'relevant person' to identify classes of persons who may directly or indirectly remit foreign income/gains of an individual, whereupon the individual is treated as having made the remittance.

A relevant person includes:

- the individual;
- the individual's spouse or civil partner;
- a minor child or grandchild of one of the above;
- a company which is close, or would be close if UK resident, where any of the above is a participator;
- the trustees of a settlement of which any of the above is a beneficiary; and
- a body connected with such a settlement.

For these purposes, 'spouse' and 'civil partner' are both extended to include a person living together with the individual 'as if they were' a spouse or civil partner. Precisely what 'living together as if they were' means is not entirely clear and could give rise to an interesting test case in the future.

9.4.2 Meaning of 'remitted to the United Kingdom'

The legislation (ITA 2007, s.809L) sets out the circumstances under which an individual is treated as remitting foreign income/gains to the United Kingdom. The more common examples are the use of the foreign income/gains to fund, whether directly or indirectly:

- money or property brought to, received or used in the United Kingdom by a relevant person;
- a service provided in the United Kingdom to or for a relevant person;
- servicing of an overseas 'relevant debt' (including interest on it) used to fund property or a service provided for a relevant person in the United Kingdom; and
- a gift to a non-relevant person which in due course is used to provide property or a service to a relevant person or service a 'relevant debt'.

A remittance is also deemed where a non-relevant person's property is brought to, received or used in the United Kingdom and is enjoyed by a relevant person, if there is an arrangement for the non-relevant person to receive consideration that is (or derives from) the individual's foreign income/gains in return for the enjoyment.

9.5 OFFSHORE STRUCTURES AND ANTI-AVOIDANCE LEGISLATION

Anti-avoidance rules exist in all aspects of the UK tax legislation. Outlined below are the IT, CGT and IHT anti-avoidance rules that must be considered in relation to dealing with offshore structures.

9.5.1 Income tax

Settlements

Regardless of the residence of a settlement, income arising to the trustees is treated as income of the settlor where he and/or his spouse (or civil partner) can benefit from the settled property directly or indirectly. It is assessable as the highest part of the settlor's total income but he has a right of recovery of tax borne from the trustees (Income Tax (Trading and Other Income) Act (ITTOIA) 2005, Part 5, Chapter 5).

If the settlor has claimed for it, then the trustee's foreign source income will be assessable on the remittance basis. The settlement will be a relevant person (see **9.4**); property derived from the trust's foreign income that is brought to, received in or enjoyed in the United Kingdom by the trustees will be a taxable remittance of the settlor.

Transfers of assets abroad

These rules apply where income tax avoidance is sought for UK ordinarily resident individuals by means of a transfer of assets and, as a result of the transfer and any associated operations, income becomes payable to a person resident or domiciled outside the United Kingdom. Although typically considered when dealing with non-UK resident trusts, there is no need for a formal structure to be in place.

Exemption from charge may be obtained if the individual can 'satisfy an officer of Revenue and Customs' that it would be wrong to infer tax avoidance as a motive based upon all the particular circumstances or that all the transactions were genuinely commercial and involved with a trade or business. It is generally considered to be extremely difficult to satisfy an officer of Revenue and Customs!

The income arising in the structure will be treated as that of the transferor (whether or not he was ordinarily resident when the transfer was made) where he or his spouse or civil partner has the 'power to enjoy' that income, which term has a very wide meaning.

Whilst these provisions have broadly the same effect as the settlement provisions for income at the trust level, set out immediately above, the settlement provisions take precedence. However, these rules will apply for income arising from transfers of assets to non-UK resident companies owned by the transferor or a close relative and, more frequently, such companies owned by an offshore trust structure.

Where the income is not taxable upon the transferor, undistributed income within the structure ('relevant income') will be matched with benefits received by individuals ordinarily resident in the United Kingdom and assessed to income tax. Benefits matched with income are treated as arising to the beneficiary in the later of the year of receipt or the year the relevant income arises. For a non-UK domiciled beneficiary claiming the remittance basis, the relevant income will be assessable on the remittance basis to the extent that the underlying income is foreign source income.

The foreign source income arising may also be dealt with under the remittance basis if the individual is competent to make the claim for it and does so.

Unless a transfer of assets from a UK-domiciled individual to a non-UK domiciled spouse or civil partner forms part of a wider arrangement for avoiding tax, HMRC would not seek to assess the transferor where the income could avoid UK taxation through the remittance basis.

Shadow director problems

A common concern arises where an individual occupies a UK property owned by a non-resident company which in turn is owned by a non-resident trust. The fear is that an income tax charge could be visited upon the individual, under the employment taxation rules, regardless of any potential income chargeable from the offshore structure, as he could be considered a 'shadow director' (a person whose instructions the directors of a company tend to follow or act upon).

Concern is often expressed that a beneficiary who is permitted to occupy a property and to take control of all matters relating to it might be deemed to be acting in the role of a shadow director. The best advice to forestall the risk of potentially substantial tax charges is to formalise the terms of occupation by a licence, forbidding the individual to effect any alteration to or change of use of the property. Thus, if the individual does undertake forbidden works, rather than acting with the blessing of the directors he will be in breach of the licence.

9.5.2 Capital gains tax

Non-UK resident companies

A proportion of the net capital gains (but not net losses) arising in a tax year to a non-UK resident company which would be 'close' if UK resident (usually meaning owned as to more than 50 per cent by five or fewer shareholders and their associates) may be taxable on any UK resident whose interest as a 'participator', together with similar interests of persons connected with him, exceeds 10 per cent (TCGA 1992, s.13). The proportion is the extent of his personal interest as a participator.

The term 'participator' is generally defined as a person having a share or interest in the capital or income of the company, but in addition to the simple case of a shareholder it includes, *inter alia*, a person with a right to acquire shares or voting rights and a loan creditor.

If an amount in respect of the chargeable gain is distributed to a participator, whether by dividend, capital distribution or on dissolution of the company, then the tax paid by him on the earlier attribution of gain may be used to reduce his UK tax liability on that distribution. However, the distribution must be made within three years from the end of the accounting year in which the gain was realised or, if earlier, four years from the date the gain accrued.

Where a non-UK resident company is controlled by an offshore trust, TCGA 1992, s.13 applies such that the company gains are attributed to the trustees and dealt with under the provisions outlined below.

Non-UK resident trusts

Net capital gains realised in a tax year by an offshore trust will be attributed (under TCGA 1992, s.86) to the UK domiciled and resident settlor (who is still alive at the end of that year) if the class of beneficiary does or can include:

- the settlor or his spouse/civil partner;
- any child (or his spouse/civil partner) of the settlor or his spouse/civil partner;
- any grandchild (or his spouse/civil partner) of the settlor or his spouse/civil partner; or
- any company (or an associated company of it is) controlled by any one or more of the above.

For a trust set up before 17 March 1998, it is usually the case that the third category above (grandchildren, etc.) can be ignored unless further property was subsequently added.

Gains attributed to the settlor are taxable on him in the year they arise but he has a statutory right of reclaim from the trustees for the CGT suffered as a result. Net capital losses in a year are carried forward to offset against subsequent trust gains.

Where the trust gains are not attributable to the settlor, they may be attributed to any beneficiary who has received a 'capital payment' (TCGA 1992, s.87). A capital payment is generally a payment which is not chargeable to income tax; as well as straightforward cash distributions, it includes the transfer of an asset or the conferring of a benefit. The more common benefits are occupation of property and beneficial loans.

The net gains for each year are computed as if the trust were resident in the United Kingdom, and are held pending a matching of amount with subsequent capital payments or brought forward unmatched capital payments. Gains matched to capital payments for non-UK resident and not ordinarily resident beneficiaries fall outside the scope of CGT (subject to the rules for temporary non-residents, see **9.1.2**) and this can be a useful planning tool to 'wash stockpiled gains'.

The beneficiary who is liable to CGT on capital payments matched with gains of an earlier year may also incur a supplementary charge on the CGT due. The charge is equivalent to notional interest on the CGT (current rate of 10 per cent has been fixed since 1991) for each tax year between the year the gain was realised and the year the capital payment was made; no charge arises where payment is made in the year following the matched gain and the number of years to be charged cannot exceed six (taking the current maximum supplementary charge to 60 per cent of the CGT due).

Prior to 6 April 2008, non-UK domiciled individuals were exempt from CGT on capital payments matched with, and thereby reducing, trust stockpiled gains. This is no longer the position and the matched sums now fall within the scope of CGT; however, such beneficiaries who are UK resident or ordinarily resident may still claim for the remittance basis to apply. Importantly, there is no 'look through' provision to automatically charge any stockpiled gain when it may have been realised on a UK situated asset.

A non-domiciled settlor is dealt with under the rules as for any other non-domiciled beneficiary in receipt of capital payments and does not have the trust gains immediately charged upon him.

The chance of retrospective taxation for non-UK domiciled individuals is removed by excluding any CGT charge for them on any pre-6 April 2008 capital payment matched with a later year's gain and any post-5 April 2008 capital payment matched with pre-6 April 2008 stockpiled gains.

Furthermore, the trustees of offshore trusts have the right to make a rebasing election that is intended to ensure that non-UK domiciled individuals will only be charged on realised trust gains accrued after 5 April 2008. This election must be made by 31 January following the first tax year in which either a capital payment is made to a UK resident beneficiary or funds are appointed into a separate settlement. For many trusts that deadline will have passed on 31 January 2010.

9.5.3 Inheritance tax

Most settlements made post-21 March 2006 and all pre-22 March 2006 discretionary trusts are subject to IHT on the 'trust assets' at each 10-year anniversary of commencement of the settlement and when they are appointed out to beneficiaries. Where a trust is settled by an individual who is non-UK domiciled for IHT purposes (see **9.1**), trust assets situated outside the United Kingdom are 'excluded property' and outside the scope of IHT. They are not brought into account in computing any IHT on the UK situated assets.

One important anti-avoidance provision deals with what is commonly referred to as gifts with reservation of benefit (GROB) and was introduced in 1986 when IHT replaced capital transfer tax.

Where an individual gifts an asset but does not give up full possession of it or reserves a right to enjoy it at a later time, the asset ('property subject to a reservation') is treated as remaining comprised in his estate at death. This would apply where the gift is made to trustees and the settlor is capable of benefiting from the settled property. However, if full possession or the right to enjoyment is subsequently given up he will be treated as making a potentially exempt transfer at that later time.

Combining these matters produces an interesting situation where a non-UK domiciled individual creates a discretionary trust from which he is capable of benefiting and he subsequently becomes UK domiciled for IHT purposes. Although the settled property comprises a GROB, the excluded property rules will continue to apply for non-UK situated assets and take precedence; so, whilst the settled assets are treated as remaining in his estate, the foreign assets will be regarded as excluded property and outside the scope of IHT. This is confirmed in the HMRC *Inheritance Tax Manual* at IHTM14396.

Non-UK situated assets include (for CGT and IHT purposes):

- bearer shares situated abroad in non-UK incorporated companies;
- registered shares in foreign companies where register is kept abroad;
- non-UK situated real property;
- foreign debts and specialty debts where the deed is held outside the United Kingdom;
- aircraft and ships situated abroad;
- intangible assets not subject to UK law;
- goodwill of a trade carried on outside the United Kingdom.

9.6 REMITTANCE BASIS IN THE CONTEXT OF DIVORCE

This section examines situations where careful consideration should be given in relation to a divorce settlement where the transferor spouse is non-UK domiciled and is claiming the remittance basis of taxation. The 2008 legislation is comparatively new with little in the way of established precedent in this area. Moreover, the legislation is widely drawn with the intention to deal with as many situations as possible and to avoid reliance upon Extra Statutory Concessions.

9.6.1 Transfer of funds for the spouse

Transfers between spouses and civil partners before decree absolute must be considered under the rules relating to relevant persons, whereas transfers after that time are covered by the rules relating to non-relevant persons (see **9.4.1**).

There are a variety of settlement arrangements that can be arrived at but the following assumes funds are transferred as a result of a court order.

Does payment settle a relevant debt?

A settlement under a court order should not be regarded as giving rise to a 'relevant debt'; it is an obligation imposed to effect the required division of the marital assets rather than a debt created by the order. Even if it were to be categorised generally as a debt, it is not one that 'relates to' the provision of property or a service (see **9.4.2**).

Does payment constitute consideration?

It may be argued that a transfer of funds between the parties under a court order represents consideration passing between them under a transaction at arm's length, thereby extinguishing the obligation. As such, funds received by the transferee only represent the transferee's personal funds received in consideration of the obligation. Accordingly, if the transferee subsequently remits those funds to the United Kingdom before decree absolute, there is no taxable remittance of the transferor's foreign income/capital gains.

HMRC may not accept this view and its interpretation depends on whether the transfer would constitute 'consideration'. As highlighted previously (see **2.2.9**), there is a conflict between the conclusions in *G* v. *G* [2002] EWHC 1339 and in *Haines* v. *Hill and another* [2007] EWCA Civ 1284, over whether such a payment constitutes 'consideration'. However, in *G* v. *G*, the payment was said to not be consideration for CGT purposes so that hold over relief was available. In *Haines* v. *Hill and another*, it was concluded that the satisfaction of a settlement was consideration.

Structuring the payment

In order to mitigate potential problems in these areas, it is advised that any payment is made to an overseas bank account for the transferee and that no funds are remitted to the United Kingdom until after decree absolute.

Furthermore, the transfer to the United Kingdom should not be used directly to benefit a minor child or grandchild of the transferor because they remain a relevant person until the age of majority. If HMRC argues that the original transfer was 'for the child/grandchild' and this constituted a taxable remittance, the preceding argument over consideration would be the best form of defence.

Examples of structuring the payment and the implications

There are various ways that the individual can make a payment from his non-UK bank account to the other party with the following implications where the funds are, or derive from, the foreign income/gains:

- a transfer to his account in the United Kingdom prior to a payment to the other party: this will be a taxable remittance, the timing of the payment is irrelevant;
- a transfer to the party's UK bank account before decree absolute: this will be a taxable remittance;
- a transfer to the party's UK bank account after decree absolute: this should not be a taxable remittance provided the original funds were not 'destined' to benefit the transferor's minor child or grandchild;
- a transfer to the other party's overseas bank account and a transfer by them to the United Kingdom before decree absolute: this will be a taxable remittance.

In simple summary, the most tax-effective procedure is for the transferee party to receive the funds into a foreign bank account on condition that they undertake not to remit them into the United Kingdom until after the decree absolute and not to earmark them directly for the benefit of relevant minor children or grandchildren.

9.6.2 Transfers for children and grandchildren

As stated previously, transfers for minor children and grandchildren will be taxable once the funds are identified as having been remitted. Care should also be taken with respect to transfers to children who have minor children of their own; if the funds are intended to be used to benefit the grandchildren in the United Kingdom then this will give rise to taxable remittance.

Transfers to adult children and grandchildren can be made without giving rise to a taxable remittance. However, as for the divorced party, it is advisable for the transfer to be made to the recipient's overseas bank account.

9.6.3 Payment of professional fees

Where professional fees are owed to a UK adviser who has provided services in the United Kingdom, payment out of foreign income/gains will generally be a taxable remittance even if settled overseas. An exemption is provided that applies where the fees are for services relating wholly or mainly to non-UK property, and payment is made to a non-UK bank account of the service provider.

In a divorce context, it may be unlikely that solicitors' fees will qualify in their entirety for this exemption. If the situation merits, overseas work should be billed separately and paid for outside the United Kingdom.

9.6.4 Creation of a trust for the spouse

If it is proposed that the individual should create a trust for the benefit of the other party (with the settlor irrevocably excluded from benefit) with funds

THE INTERNATIONAL DIMENSION

comprising his foreign income/gains, the tax consequences under the remittance basis depend upon whether or not the trust is a 'relevant person'. For these purposes, the residence status of the trust does not matter.

A trust is a relevant person if any of its beneficiaries are relevant persons. This means the trust will be a relevant person only until the decree absolute. If the transferor's children or grandchildren are also beneficiaries, then the trust will continue to be a relevant person for so long as one of these beneficiaries is below the age of 18.

Whether or not the trust is a relevant person, it is recommended that the settlement is made to an overseas bank account of the trust.

If the trustees bring, use or enjoy the funds in the United Kingdom while the trust is a relevant person, then this will constitute a taxable remittance for the settlor. This will be the case, for example, if the trustees engage a UK based investment manager and transfer the funds into a UK account with him.

While the trust is not a relevant person, simply bringing the funds into the United Kingdom will not constitute a taxable remittance for the settlor. By definition, none of the beneficiaries of such a trust will be relevant persons, but if there is a breach of trust such that a relevant person does receive a distribution, there may be a UK tax charge on the settlor in respect of the remitted amount.

9.7 COMMONLY ENCOUNTERED OFFSHORE STRUCTURES

Where there are offshore trusts and companies included in the couple's assets, it will be necessary to seek specialist advice on the implications of extracting the agreed funds to satisfy the court order. However, there are a couple of structures through which property, both in the United Kingdom and overseas, may be owned that can be the subject of general comments.

Other structures will require the application of the rules laid out in this chapter.

9.7.1 Offshore trust owns offshore company owning UK property

These structures are commonly established by non-UK domiciled individuals to own their UK home to be occupied rent-free under licence. The property falls outside the scope of IHT because it is the company shares which are considered when looking at the trust and they are 'excluded property' for IHT purposes. With a purpose trust such as this, there should be no income arising in the structure.

Until 5 April 2008, gains on the property were irrelevant as capital payments (in the form of benefit from the occupation) to non-UK domiciled beneficiaries as they were exempt from CGT. Since 6 April 2008, capital payments to non-UK domiciled beneficiaries cannot be ignored but there is the possibility for trustees of an offshore settlement in existence before then of making the rebasing election to eliminate a non-UK domiciled beneficiary's exposure to CGT on realised and unrealised gains accruing up to 5 April 2008.

Where a non-UK domiciled individual established such a trust some time previously, but as part of the divorce proceedings it is considered that the benefit of the property should rest with the other UK domiciled party, various possibilities might be considered as to how to deal with this. The basic options are for the structure to remain intact or to be terminated with the property being transferred to the UK domiciled party.

If the structure is left intact but with only the UK domiciled party continuing to occupy the property, the following tax issues arise. Provided the 'shadow director' rules do not apply (see **9.5.1**), the benefit of the annual rent-free occupation would be attributed as a capital payment at the market rent foregone. Assuming no other gains have been realised in the structure, the capital payment will remain unmatched and carry forward to match to future trust gains, i.e. when the property is finally sold.

The capital payments built up over the years would be matched with the company's capital gain (apportioned to the trust) and assessed on the UK domiciled party. The position could be worsened if the company were liquidated as well, because the trustees would also realise their own gain on the shares.

There will be no CGT principal private residence relief for occupation by the trust beneficiary as the property was owned by the company.

The preferred option, assuming the trustees were in time to make the rebasing election, would be to wind up the company and terminate the trust via an appointment of the property to the non-UK domiciled settlor. Depending on the value of the property as at 5 April 2008 against its market value, there may be little or no gains to match against capital payments restricted to the period from 6 April 2008 for the non-UK domiciled beneficiary/settlor. The property can then be transferred to the UK domiciled spouse for personal ownership.

9.7.2 Offshore company owns foreign holiday property

UK resident individuals often acquire foreign properties through offshore companies for non-tax reasons, such as to avoid local forced heirship rules or property tax reasons.

Since 2008, a UK resident but non-UK domiciled shareholder is exposed to CGT on gains made if the property is sold by the company, although he will be able to claim the remittance basis and perhaps avoid any liability to CGT. However, if the company shares are transferred to the UK domiciled partner, the future gain will be fully assessable on an arising basis. Therefore, the implications of such a transfer of shares must be considered carefully.

As with a UK property owned by an offshore company, HMRC has previously considered pursuing some owners of these structures under the 'shadow director' rules with a view to raising an income tax charge in respect of occupation of the property. However, retrospective exempting legislation was enacted in 2008 to prevent such charge for overseas property held by an overseas company but subject to certain criteria broadly relating to holiday homes:

- the property is owned by a company that is owned by individuals;
- the company's only activities are incidental to its ownership of the property;
- the property is the company's only or main asset; and
- the property is not funded directly or indirectly by a connected company.

It is understood that the relief cannot apply where the company shares are owned by trustees.

Combining all of this, it would seem that the best tactic to take all possible tax advantages would be for the UK domiciled partner to acquire the property through a new offshore company. Subject to local jurisdictional matters, the property could be transferred from the existing company at a low value with any debt written off after decree absolute.

CHAPTER 9 CHECKLIST

1. Identify the situs of chargeable assets (**9.1.2**).
2. Consider IHT planning actions before an individual acquires a deemed UK domicile after a prolonged period of tax residence (17 out of last 20 tax years) (**9.1.3**).
3. Identify the residence and domicile status of the relevant individuals (**9.2.1** and **9.2.3**).
4. Consider planning for the remittance basis before exposure to the remittance basis charge after a prolonged period of tax residence (seven out of last nine tax years) (**9.3.2**).
5. Revisit all offshore structures on a regular basis to ensure best practice is being followed, particularly in light of separation, divorce or dissolution (**9.7**).

CHAPTER 10

Valuation in the context of tax and family breakdown

> **KEY CONCEPTS**
>
> Market value for tax purposes is not necessarily the same as the value which may be agreed or determined for the purposes of separation or court proceedings.

10.1 MARKET VALUE

Reference is made in several chapters to 'market value' and in particular where assets are transferred between couples on family breakdown. Where relevant, market value is a significant determinative factor in establishing potential liability to tax on transfers between parties who are separated, and both actual and contingent capital gains tax and other liabilities are deductible when arriving at net values for the purposes of Form E (see **1.2** and **Appendix 7**). A valuation of the couple's assets will often be necessary, whether done informally or, in more complex and substantial cases, by instructing suitably qualified independent experts to carry out valuations of property, shares in private companies or other assets. It is often said that valuation is an art not a science, and various court cases confirm that it is not an arithmetic exercise but a matter of applying professional judgement based on experience and examination of the specific facts of each case. As such, it is not uncommon for independent valuers to arrive at different valuations for the same asset, or for there to be a range of possible values depending on the methodology adopted and assumptions made, for example, in the case of trading companies, as to future trading prospects and risks attached to the business concerned.

A factor which will often influence the approach to tax valuations is the requirement for them to be negotiated and agreed with HMRC's Share and Asset Valuation Division. Depending on the most favourable valuation outcome being sought for the client (i.e. that which gives the lowest overall tax liability), and where there is a range of possible valuations, a valuer will usually put forward their lowest or highest value or values, as appropriate, to allow scope for negotiation with HMRC.

It cannot automatically be assumed that market value for tax purposes (and agreed by HMRC) is or would be the same as the market value which is or would be agreed or determined by a court for the purposes of family breakdown. This is because the valuing of assets for tax purposes makes some specific fiscal assumptions, whereas the Family Division of the court does not, although there may well be some similarities in the valuation process. Even so, a valuation agreed for the purposes of family proceedings may have tax implications for the future even if no immediate transfer takes place, since a value has been established at that point in time to which HMRC might have regard.

10.2 CAPITAL GAINS TAX

For CGT purposes, there is a statutory definition of market value which is to be found in Taxation of Chargeable Gains Act (TCGA) 1992, s.272.

10.2.1 Assets generally

The general rule is that market value means the price which those assets might reasonably be expected to fetch on a sale in the open market. In estimating the market value of any asset, no reduction can be made on the assumption that the whole of the asset is to be placed on the market at the same time, i.e. no reduction is allowed to reflect any market forces due to flooding the market.

There are separate valuation rules for a small category of other assets which are listed below.

10.2.2 Listed securities

For securities and shares listed on a recognised stock exchange, the normal rule is to take the lower of the two prices shown in the quotations on the relevant date plus one-quarter of the difference between those figures, or halfway between the highest and lowest prices at which bargains (ignoring bargains at special prices) were recorded on the relevant date, assuming such bargains were recorded on the relevant date. The lower figure of these two measures is the figure to be taken for market value.

These provisions are due to be replaced from a date to be appointed by Treasury order and similar or different provisions may be set out by Treasury regulations for different cases (Finance Act 2007, Sched.26, para.4).

10.2.3 Unit trusts

For units in a unit trust, the market value is the buying price (that is, the lower price) published on the relevant date or if none on that date, the latest date prior to then.

10.2.4 Unquoted securities (including Alternative Investment Market (AIM) shares)

In any case where the market value of unquoted shares and securities falls to be determined by the general rule set out above, it is assumed that in the open market there is available to any prospective purchaser of the asset in question all the information which a prudent prospective purchaser of the asset might reasonably require if he were proposing to purchase from a willing vendor by private treaty and at arm's length (TCGA 1992, s.273).

The above assumptions therefore provide for an information standard which is available and reasonably required for a prospective purchaser of unquoted shares acting prudently. This would include information from all sources, including confidential information which would not necessarily be disclosed in the real world. In terms of what is reasonably required, this will turn on the size of the holding and amount of money involved. Thus, for a majority holding a purchaser acting prudently will be assumed to have carried out proper due diligence on the company. What is reasonable in relation to a minority holding is likely to depend on the amount of money being invested and put at risk, together with the size of the minority holding. As a bare minimum and irrespective of the size of holding, it would be reasonable to have information about the current position of the company and its future prospects.

For tax purposes, a hypothetical sale is assumed to take place in a hypothetical open market between a willing vendor and a willing purchaser which excludes no one, including any special purchaser (*Re Lynall* [1972] AC 680). It is, however, assumed to take place in the real world (*Walton (Executor of Walton (dec'd))* v. *IRC* [1996] STC 68). Case law establishes that a willing vendor is someone who must sell and at the highest price that willing purchasers are available to offer at the time of valuation. If a special purchaser exists at the date of valuation who may affect the price obtainable for the property in question, the special purchaser must be an identified person and be in a special position in relation to the property in question. It is not sufficient merely to postulate the existence of a special purchaser.

10.2.5 Transactions between connected parties

For transactions between connected persons (broadly, this includes spouses, civil partners, brothers, sisters, ancestors and lineal descendants), it is specifically provided that the transaction will be treated 'otherwise than by way of a bargain at arm's length' and the market value taken as the sole consideration for CGT purposes (TCGA 1992, s.18).

Trustees are also connected with the settlor and with persons connected with the settlor and with any company connected to the settlement. There are further provisions relating to persons deemed to be connected to companies (TCGA 1992, s.286).

As discussed earlier, market value will be relevant to capital gains transactions between husbands and wives and between civil partners after the tax year of separation as a result of their remaining connected for tax purposes but not being able to benefit from the no gain, no loss rule as they are no longer living together. Similarly, market value will be relevant for transfers which amount to the creation of a trust or settlement on separation, etc., as well as in other circumstances.

For connected persons, it is also provided that if the person making the disposal (or a connected person) has power to enforce a right or restriction in respect of the asset transferred, the market value of the asset is determined initially free of any such encumbrance and is then reduced by 'the market value of the right or restriction or the amount by which its extinction would enhance the value of the asset to its owner, whichever is the less' (TCGA 1992, s.18(6)(b)). However, such rights are ignored for these purposes if, upon enforcement, the asset's value would be effectively destroyed or substantially impaired and no advantage would accrue to the person making the disposal (or a connected person) (TCGA 1992, s.18(6)).

There is also an anti-avoidance rule to defeat a series of smaller asset transfers by way of gift, or otherwise, out of a larger asset holding to one or more connected persons in any six-year period ending on the date of the transfer under consideration. If this rule applies, market value is applied to the aggregate of all the transfers as if disposed of together and the value of the smaller transfers is recalculated accordingly. Common examples are a set of antique furniture or paintings or a substantial shareholding in an unquoted company. These provisions do not apply to a transaction between spouses or civil partners except those made after the tax year of separation and to any other transactions made in the same series where other connected persons are involved.

10.2.6 Transactions between unconnected persons

Transactions between unconnected persons, however, are not subject to the connected persons rules but as described elsewhere if the transaction is not a bargain otherwise than at arm's length, market value then also applies for CGT purposes (TCGA 1992, s.17).

10.2.7 HMRC agreement to the market value

Individuals are required to self-assess their tax position each year, so in completing their tax return for the relevant year in which there is an event giving rise to a transfer or disposal at market value, disclosure would need to be made of the event and of the estimated valuation. In this case, the estimated valuation can only be queried and negotiated under the normal self-assessment compliance and enquiry process. HMRC inspectors are instructed to refer to appropriate specialists in all cases where it is necessary to determine the market value of assets other than quoted shares (HMRC *Capital Gains Tax Manual* at CG16233).

Alternatively, if an individual requires certainty over the valuation, HMRC has a post-transaction valuation check process. This requires Form CG34 (see **Appendix 6**) to be completed with relevant accompanying documents, and must be carried out in advance of the tax return for the year being completed. If the asset in question is unquoted shares, Form CG34, which is initially sent to the tax district dealing with the individual's tax return, will be forwarded on to HMRC Shares and Assets Valuation Division. Land and buildings in the United Kingdom are dealt with by the district valuer.

If the valuation is not yet agreed under the post-transaction valuation check process, and the tax return has been filed, an enquiry into the valuation can still be raised before the period for notice of enquiry into the return ceases, which is normally 12 months after the due date for filing the tax return (the due date being 31 January following the end of the tax year). Where a tax return for a period remains open after the expiry of the notice period to enquire into a return solely because of an as yet to be agreed CGT valuation, HMRC will not, save in exceptional circumstances, raise any enquiries into the return unrelated to the valuation or the CGT computation (Statement of Practice 1/99).

If CGT hold over relief is claimed, it may not be necessary to agree a market value with HMRC, as discussed in **2.2**.

10.3 INHERITANCE TAX

Almost identical definitions for market value as for CGT purposes are to be found at Inheritance Tax Act (IHTA) 1984, s.160 (general rule for assets) and IHTA 1984, s.168 (unquoted shares and securities) for IHT purposes, adopting similar valuation assumptions as appropriate.

However, the value of a transfer for IHT purposes is not taken as the value for CGT. For IHT purposes, the value transferred by a chargeable lifetime gift is the diminution in value of the donor's estate (IHTA 1984, s.3(1)). Disposals of assets for CGT purposes which may also be transfers of value for IHT purposes will principally be those involving transfers into and out of trusts, and transfers by individuals which are potentially exempt transfers (PETs) but which subsequently become chargeable because of the death of the transferor within seven years.

For example, where a disposal of a minority interest in shares out of a substantial majority shareholding results in the transferor retaining either a majority or minority shareholding, the diminution in value principle applied to the donor's estate can result in a disparity in valuations which creates a larger IHT liability than would be the case if the transferred shares were capable of being valued in isolation. Furthermore, for CGT purposes it is the transferred shares alone which are valued, creating a disparity between the taxes even though effectively the same transfer is being valued.

EXAMPLE 10A

Bill owns 70% of the issued share capital of Flowerpots Ltd. He gifted half of his shareholding to his brother Ben. Unfortunately, two years later Bill dies.

For IHT purposes, the value transferred by the gift is the diminution in the value of Bill's estate, i.e. the difference between the value of a 70% shareholding and the value of a 35% shareholding. This is not the same as the value of a 35% shareholding, because of the overall loss of control of Flowerpots Ltd for Bill (i.e. his shareholding falling below 50%).

For CGT purposes, the amount of consideration deemed to have been received by Bill for the gift is the market value of the 35% shareholding transferred.

Where the value of any property is in isolation less than the value it would have had if it and property held by a spouse or civil partner were valued together and that value is apportioned between them, the larger value is taken. This might typically apply to land and property held jointly by spouses or to shares held in family owned companies.

10.4 VALUATION OF PRIVATE COMPANY SHARES: AGREED VALUATION BINDING ON BOTH PARTIES FOR TAX PURPOSES

If a person disposes of unquoted shares or securities to a connected person or otherwise than by way of a bargain at arm's length, HMRC will negotiate the value with that person or the agent acting for him.

There are, however, regulations which allow any person whose CGT liability is affected by the valuation to be joined in the formal determination of the value. This would apply where, for example, there is a transfer of unquoted shares between spouses who are separated after the tax year of separation, or between cohabitees, and where the benefit of hold over relief has not been claimed, so that the transferor spouse is treated as disposing of the asset at market value. In these circumstances, the transferee can apply to be joined in the proceedings. If such an application is made, HMRC is required to negotiate a value with both the transferor and transferee (or their agents). This might be the case where the transferor is seeking a low (tax) valuation for the shares (to minimise any immediate CGT charge) but the transferee is seeking a high (tax) valuation (to minimise any future CGT on a subsequent disposal).

The relevant provisions are found in the Capital Gains Tax Regulations 1967, SI 1967/149, which provide that any person who is affected by a determination of market value for CGT purposes can be a party to such a determination and can be bound by it. The aim of the Regulations is to ensure that where the market value of an asset on a particular date, or an apportionment of any valuation or amount, affects the CGT liability of more than one person, then each such person has the opportunity to have a say in determining that market value or apportionment, that the same market value or apportionment is used in each of their computations, and that market value or apportionment is determined as soon as possible. The market value or apportionment is binding on each party who has been given an opportunity to be joined, and provided the Regulations have been followed this will be so whether or not they have taken that opportunity.

Whilst such applications are likely to be very infrequent in practice, it is possible that in the circumstances of family breakdown both parties wish to put forward their own evidence as to the valuation.

10.5 BRIEF OVERVIEW OF MAIN VALUATION BASES FOR PRIVATE COMPANY SHARES

In general it will be necessary to consider the following factors as a bare minimum in any share valuation:

- the information that would be available to a prospective purchaser (which will depend on the circumstances) along with evidence of any dealings in the shares and any previous agreements as to valuation;
- any rights or restrictions attaching to the shares in the memorandum and articles and any shareholders' or other agreement (since there can be many classes of shares with different rights as to votes, dividends or surplus on a winding up and restrictions on transfer);
- the size of the holding and most appropriate method or methods of valuation, which will depend on the facts of the case and importance of any one or more particular factor;
- any special factors, which will include company commercial matters, shareholder aspects (for example, how the other shares are held and the relationship between the shareholders), and the economic and political climate in which the company operates.

10.5.1 Profitable trading companies

The following assumes that the shares to be valued are ordinary shares which have the same entitlement as to votes, dividends and surplus on a winding up and no other different classes of shares in issue. This is likely to be so in the majority of cases encountered in practice.

Influential (more than 25 per cent) or majority (more than 50 per cent) shareholdings: earnings basis of valuation

For influential or majority shareholdings, a generally accepted method of valuation for a profitable trading company is an earnings based valuation applying an appropriate multiple to an estimate of maintainable profits. HMRC would normally expect the valuation of a shareholding of more than 25 per cent to be earnings related.

An earnings basis of valuation can be based on either pre/post-tax profits, on earnings before interest and tax (EBIT), or on earnings before interest, tax, depreciation and amortisation (EBITDA). The principal stages of an earnings based valuation may then be summarised as follows:

(a) identification of the level of maintainable profits (and, if appropriate, separation of assets which are not relevant to the principal profit-generating activities of the company); and
(b) capitalisation of maintainable profits by selecting an appropriate multiple to apply to those profits.

Arriving at a level of maintainable profits is not usually a straightforward matter, and is often taken as the current level of the company's profit-generating capacity. This definition is not wholly appropriate, however, if profits are expected to decline, in which case any anticipated reduction should be recognised unless such decline is considered only temporary. Similarly, any anticipated increase should equally be reflected. A prospective purchaser would have regard to the latest management accounts and any budgets/forecasts in addition to a recent history of profits where they can reasonably be relied upon as a guide to future profits. It is also necessary to exclude from maintainable profits any items of income and expenditure which would not recur on the assumption of new ownership.

An EBIT or EBITDA valuation is often used in analysing the profitability of a company in commercial deals because it eliminates the effects of financing and accounting decisions and concentrates on the business of the company. However, pre/post-tax earnings are also often used in a multiples based approach with the application of a suitable and adjusted price/earnings (P/E) multiple, which is often based on the current share price of comparable listed companies operating in the same sector and/or recent private company acquisitions of similar businesses where those comparables exist, and using other third party information sources. From any listed company comparable P/E identified, a discount is normally applied to reflect, *inter alia*, any potential risks or differences associated with the private company to be valued. A further discount may then be applied to reflect the marketability of the size of the shareholding being valued, having regard to all surrounding circumstances.

If the company has assets which are not relevant to the principal profit-generating activities of the company (see above), these would need to valued separately and added to the valuation of the company on the earnings basis to arrive at a valuation of the company as a whole.

In the context of commercial deals, a discounted cash flow (DCF) approach may also be used and is typically applied to businesses where there are fragmented non-recurring 'project based' revenue streams or where there is uncertainty surrounding the levels of maintainable earnings into the future (e.g. early stage or start up companies). The DCF approach estimates the value of a business as the present value of the aggregated future free cash flows arising from the use of the working assets of the business, i.e. those which derive from the flow of income or earnings. The current value of surplus assets (or net debt) is then added to (subtracted from) this net present value to derive the equity value of the business. The rate at which the future free cash flows are discounted to derive their present value is known as the weighted average cost of capital (WACC). The WACC represents the opportunity cost of purchasing those cash flows in deriving a fair value of the business and is the weighted average of this opportunity cost to both equity and debt investors. In other words, this is the risk a potential acquirer attributes to the cash flows projected for the business versus the risk of investing in another asset.

10.5.2 Non-trading companies and trading companies in certain circumstances

Influential (more than 25 per cent) or majority (more than 50 per cent) shareholdings: assets basis of valuation

An assets basis of valuation may be considered a generally accepted method of valuation for:

- investment or property investment holding companies;
- trading companies which are about to go into liquidation;
- trading companies where the assets are under-utilised and the company is loss making (with no reasonable prospect of a foreseeable turnaround) or landed estate or farming companies where the principal value derives from the asset value of their underlying land and buildings;
- where there are significant assets which could be sold without affecting the trade of the company.

In arriving at the net asset value, the latest balance sheet assets and liabilities will need to be investigated in order to consider whether the assets properly reflect current market value (or if there are assets such as 'goodwill' which should be recognised and are not) and whether there are any actual or contingent liabilities which also need to be considered and recognised. An assets basis is not generally appropriate to a profitable trading company valued on a going concern basis since the asset value does not recognise the profits generated by the company.

Certain property related businesses, such as hotels, nursing homes, pubs and leisure amenities, would generally be valued on a going concern net asset basis by expert property surveyors or valuers who specialise in the buying and selling of such businesses. In arriving at the market value of the existing use of the freehold or leasehold premises from which the business is being conducted, the property valuer will normally consider a profits based multiples approach having regard to purchases and sales of comparable property related businesses. The market value of the freehold/leasehold business will then be substituted in the balance sheet of the company, as appropriate. The company may have other assets and liabilities in its balance sheet which have not been taken into account by the property valuer which will need to be considered in order to arrive at a valuation of the company.

Uninfluential shareholdings (no more than 25 per cent)

A dividend yield basis of valuation is a generally accepted method of valuation for uninfluential minority interest shareholdings where the only practical benefit of the shareholding is the right to receive dividends out of annual profits of the company and there is no foreseeable prospect of realising a capital value from the shares, for example, by way of a sale of the whole company and pro rata share of sale proceeds. Typically, a dividend yield basis of valuation will generally be relevant to very small minority interests in dividend paying companies where there is no foreseeable prospect of an exit.

However, it is not uncommon for private companies to have no historic or any current and sustainable dividend policy, nor for there to be any reasonable expectation of future dividends. In those circumstances, it may be that any value will be derived from a foreseeable future sale or liquidation. Various different, or hybrid, valuation approaches may therefore need to be considered in these circumstances, e.g. by reference to earnings or assets, initially depending on the company concerned but then suitably discounted.

In commercial circumstances, sales and purchases of very small minority shareholdings in private unquoted companies (10 per cent or less) between third parties are rarely encountered in practice, since high levels of discount from a pro rata value for the whole company are likely, as this generally means being locked into a minority position and thus protected only by the unfair prejudice jurisdiction of the Companies Court.

From a commercial perspective, a minority family shareholder in a family owned company may be deriving benefits from the fact that the company is run for the family's mutual group benefit, whether those benefits accrue to that shareholder now or in the future, and as to income, capital, mitigation of family tax liabilities or inheritance, depending on the circumstances.

Again, commercially, there are many non-family owned companies where the minority shareholders either participate in the business of the company as directors or employees, having perhaps been incentivised by shares, and/ or where there is a reasonable prospect or exit strategy for the sale of the whole company in the foreseeable future. In such cases, those shareholders will not normally be inclined to sell their minority shareholdings at a high discount unless ordered to do so to satisfy a court order, or required to sell on leaving the company, but would prefer to hold on to them in the expectation that, in the event of a future sale, they will receive a pro rata share of sale proceeds.

For tax purposes, given the statutory fiscal basis of valuation, it is the author's experience that HMRC will normally agree to high levels of discounts for uninfluential minority interest shareholdings.

Shareholdings of less than 100 per cent

Where private company valuations are concerned, it is usual to apply a discount from the valuation of the whole company (arrived at, e.g., on an earnings basis or net asset basis) for the size of the shareholding in question to reflect the lack of marketability of the private company shares.

The aim is to choose a discount, or a range of discounts, that best reflects the level of marketability associated with the specific shareholding in question, having regard to the desirability of the company and all the concomitant surrounding circumstances.

HMRC *Shares and Assets Valuation Manuals* have previously suggested the following range of discounts from net asset value for property investment companies (which should be regarded as indicative averages only).

for a holding of 90% or above	nil
under 90% down to 75%	0–5%
under 75% but above 50%	5–15%
50%	20–30%
under 50% but above 25%	25–40%
less than 25%	50–80% (dividend yield basis applicable also)

There have been various share valuation cases for unquoted companies involving minority interests which have come before the Special Commissioners (now known as the First Tier Tribunal (Tax)) following appeals by the taxpayer.

In *Cash and Carry* v. *Inspector of Taxes* [1998] STC 1120, where it was necessary to value a 24 per cent holding in a trading company, a valuation of the total company was agreed but there was a dispute about the amount by which that value should be discounted to reflect a minority holding. The Special Commissioner decided that the discount should be 55 per cent based on the following information, which should have been available to a prospective purchaser: (a) no dividends had been paid or were likely to be paid;

(b) profits were unlikely to increase in the near future; and (c) there was a likelihood that the company would be sold.

In *Administrators of the Estate of Caton (dec'd)* v. *Couch* [1995] STC (SCD) 34, it was held that the value of a 14 per cent shareholding in a successful trading company should be valued after a 50 per cent discount from the pro rata value for all the shares in the company, as there were good prospects of a sale within a year.

In a more recent case of *MacArthur (dec'd)* v. *HMRC* [2008] STC 1100, it was held that a discount of 45 per cent was appropriate to the valuation of a 26.8 per cent shareholding in a family investment company.

Whilst noting the above, each case must be considered on its own particular facts.

10.6 QUASI-PARTNERSHIP COMPANIES: HMRC VIEW

The typical characteristics of a quasi-partnership company are that there should be a business association formed or continued on the basis of a personal relationship of mutual trust and confidence, an understanding or agreement that all of the shareholders should participate in the management of the business, and restrictions on the transfer of shares, so that a member cannot realise his stake if he is excluded from the business.

These elements are typical but not exhaustive and where there is a breakdown in the relationship and the quasi-partner majority wish to exclude a quasi-partner minority, the valuation is then based on a notional sale of the business as a whole to an outside purchaser, i.e. the whole of the share capital, not one of the parties' interests.

In the case of a company possessing the relevant characteristics and where there is a breakdown in relationship, the majority wishing to exclude one of the quasi-partners must offer a fair price for his or her shares based on a pro rata amount of the business as a whole, thereby achieving the same freedom to manage the business as a whole to an outsider (see *Bird Precision Bellows Ltd, Re; Company (No.003420 of 1981), Re* [1986] Ch. 658). Thus, in cases where there is unfairly prejudicial conduct by the dominant shareholder(s), the minority shareholders are entitled to petition the court for an appropriate order which may include the purchase of their shares by the other members or by the company itself (see Companies Act 2006, s.994, formerly Companies Act 1985, s.459).

In the Shares Valuation Fiscal Forum Minutes of 8 April 2003, Fred Cook of HMRC stated the HMRC Shares Valuation view on quasi-partnerships thus:

- Whether a company is a quasi-partnership is a matter of fact and evidence.
- Even if a company is a quasi-partnership, it does not necessarily follow that the fiscal (i.e. tax) value of a minority holding is other than at a

- discount pro rata to the full going concern or break-up value of the company.
- Each case has to be considered on its merits and the facts and history need to be considered closely.
- Since fiscal valuation involves a hypothetical vendor and a hypothetical purchaser, it cannot necessarily be assumed that either of these parties was or will become a quasi-partner.
- The potential exits (if any) need to be considered.
- The courts have handed down decisions in cases of unfairly prejudicial behaviour. The courts have distinguished these decisions from deciding on market value. It is wrong to assume that a purchaser of shares will find a situation where unfairly prejudicial behaviour gives rise to an exit opportunity.

10.7 VALUATION OF FAMILY COMPANIES IN THE CONTEXT OF COURT PROCEEDINGS

As regards valuation in the context of family breakdown cases, the overriding approach is one of fairness and therefore a valuation determined for tax purposes which imposes a statutory fiscal framework for the valuation may well be different from a valuation which has been determined by the courts as part of a financial settlement.

In *Charman v. Charman* [2006] EWHC 1879 (Fam), the High Court (Family Division) noted that (para.85):

> The approach to valuation issues in this Division is and always has been to look at the reality of the situation in any given case. For decades the Court has set its face against hypothetical valuations produced for different purposes (income tax, probate etc.). Any other approach is, quite simply, unfair. Indeed the rigid adoption of CETVs in pension cases sometimes has that effect, albeit that it is expedient for other reasons. Of course, this often leads to spirited debate. So where, for instance, a case proceeds on the basis that a sale at less than true market value is inevitable to satisfy a likely court order then discounts at high levels are often appropriate. But where a sale can be avoided or delayed to enable full value to be extracted over a reasonable time that too must, in fairness, be properly reflected in valuation.

Therefore, there is a requirement to adopt a commercial approach specific to the facts in relation to valuing interests in private companies in family cases: 'Exactly the same kind of considerations apply when looking e.g. at discounts for valuation of minority interests in private companies. Sometimes they apply, sometimes, especially in family situations, they do not. See *G v. G (Financial Provision: Equal Division)* [2002] 2 FLR 1143' (see *Charman v. Charman* [2006] EWHC 1879 (Fam), para.86 and Court of Appeal, [2007] EWCA Civ 503, para.102).

In the case of a family owned property company in *NA* v. *MA* [2006] EWHC 2900 (Fam), the court noted that:

> Although the relationships in the family are (and always have been) strained they have always acted in concert when it comes to realising assets. I am satisfied that, in financial matters, they act for their mutual, group benefit. Accordingly, I do not consider that any application of a minority discount is appropriate for the properties held by the family. This approach accords with the recent decision by Coleridge J in *Charman* v. *Charman* and also accords with the long established practice in this Division, that underlying reality is the relevant test. As history indicates, the Husband will obtain his full share without a discount when family owned assets are sold.

In *D* v. *D & B Ltd* [2007] EWHC 278 (Fam), the High Court also noted points which would likely be of relevance with respect to the sale of a private trading company and this case contains a useful exposition of some of the commercial considerations and uncertainties involved in valuing private trading companies in practice.

In the case of any company which may potentially have the characteristics of a quasi-partnership, and, for example, companies where there is deadlock and the spouses or civil partners who are also directors own the company 50:50, it is for the court to decide whether or not a quasi-partnership exists and a question of law for the court to decide whether or not there should be a discount to the pro rata value. If a discount is to apply, the size of the discount is a matter of valuation. The principles of quasi-partnership appear to impact considerably in divorce cases where family shareholdings are in point.

In the commercial case of *Irvine* v. *Irvine* [2006] EWHC 1875, the minority shareholder found that even a holding of 49.96 per cent was subject to a minority discount when valued for sale following a successful petition under Companies Act 1985, s.459. This was despite the fact that the difference in shareholding arose from the gift of a single share, and the outcome was an acquisition by the majority shareholder at a 30 per cent discount.

In this case, the minority shareholder's Companies Act 1985, s.459 petition was successful and the court has flexible powers to grant a remedy to a successful petitioner. A common remedy is to order a buy-out of the minority shareholder's interest. Having ordered a buy-out, it was necessary for the shareholding to be valued. The first issue before the court was whether the value of the shares was simply the pro rata value, or whether there should be any discount to reflect the fact that the sale was of a minority shareholding. In this case, the court held that the shareholding must be valued for what it was, namely less than 50 per cent of the company's shares, and discounted accordingly.

Having decided to apply a discount, the court then went on to consider the level of discount appropriate on the facts. The court heard evidence from experts for both parties as to the value of the business and the level of discount and held that:

- although the holding was 49.96 per cent, this did not give any more control over the majority shareholder and the conduct of the business than if the holding had been a lower amount also sufficient to prevent the passing of a special resolution;
- the assumption was that the sale was to a third party purchaser so it was irrelevant that the effect of the sale would be to give the majority shareholder control over all the shares and free him from further shareholder criticism of his conduct of affairs. There was therefore no premium value to reflect the fact this would be the actual effect of the sale.

The decision illustrates that even a small variation between shareholdings can result in a dramatic difference in the levels of control that may be exerted over a company's affairs, and ultimately in the value of the respective shareholdings.

There is no general or universal rule determining valuation in the circumstances of a Companies Act 1985, s.459 petition: everything depends on the circumstances of the case, although the court will be concerned to be fair between the parties. In this case, in assessing the minority discount the court felt that the level of actual control permitted by the shareholding was relevant, but disregarded the identity of the actual purchaser in favour of an assumed third party. The court did not therefore assign the shares a premium to reflect the fact that the actual purchaser would gain control. However, in an earlier case, *Re Eurofinance Group Ltd* [2001] BCC 551, the court found that when arriving at a fair value in the absence of a market, fairness between the parties required an assumption that the notional sale was taking place between the actual participants and the assumption of a third party purchaser was held to be inappropriate. The question before the courts was, however, different as in the former, the court was assessing the minority discount, but in the latter, the sale was of the majority shareholding and the issue was to assess the fair value of that holding.

The overriding consideration in all the cases is to achieve 'fairness'. This is further illustrated by cases where the relationship between the parties is of a quasi-partnership nature. In such cases, shares will generally be ordered to be purchased on a non-discounted basis. In *Strahan* v. *Wilcock* [2006] EWCA Civ 13, Arden LJ remarked 'It is difficult to conceive of circumstances in which a non-discounted basis of valuation would be appropriate where there was unfair prejudice for the purposes of the 1985 Act but such a relationship did not exist'. However, she continued that in the case before her she did not need to express a final view on what those circumstances might be.

10.8 UNDIVIDED SHARES IN JOINTLY HELD LAND AND PROPERTY

The value of a share of a house or land that is owned jointly depends on:

(a) the size of the share that the person holds;
(b) who the other owner(s) is (are).

For tax purposes, it is necessary to find out the market value of the whole property and then to work out the value of the share based on the proportion of the property the person owned. If the property is jointly owned with someone who is not the person's spouse or civil partner, HMRC will as a starting point accept a reduction in the value of the share by 10 per cent. This may need to be agreed with the district valuer. The reduction HMRC initially accepts reflects:

- the difficulty in selling a jointly owned share of a property; and
- the fact that the value of a joint owner's share may be reduced because the other owner has the right to go on living in the property.

EXAMPLE 10B

Brian is married but separated from his wife Jo. He owns an investment property jointly with his brother Arthur in Wales. The house is worth £500,000. Brian's share would generally be valued for tax purposes (and possibly also for the purposes of any court proceedings) at £225,000 (half of £500,000 less a 10% discount).

Where the other co-owner(s) is (are) not in occupation but has (have) a clear right to occupy as their main residence and the purpose behind the arrangement still exists, or where the other co-owner(s) is (are) in occupation as their main residence, higher discounts of, say, 15 per cent may be accepted (see e.g. Valuation Office Agency, *Inheritance Tax Practice Manual*, Practice Note 2, undivided shares).

Where land held by joint tenants is disposed of, each tenant is entitled to an equal share of the net sale proceeds. This rule applies even if the joint tenants have not contributed equally to the cost of acquiring the land. In relation to the severing of a joint tenancy or its conversion into a tenancy in common without a disposal of the property, this will only have CGT consequences if one or more of the former joint tenants have reduced their interests in the land.

Where land is disposed of by joint tenants, the chargeable gain, or allowable loss, arising on the disposal of land held on a joint tenancy should be computed in accordance with the above rule. However, if the joint tenants divide the proceeds in accordance with their contributions to the cost of the land, HMRC advises that that division can be accepted for CGT purposes, provided that all the joint tenants signify their agreement in writing.

10.9 VALUATION OF PARTNERSHIP INTERESTS

For tax purposes, partnership interests are valued on a pro rata basis with no discount for the fact that the partner's interest is less than a 100 per cent interest in the whole of the partnership's assets. As such, the assets of the partnership are valued according to what the partnership owns as a whole and apportioned pro rata to the partners.

In *Gray* v. *IRC* [1994] STC 360, Hoffmann LJ stated that:

> As between themselves, partners are not entitled individually to exercise proprietary rights over any of the partnership assets. This is because they have subjected their proprietary interests to the terms of the partnership deed which provides that the assets shall be employed in the partnership business and on dissolution realised for the purposes of paying debts and distributing any surplus. As regards the outside world, however, the partnership deed is irrelevant. The partners are collectively entitled to each and every asset of the partnership, in which each of them therefore has an undivided share.

Consequently, the valuation of an interest in a business carried on as a partnership should be by reference to the value of the appropriate share of each asset and furthermore with no discount for the costs of sale based on the general law definition of a partnership share as a proportionate interest in the partnership assets after they have been converted into money, and all the partnership debts and liabilities have been paid and discharged.

10.10 CONTINGENT CORPORATION TAX

Typically, contingent corporation tax is encountered in net asset based valuations of shareholdings in property investment companies or trading companies with investment assets. As mentioned in **10.5.2**, in arriving at the net asset value of a property investment company, the latest balance sheet assets and liabilities need to be investigated in order to consider whether the assets properly reflect current market value and whether there are any additional actual or contingent liabilities which need also to be considered and recognised. In reflecting the current market value of any balance sheet assets, corporation tax on any inherent unrealised capital gains on those assets is one such liability to be considered.

For example, a purchaser of the shares of a company owning freehold investment property (as opposed to a purchaser of the underlying property direct) may, when seeking to negotiate the price of the company shares, seek to discount the value of the company to take account of the contingent corporation tax liability on any inherent unrealised capital gain on, say, any freehold investment properties at the prevailing UK corporation tax rate (currently up to 28 per cent). This tax is only contingent, however, since a sale of the properties is assumed not to be in immediate prospect by a hypothetical prospective purchaser of shares. Depending on the nature and identity of the purchaser, any such gain may potentially also be further deferred.

Therefore, when considering the possible reduction in the value of shares in the company due to the contingent tax charge, the value of the reduction is not the full potential corporation tax liability computed as if the disposal occurred now. Instead, the liability is discounted to reflect the fact that the sale may not be imminent, if indeed anticipated at all. A customary starting point with regard to agreeing a figure with HMRC is for a 50 per cent discount to be applied to the figure for corporation tax; however, where the asset/investment is unlikely to be sold or where tax reliefs are available to roll over/hold over or defer the gain, the discount to be applied may be even greater, reflecting the probability of the contingency materialising within the foreseeable future.

By way of further reference, prior to its withdrawal the HMRC *Shares and Assets Valuation Manual* formerly commented as follows:

> Market practice, in the form of both actual deals involving property investment companies, and in the treatment by auditors of companies' accounts, indicates that the full deduction for the contingent tax liability arising as a result of the increased value of the company's properties is rarely, if ever, allowed for. Deals in the market reveal that where the purchaser has no intention of disposing of the properties, the allowance made for any inbuilt Corporation Tax liability is likely to be small. Where there is the possibility of a sale, some allowance seems to be appropriate although it is almost impossible to quantify the exact deduction taken for the potential tax liability in an actual sale in the open market since the ultimate sale price more often than not reflects a composite discount made up of several factors, only one of which is the allowance for the contingent tax.

See also, for an example of a property owning business, the tax case of *Shinebond Ltd v. Carrol (Inspector of Taxes)* [2006] STC (SCD) 147.

CHAPTER 10 CHECKLIST

1. Are chargeable assets to be transferred between a separating couple which will require determination of market value for tax purposes? **(10.2.7)**
2. If there is a valuation required for tax purposes, does a post-transaction valuation check need to be considered? **(10.2.7)**
3. To what extent should the parties be advised to seek an agreed HMRC valuation which is binding on both parties? **(10.4)**

APPENDIX 1

Inheritance (Provision for Family and Dependants) Act 1975

1 Application for financial provision from deceased's estate

(1) Where after the commencement of this Act a person dies domiciled in England and Wales and is survived by any of the following persons –

  (a) the spouse or civil partner of the deceased;
  (b) a former spouse or former civil partner of the deceased, but not one who has formed a subsequent marriage or civil partnership;
  (ba) any person (not being a person included in paragraph (a) or (b) above) to whom subsection (1A) or (1B) below applies;
  (c) a child of the deceased;
  (d) any person (not being a child of the deceased) who, in the case of any marriage or civil partnership to which the deceased was at any time a party, was treated by the deceased as a child of the family in relation to that marriage or civil partnership;
  (e) any person (not being a person included in the foregoing paragraphs of this subsection) who immediately before the death of the deceased was being maintained, either wholly or partly, by the deceased;

that person may apply to the court for an order under section 2 of this Act on the ground that the disposition of the deceased's estate effected by his will or the law relating to intestacy, or the combination of his will and that law, is not such as to make reasonable financial provision for the applicant.

(1A) This subsection applies to a person if the deceased died on or after 1st January 1996 and, during the whole of the period of two years ending immediately before the date when the deceased died, the person was living –

  (a) in the same household as the deceased, and
  (b) as the husband or wife of the deceased.

(1B) This subsection applies to a person if for the whole of the period of two years ending immediately before the date when the deceased died the person was living –

  (a) in the same household as the deceased, and
  (b) as the civil partner of the deceased.

(2) In this Act 'reasonable financial provision' –

  (a) in the case of an application made by virtue of subsection (1)(a) above by the husband or wife of the deceased (except where the marriage with the deceased was the subject of a decree of judicial separation and at the date of death the decree was in force and the separation was continuing), means such financial provision as it would be reasonable in all the circumstances of the case for a husband or wife to receive, whether or not that provision is required for his or her maintenance;

(aa) in the case of an application made by virtue of subsection (1)(a) above by the civil partner of the deceased (except where, at the date of death, a separation order under Chapter 2 of Part 2 of the Civil Partnership Act 2004 was in force in relation to the civil partnership and the separation was continuing), means such financial provision as it would be reasonable in all the circumstances of the case for a civil partner to receive, whether or not that provision is required for his or her maintenance;

(b) in the case of any other application made by virtue of subsection (1) above, means such financial provision as it would be reasonable in all the circumstances of the case for the applicant to receive for his maintenance.

(3) For the purposes of subsection (1)(e) above, a person shall be treated as being maintained by the deceased, either wholly or partly, as the case may be, if the deceased, otherwise than for full valuable consideration, was making a substantial contribution in money or money's worth towards the reasonable needs of that person.

2 Powers of court to make orders

(1) Subject to the provisions of this Act, where an application is made for an order under this section, the court may, if it is satisfied that the disposition of the deceased's estate effected by his will or the law relating to intestacy, or the combination of his will and that law, is not such as to make reasonable financial provision for the applicant, make any one or more of the following orders –

(a) an order for the making to the applicant out of the net estate of the deceased of such periodical payments and for such term as may be specified in the order;

(b) an order for the payment to the applicant out of that estate of a lump sum of such amount as may be so specified;

(c) an order for the transfer to the applicant of such property comprised in that estate as may be so specified;

(d) an order for the settlement for the benefit of the applicant of such property comprised in that estate as may be so specified;

(e) an order for the acquisition out of property comprised in that estate of such property as may be so specified and for the transfer of the property so acquired to the applicant or for the settlement thereof for his benefit;

(f) an order varying any ante-nuptial or post-nuptial settlement (including such a settlement made by will) made on the parties to a marriage to which the deceased was one of the parties, the variation being for the benefit of the surviving party to that marriage, or any child of that marriage, or any person who was treated by the deceased as a child of the family in relation to that marriage;

(g) an order varying any settlement made –

(i) during the subsistence of a civil partnership formed by the deceased, or

(ii) in anticipation of the formation of a civil partnership by the deceased,

on the civil partners (including such a settlement made by will), the variation being for the benefit of the surviving civil partner, or any child of

APPENDIX 1

both the civil partners, or any person who was treated by the deceased as a child of the family in relation to that civil partnership.

(2) An order under subsection (1)(a) above providing for the making out of the net estate of the deceased of periodical payments may provide for –

(a) payments of such amount as may be specified in the order,
(b) payments equal to the whole of the income of the net estate or of such portion thereof as may be so specified,
(c) payments equal to the whole of the income of such part of the net estate as the court may direct to be set aside or appropriated for the making out of the income thereof of payments under this section,

or may provide for the amount of the payments or any of them to be determined in any other way the court thinks fit.

(3) Where an order under subsection (1)(a) above provides for the making of payments of an amount specified in the order, the order may direct that such part of the net estate as may be so specified shall be set aside or appropriated for the making out of the income thereof of those payments; but no larger part of the net estate shall be so set aside or appropriated than is sufficient, at the date of the order, to produce by the income thereof the amount required for the making of those payments.

(4) An order under this section may contain such consequential and supplemental provisions as the court thinks necessary or expedient for the purpose of giving effect to the order or for the purpose of securing that the order operates fairly as between one beneficiary of the estate of the deceased and another and may, in particular, but without prejudice to the generality of this subsection –

(a) order any person who holds any property which forms part of the net estate of the deceased to make such payment or transfer such property as may be specified in the order;
(b) vary the disposition of the deceased's estate effected by the will or the law relating to intestacy, or by both the will and the law relating to intestacy, in such manner as the court thinks fair and reasonable having regard to the provisions of the order and all the circumstances of the case;
(c) confer on the trustees of any property which is the subject of an order under this section such powers as appear to the court to be necessary or expedient.

3 Matters to which court is to have regard in exercising powers under s 2

(1) Where an application is made for an order under section 2 of this Act, the court shall, in determining whether the disposition of the deceased's estate effected by his will or the law relating to intestacy, or the combination of his will and that law, is such as to make reasonable financial provision for the applicant and, if the court considers that reasonable financial provision has not been made, in determining whether and in what manner it shall exercise its powers under that section, have regard to the following matters, that is to say –

(a) the financial resources and financial needs which the applicant has or is likely to have in the foreseeable future;
(b) the financial resources and financial needs which any other applicant for an order under section 2 of this Act has or is likely to have in the foreseeable future;

INHERITANCE (PROVISION FOR FAMILY AND DEPENDANTS) ACT 1975

(c) the financial resources and financial needs which any beneficiary of the estate of the deceased has or is likely to have in the foreseeable future;
(d) any obligations and responsibilities which the deceased had towards any applicant for an order under the said section 2 or towards any beneficiary of the estate of the deceased;
(e) the size and nature of the net estate of the deceased;
(f) any physical or mental disability of any applicant for an order under the said section 2 or any beneficiary of the estate of the deceased;
(g) any other matter, including the conduct of the applicant or any other person, which in the circumstances of the case the court may consider relevant.

(2) This subsection applies, without prejudice to the generality of paragraph (g) of subsection (1) above, where an application for an order under section 2 of this Act is made by virtue of section 1(1)(a) or (b) of this Act.
The court shall, in addition to the matters specifically mentioned in paragraphs (a) to (f) of that subsection, have regard to –

(a) the age of the applicant and the duration of the marriage or civil partnership;
(b) the contribution made by the applicant to the welfare of the family of the deceased, including any contribution made by looking after the home or caring for the family.

In the case of an application by the wife or husband of the deceased, the court shall also, unless at the date of death a decree of judicial separation was in force and the separation was continuing, have regard to the provision which the applicant might reasonably have expected to receive if on the day on which the deceased died the marriage, instead of being terminated by death, had been terminated by a decree of divorce.

In the case of an application by the civil partner of the deceased, the court shall also, unless at the date of the death a separation order under Chapter 2 of Part 2 of the Civil Partnership Act 2004 was in force and the separation was continuing, have regard to the provision which the applicant might reasonably have expected to receive if on the day on which the deceased died the civil partnership, instead of being terminated by death, had been terminated by a dissolution order.

(2A) Without prejudice to the generality of paragraph (g) of subsection (1) above, where an application for an order under section 2 of this Act is made by virtue of section 1(1)(ba) of this Act, the court shall, in addition to the matters specifically mentioned in paragraphs (a) to (f) of that subsection, have regard to –

(a) the age of the applicant and the length of the period during which the applicant lived as the husband or wife or civil partner of the deceased and in the same household as the deceased;
(b) the contribution made by the applicant to the welfare of the family of the deceased, including any contribution made by looking after the home or caring for the family.

(3) Without prejudice to the generality of paragraph (g) of subsection (1) above, where an application for an order under section 2 of this Act is made by virtue of section 1(1)(c) or 1(1)(d) of this Act, the court shall, in addition to the matters specifically mentioned in paragraphs (a) to (f) of that subsection,

APPENDIX 1

have regard to the manner in which the applicant was being or in which he might expect to be educated or trained, and where the application is made by virtue of section 1(1)(d) the court shall also have regard –

(a) to whether the deceased had assumed any responsibility for the applicant's maintenance and, if so, to the extent to which and the basis upon which the deceased assumed that responsibility and to the length of time for which the deceased discharged that responsibility;

(b) to whether in assuming and discharging that responsibility the deceased did so knowing that the applicant was not his own child;

(c) to the liability of any other person to maintain the applicant.

(4) Without prejudice to the generality of paragraph (g) of subsection (1) above, where an application for an order under section 2 of this Act is made by virtue of section 1(1)(e) of this Act, the court shall, in addition to the matters specifically mentioned in paragraphs (a) to (f) of that subsection, have regard to the extent to which and the basis upon which the deceased assumed responsibility for the maintenance of the applicant, and to the length of time for which the deceased discharged that responsibility.

(5) In considering the matters to which the court is required to have regard under this section, the court shall take into account the facts as known to the court at the date of the hearing.

(6) In considering the financial resources of any person for the purposes of this section the court shall take into account his earning capacity and in considering the financial needs of any person for the purposes of this section the court shall take into account his financial obligations and responsibilities.

4 Time-limit for applications

An application for an order under section 2 of this Act shall not, except with the permission of the court, be made after the end of the period of six months from the date on which representation with respect to the estate of the deceased is first taken out.

5 Interim orders

(1) Where on an application for an order under section 3 of this Act it appears to the court –

(a) that the applicant is in immediate need of financial assistance, but it is not yet possible to determine what order (if any) should be made under that section; and

(b) that property forming part of the net estate of the deceased is or can be made available to meet the need of the applicant;

the court may order that, subject to such conditions or restrictions, if any, as the court may impose and to any further order of the court, there shall be paid to the applicant out of the net estate of the deceased such sum or sums and (if more than one) at such intervals as the court thinks reasonable; and the court may order that, subject to the provisions of this Act, such payments are to be made until such date as the court may specify, not being later than the date on which the court either makes an order under the said section 2 or decides not to exercise its powers under that section.

(2) Subsections (2), (3) and (4) of section 2 of this Act shall apply in relation to an order under this section as they apply in relation to an order under that section.

(3) In determining what order, if any, should be made under this section the court shall, so far as the urgency of the case admits, have regard to the same matters as those to which the court is required to have regard under section 3 of this Act.

(4) An order made under section 2 of this Act may provide that any sum paid to the applicant by virtue of this section shall be treated to such an extent and in such manner as may be provided by that order as having been paid on account of any payment provided for by that order.

6 Variation, discharge, etc of orders for periodical payments

(1) Subject to the provisions of this Act, where the court has made an order under section 2(1)(a) of this Act (in this section referred to as 'the original order') for the making of periodical payments to any person (in this section referred to as 'the original recipient'), the court, on an application under this section, shall have power by order to vary or discharge the original order or to suspend any provision of it temporarily and to revive the operation of any provision so suspended.

(2) Without prejudice to the generality of subsection (1) above, an order made on an application for the variation of the original order may –

   (a) provide for the making out of any relevant property of such periodical payments and for such term as may be specified in the order to any person who has applied, or would but for section 4 of this Act be entitled to apply, for an order under section 2 of this Act (whether or not, in the case of any application, an order was made in favour of the applicant);

   (b) provide for the payment out of any relevant property of a lump sum of such amount as may be so specified to the original recipient or to any such person as is mentioned in paragraph (a) above;

   (c) provide for the transfer of the relevant property, or such part thereof as may be so specified, to the original recipient or to any such person as is so mentioned.

(3) Where the original order provides that any periodical payments payable thereunder to the original recipient are to cease on the occurrence of an event specified in the order (other than the formation of a subsequent marriage or civil partnership by a former spouse or former civil partner) or on the expiration of a period so specified, then, if, before the end of the period of six months from the date of the occurrence of that event or of the expiration of that period, an application is made for an order under this section, the court shall have power to make any order which it would have had power to make if the application had been made before the date (whether in favour of the original recipient or any such person as is mentioned in subsection (2)(a) above and whether having effect from that date or from such later date as the court may specify).

(4) Any reference in this section to the original order shall include a reference to an order made under this section and any reference in this section to the original recipient shall include a reference to any person to whom periodical payments are required to be made by virtue of an order under this section.

(5) An application under this section may be made by any of the following persons, that is to say –

   (a) any person who by virtue of section 1(1) of this Act has applied, or would but for section 4 of this Act be entitled to apply, for an order under section 2 of this Act,

APPENDIX 1

    (b) the personal representatives of the deceased,
    (c) the trustees of any relevant property, and
    (d) any beneficiary of the estate of the deceased.

(6) An order under this section may only affect –

    (a) property the income of which is at the date of the order applicable wholly or in part for the making of periodical payments to any person who has applied for an order under this Act, or
    (b) in the case of an application under subsection (3) above in respect of payments which have ceased to be payable on the occurrence of an event or the expiration of a period, property the income of which was so applicable immediately before the occurrence of that event or the expiration of that period, as the case may be,

and any such property as is mentioned in paragraph (a) or (b) above is in subsections (2) and (5) above referred to as 'relevant property'.

(7) In exercising the powers conferred by this section the court shall have regard to all circumstances of the case, including any change in any of the matters to which the court was required to have regard when making the order to which the application relates.

(8) Where the court makes an order under this section, it may give such consequential directions as it thinks necessary or expedient having regard to the provisions of the order.

(9) No such order as is mentioned in section 2(1)(d), (e) or (f), 9, 10 or 11 of this Act shall be made on an application under this section.

(10) For the avoidance of doubt it is hereby declared that, in relation to an order which provides for the making of periodical payments which are to cease on the occurrence of an event specified in the order (other than the formation of a subsequent marriage or civil partnership by a former spouse or former civil partner) or on the expiration of a period so specified, the power to vary an order includes power to provide for the making of periodical payments after the expiration of that period or the occurrence of that event.

7 Payment of lump sums by instalments

(1) An order under section 2(1)(b) or 6(2)(b) of this Act for the payment of a lump sum may provide for the payment of that sum by instalments of such amount as may be specified in the order.

(2) Where an order is made by virtue of subsection (1) above, the court shall have power, on an application made by the person to whom the lump sum is payable, by the personal representatives of the deceased or by the trustees of the property out of which the lump sum is payable, to vary that order by varying the number of instalments payable, the amount of any instalment and the date on which any instalment becomes payable.

Property available for financial provision

8 Property treated as part of 'net estate'

(1) Where a deceased person has in accordance with the provisions of any enactment nominated any person to receive any sum of money or other property on his death and that nomination is in force at the time of his death, that sum of money, after deducting therefrom any inheritance tax payable in respect thereof, or that other property, to the extent of the value thereof at the

date of the death of the deceased after deducting therefrom any inheritance tax so payable, shall be treated for the purposes of this Act as part of the net estate of the deceased; but this subsection shall not render any person liable for having paid that sum or transferred that other property to the person named in the nomination in accordance with the directions given in the nomination.
(2) Where any sum of money or other property is received by any person as a donatio mortis causa made by a deceased person, that sum of money, after deducting therefrom any inheritance tax payable thereon, or that other property, to the extent of the value thereof at the date of the death of the deceased after deducting therefrom any inheritance tax so payable, shall be treated for the purposes of this Act as part of the net estate of the deceased; but this subsection shall not render any person liable for having paid that sum or transferred that other property in order to give effect to that donatio mortis causa.
(3) The amount of inheritance tax to be deducted for the purposes of this section shall not exceed the amount of that tax which has been borne by the person nominated by the deceased or, as the case may be, the person who has received a sum of money or other property as a donatio mortis causa.

9 Property held on a joint tenancy

(1) Where a deceased person was immediately before his death beneficially entitled to a joint tenancy of any property, then, if, before the end of the period of six months from the date on which representation with respect to the estate of the deceased was first taken out, an application is made for an order under section 2 of this Act, the court for the purpose of facilitating the making of financial provision for the applicant under this Act may order that the deceased's severable share of that property, at the value thereof immediately before his death, shall, to such extent as appears to the court to be just in all the circumstances of the case, be treated for the purposes of this Act as part of the net estate of the deceased.
(2) In determining the extent to which any severable share is to be treated as part of the net estate of the deceased by virtue of an order under subsection (1) above, the court shall have regard to any inheritance tax payable in respect of that severable share.
(3) Where an order is made under subsection (1) above, the provisions of this section shall not render any person liable for anything done by him before the order was made.
(4) For the avoidance of doubt it is hereby declared that for the purposes of this section there may be a joint tenancy of a chose in action.

Powers of court in relation to transactions intended to defeat applications for financial provision

10 Dispositions intended to defeat applications for financial provision

(1) Where an application is made to the court for an order under section 2 of this Act, the applicant may, in the proceedings on that application, apply to the court for an order under subsection (2) below.
(2) Where on an application under subsection (1) above the court is satisfied –
   (a) that, less than six years before the date of the death of the deceased, the deceased with the intention of defeating an application for financial provision under this Act made a disposition, and

APPENDIX 1

    (b) that full valuable consideration for that disposition was not given by the person to whom or for the benefit of whom the disposition was made (in this section referred to as 'the donee') or by any other person, and

    (c) that the exercise of the powers conferred by this section would facilitate the making of financial provision for the applicant under this Act,

then, subject to the provisions of this section and of sections 12 and 13 of this Act, the court may order the donee (whether or not at the date of the order he holds any interest in the property disposed of to him or for his benefit by the deceased) to provide, for the purpose of the making of that financial provision, such sum of money or other property as may be specified in the order.

(3) Where an order is made under subsection (2) above as respects any disposition made by the deceased which consisted of the payment of money to or for the benefit of the donee, the amount of any sum of money or the value of any property ordered to be provided under that subsection shall not exceed the amount of the payment made by the deceased after deducting therefrom any inheritance tax borne by the donee in respect of that payment.

(4) Where an order is made under subsection (2) above as respects any disposition made by the deceased which consisted of the transfer of property (other than a sum of money) to or for the benefit of the donee, the amount of any sum of money or the value of any property ordered to be provided under that subsection shall not exceed the value at the date of the death of the deceased of the property disposed of by him to or for the benefit of the donee (or if that property has been disposed of by the person to whom it was transferred by the deceased, the value at the date of that disposal thereof) after deducting therefrom any inheritance tax borne by the donee in respect of the transfer of that property by the deceased.

(5) Where an application (in this subsection referred to as 'the original application') is made for an order under subsection (2) above in relation to any disposition, then, if on an application under this subsection by the donee or by any applicant for an order under section 2 of this Act the court is satisfied –

    (a) that, less than six years before the date of the death of the deceased, the deceased with the intention of defeating an application for financial provision under this Act made a disposition other than the disposition which is the subject of the original application, and

    (b) that full valuable consideration for that other disposition was not given by the person to whom or for the benefit of whom that other disposition was made or by any other person,

the court may exercise in relation to the person to whom or for the benefit of whom that other disposition was made the powers which the court would have had under subsection (2) above if the original application had been made in respect of that other disposition and the court had been satisfied as to the matters set out in paragraphs (a), (b) and (c) of that subsection; and where any application is made under this subsection, any reference in this section (except in subsection (2)(b)) to the donee shall include a reference to the person to whom or for the benefit of whom that other disposition was made.

(6) In determining whether and in what manner to exercise its powers under this section, the court shall have regard to the circumstances in which any disposition was made and any valuable consideration which was given therefor, the relationship, if any, of the donee to the deceased, the conduct and financial resources of the donee and all the other circumstances of the case.

(7) In this section 'disposition' does not include –

  (a) any provision in a will, any such nomination as is mentioned in section 8(1) of this Act or any donatio mortis causa, or
  (b) any appointment of property made, otherwise than by will, in the exercise of a special power of appointment,

  but, subject to these exceptions, includes any payment of money (including the payment of a premium under a policy of assurance) and any conveyance, assurance, appointment or gift of property of any description, whether made by an instrument or otherwise.

(8) The provisions of this section do not apply to any disposition made before the commencement of this Act.

11 Contracts to leave property by will

(1) Where an application is made to a court for an order under section 2 of this Act, the applicant may, in the proceedings on that application, apply to the court for an order under this section.

(2) Where on an application under subsection (1) above the court is satisfied –

  (a) that the deceased made a contract by which he agreed to leave by his will a sum of money or other property to any person or by which he agreed that a sum of money or other property would be paid or transferred to any person out of his estate, and
  (b) that the deceased made that contract with the intention of defeating an application for financial provision under this Act, and
  (c) that when the contract was made full valuable consideration for that contract was not given or promised by the person with whom or for the benefit of whom the contract was made (in this section referred to as 'the donee') or by any other person, and
  (d) that the exercise of the powers conferred by this section would facilitate the making of financial provision for the applicant under this Act,

  then, subject to the provisions of this section and of sections 12 and 13 of this Act, the court may make any one or more of the following orders, that is to say –

  (i) if any money has been paid or any other property has been transferred to or for the benefit of the donee in accordance with the contract, an order directing the donee to provide, for the purpose of the making of that financial provision, such sum of money or other property as may be specified in the order;
  (ii) if the money or all the money has not been paid or the property or all the property has not been transferred in accordance with the contract, an order directing the personal representatives not to make any payment or transfer any property, or not to make any further payment or transfer any further property, as the case may be, in accordance therewith or directing the personal representatives only to make such payment or transfer such property as may be specified in the order.

(3) Notwithstanding anything in subsection (2) above, the court may exercise its powers thereunder in relation to any contract made by the deceased only to the extent that the court considers that the amount of any sum of money paid or to be paid or the value of any property transferred or to be transferred in accordance with the contract exceeds the value of any valuable consideration

APPENDIX 1

given or to be given for that contract, and for this purpose the court shall have regard to the value of property at the date of the hearing.

(4) In determining whether and in what manner to exercise its powers under this section, the court shall have regard to the circumstances in which the contract was made, the relationship, if any, of the donee to the deceased, the conduct and financial resources of the donee and all the other circumstances of the case.

(5) Where an order has been made under subsection (2) above in relation to any contract the rights of any person to enforce that contract or to recover damages or to obtain other relief for the breach thereof shall be subject to any adjustment made by the court under section 12(3) of this Act and shall survive to such extent only as is consistent with giving effect to the terms of that order.

(6) The provisions of this section do not apply to a contract made before the commencement of this Act.

12 Provisions supplementary to ss 10 and 11

(1) Where the exercise of any of the powers conferred by section 10 or 11 of this Act is conditional on the court being satisfied that a disposition or contract was made by a deceased person with the intention of defeating an application for financial provision under this Act, that condition shall be fulfilled if the court is of the opinion that, on a balance of probabilities, the intention of the deceased (though not necessarily his sole intention) in making the disposition or contract was to prevent an order for financial provision being made under this Act or to reduce the amount of the provision which might otherwise be granted by an order thereunder.

(2) Where an application is made under section 11 of this Act with respect to any contract made by the deceased and no valuable consideration was given or promised by any person for that contract then, notwithstanding anything in subsection (1) above, it shall be presumed, unless the contrary is shown, that the deceased made that contract with the intention of defeating an application for financial provision under this Act.

(3) Where the court makes an order under section 10 or 11 of this Act it may give such consequential directions as it thinks fit (including directions requiring the making of any payment or the transfer of any property) for giving effect to the order or for securing a fair adjustment of the rights of the persons affected thereby.

(4) Any power conferred on the court by the said section 10 or 11 to order the donee, in relation to any disposition or contract, to provide any sum of money or other property shall be exercisable in like manner in relation to the personal representative of the donee, and –

    (a) any reference in section 10(4) to the disposal of property by the donee shall include a reference to disposal by the personal representative of the donee, and

    (b) any reference in section 10(5) to an application by the donee under that subsection shall include a reference to an application by the personal representative of the donee;

but the court shall not have power under the said section 10 or 11 to make an order in respect of any property forming part of the estate of the donee which has been distributed by the personal representative; and the personal representative shall not be liable for having distributed any such property before he has notice of the making of an application under the said section 10 or 11 on the ground that he ought to have taken into account the possibility that such an application would be made.

13 Provisions as to trustees in relation to ss 10 and 11

(1) Where an application is made for –

(a) an order under section 10 of this Act in respect of a disposition made by the deceased to any person as a trustee, or
(b) an order under section 11 of this Act in respect of any payment made or property transferred, in accordance with a contract made by the deceased, to any person as a trustee,

the powers of the court under the said section 10 or 11 to order that trustee to provide a sum of money or other property shall be subject to the following limitation (in addition, in a case of an application under section 10, to any provision regarding the deduction of inheritance tax) namely, that the amount of any sum of money or the value of any property ordered to be provided –

(i) in the case of an application in respect of a disposition which consisted of the payment of money or an application in respect of the payment of money in accordance with a contract, shall not exceed the aggregate of so much of that money as is at the date of the order in the hands of the trustee and the value at that date of any property which represents that money or is derived therefrom and is at that date in the hands of the trustee;
(ii) in the case of an application in respect of a disposition which consisted of the transfer of property (other than a sum of money) or an application in respect of the transfer of property (other than a sum of money) in accordance with a contract, shall not exceed the aggregate of the value at the date of the order of so much of that property as is at that date in the hands of the trustee and the value at that date of any property which represents the first mentioned property or is derived therefrom and is at that date in the hands of the trustee.

(2) Where any such application is made in respect of a disposition made to any person as a trustee or in respect of any payment made or property transferred in pursuance of a contract to any person as a trustee, the trustee shall not be liable for having distributed any money or other property on the ground that he ought to have taken into account the possibility that such an application would be made.

(3) Where any such application is made in respect of a disposition made to any person as a trustee or in respect of any payment made or property transferred in accordance with a contract to any person as a trustee, any reference in the said section 10 or 11 to the donee shall be construed as including a reference to the trustee or trustees for the time being of the trust in question and any reference in subsection (1) or (2) above to a trustee shall be construed in the same way.

Special provisions relating to cases of divorce, separation etc.

14 Provision as to cases where no financial relief was granted in divorce proceedings, etc

(1) Where, within twelve months from the date on which a decree of divorce or nullity of marriage has been made absolute or a decree of judicial separation has been granted, a party to the marriage dies and –

APPENDIX 1

    (a) an application for a financial provision order under section 23 of the Matrimonial Causes Act 1973 or a property adjustment order under section 24 of that Act has not been made by the other party to that marriage, or

    (b) such an application has been made but the proceedings thereon have not been determined at the time of the death of the deceased,

then, if an application for an order under section 2 of this Act is made by that other party, the court shall, notwithstanding anything in section 1 or section 3 of this Act, have power, if it thinks it just to do so, to treat that party for the purposes of that application as if the decree of divorce or nullity of marriage had not been made absolute or the decree of judicial separation had not been granted, as the case may be.

(2) This section shall not apply in relation to a decree of judicial separation unless at the date of the death of the deceased the decree was in force and the separation was continuing.

14A Provision as to cases where no financial relief was granted in proceedings for the dissolution etc of a civil partnership

(1) Subsection (2) below applies where –

    (a) a dissolution order, nullity order, separation order or presumption of death order has been made under Chapter 2 of Part 2 of the Civil Partnership Act 2004 in relation to a civil partnership,

    (b) one of the civil partners dies within twelve months from the date on which the order is made, and

    (c) either –

        (i) an application for a financial provision order under Part 1 of Schedule 5 to that Act or a property adjustment order under Part 2 of that Schedule has not been made by the other civil partner, or

        (ii) such an application has been made but the proceedings on the application have not been determined at the time of the death of the deceased.

(2) If an application for an order under section 2 of this Act is made by the surviving civil partner, the court shall, notwithstanding anything in section 1 or section 3 of this Act, have power, if it thinks it just to do so, to treat the surviving civil partner as if the order mentioned in subsection (1)(a) above had not been made.

(3) This section shall not apply in relation to a separation order unless at the date of the death of the deceased the separation order was in force and the separation was continuing.

15 Restriction imposed in divorce proceedings, etc on application under this Act

(1) On the grant of a decree of divorce, a decree of nullity of marriage or a decree of judicial separation or at any time thereafter the court, if it considers it just to do so, may, on the application of either party to the marriage, order that the other party to the marriage shall not on the death of the applicant be entitled to apply for an order under section 2 of this Act.

In this subsection 'the court' means the High Court or, where a county court has jurisdiction by virtue of Part V of the Matrimonial and Family Proceedings Act 1984, a county court.

(2) In the case of a decree of divorce or nullity of marriage an order may be made under subsection (1) above before or after the decree is made absolute, but if it is made before the decree is made absolute it shall not take effect unless the decree is made absolute.

(3) Where an order made under subsection (1) above on the grant of a decree of divorce or nullity of marriage has come into force with respect to a party to a marriage, then, on the death of the other party to that marriage, the court shall not entertain any application for an order under section 2 of this Act made by the first-mentioned party.

(4) Where an order made under subsection (1) above on the grant of a decree of judicial separation has come into force with respect to any party to a marriage, then, if the other party to that marriage dies while the decree is in force and the separation is continuing, the court shall not entertain any application for an order under section 2 of this Act made by the first-mentioned party.

15ZA Restriction imposed in proceedings for the dissolution etc of a civil partnership on application under this Act

(1) On making a dissolution order, nullity order, separation order or presumption of death order under Chapter 2 of Part 2 of the Civil Partnership Act 2004, or at any time after making such an order, the court, if it considers it just to do so, may, on the application of either of the civil partners, order that the other civil partner shall not on the death of the applicant be entitled to apply for an order under section 2 of this Act.

(2) In subsection (1) above 'the court' means the High Court or, where a county court has jurisdiction by virtue of Part 5 of the Matrimonial and Family Proceedings Act 1984, a county court.

(3) In the case of a dissolution order, nullity order or presumption of death order ('the main order') an order may be made under subsection (1) above before (as well as after) the main order is made final, but if made before the main order is made final it shall not take effect unless the main order is made final.

(4) Where an order under subsection (1) above made in connection with a dissolution order, nullity order or presumption of death order has come into force with respect to a civil partner, then, on the death of the other civil partner, the court shall not entertain any application for an order under section 2 of this Act made by the surviving civil partner.

(5) Where an order under subsection (1) above made in connection with a separation order has come into force with respect to a civil partner, then, if the other civil partner dies while the separation order is in force and the separation is continuing, the court shall not entertain any application for an order under section 2 of this Act made by the surviving civil partner.

15A Restriction imposed in proceedings under Matrimonial and Family Proceedings Act 1984 on application under this Act

(1) On making an order under section 17 of the Matrimonial and Family Proceedings Act 1984 (orders for financial provision and property adjustment following overseas divorces, etc) the court, if it considers it just to do so, may, on the application of either party to the marriage, order that the other party to the marriage shall not on the death of the applicant be entitled to apply for an order under section 2 of this Act.

In this subsection 'the court' means the High Court or, where a county court has jurisdiction by virtue of Part V of the Matrimonial and Family Proceedings Act 1984, a county court.

APPENDIX 1

(2) Where an order under subsection (1) above has been made with respect to a party to a marriage which has been dissolved or annulled, then, on the death of the other party to that marriage, the court shall not entertain an application under section 2 of this Act made by the first-mentioned party.

(3) Where an order under subsection (1) above has been made with respect to a party to a marriage the parties to which have been legally separated, then, if the other party to the marriage dies while the legal separation is in force, the court shall not entertain an application under section 2 of this Act made by the first-mentioned party.

15B Restriction imposed in proceedings under Schedule 7 to the Civil Partnership Act 2004 on application under this Act

(1) On making an order under paragraph 9 of Schedule 7 to the Civil Partnership Act 2004 (orders for financial provision, property adjustment and pension-sharing following overseas dissolution etc of civil partnership) the court, if it considers it just to do so, may, on the application of either of the civil partners, order that the other civil partner shall not on the death of the applicant be entitled to apply for an order under section 2 of this Act.

(2) In subsection (1) above 'the court' means the High Court or, where a county court has jurisdiction by virtue of Part 5 of the Matrimonial and Family Proceedings Act 1984, a county court.

(3) Where an order under subsection (1) above has been made with respect to one of the civil partners in a case where a civil partnership has been dissolved or annulled, then, on the death of the other civil partner, the court shall not entertain an application under section 2 of this Act made by the surviving civil partner.

(4) Where an order under subsection (1) above has been made with respect to one of the civil partners in a case where civil partners have been legally separated, then, if the other civil partner dies while the legal separation is in force, the court shall not entertain an application under section 2 of this Act made by the surviving civil partner.

16 Variation and discharge of secured periodical payments orders made under Matrimonial Causes Act 1973

(1) Where an application for an order under section 2 of this Act is made to the court by any person who was at the time of the death of the deceased entitled to payments from the deceased under a secured periodical payments order made under the Matrimonial Causes Act 1973 or Schedule 5 to the Civil Partnership Act 2004, then, in the proceedings on that application, the court shall have power, if an application is made under this section by that person or by the personal representative of the deceased, to vary or discharge that periodical payments order or to revive the operation of any provision thereof which has been suspended under section 31 of that Act of 1973 or Part 11 of that Schedule.

(2) In exercising the powers conferred by this section the court shall have regard to all the circumstances of the case, including any order which the court proposes to make under section 2 or section 5 of this Act and any change (whether resulting from the death of the deceased or otherwise) in any of the matters to which the court was required to have regard when making the secured periodical payments order.

(3) The powers exercisable by the court under this section in relation to an order shall be exercisable also in relation to any instrument executed in pursuance of the order.

17 Variation and revocation of maintenance agreements

(1) Where an application for an order under section 2 of this Act is made to the court by any person who was at the time of the death of the deceased entitled to payments from the deceased under a maintenance agreement which provided for the continuation of payments under the agreement after the death of the deceased, then, in the proceedings on that application, the court shall have power, if an application is made under this section by that person or by the personal representative of the deceased, to vary or revoke that agreement.

(2) In exercising the powers conferred by this section the court shall have regard to all the circumstances of the case, including any order which the court proposes to make under section 2 or section 5 of this Act and any change (whether resulting from the death of the deceased or otherwise) in any of the circumstances in the light of which the agreement was made.

(3) If a maintenance agreement is varied by the court under this section the like consequences shall ensue as if the variation had been made immediately before the death of the deceased by agreement between the parties and for valuable consideration.

(4) In this section 'maintenance agreement', in relation to a deceased person, means any agreement made, whether in writing or not and whether before or after the commencement of this Act, by the deceased with any person with whom he formed a marriage or civil partnership, being an agreement which contained provisions governing the rights and liabilities towards one another when living separately of the parties to that marriage or of the civil partners (whether or not the marriage or civil partnership has been dissolved or annulled) in respect of the making or securing of payments or the disposition or use of any property, including such rights and liabilities with respect to the maintenance or education of any child, whether or not a child of the deceased or a person who was treated by the deceased as a child of the family in relation to that marriage or civil partnership.

18 Availability of court's powers under this Act in applications under ss 31 and 36 of the Matrimonial Causes Act 1973

(1) Where –

   (a) a person against whom a secured periodical payments order was made under the Matrimonial Causes Act 1973 has died and an application is made under section 31(6) of that Act for the variation or discharge of that order or for the revival of the operation of any provision thereof which has been suspended, or

   (b) a party to a maintenance agreement within the meaning of section 34 of that Act has died, the agreement being one which provides for the continuation of payments thereunder after the death of one of the parties, and an application is made under section 36(1) of that Act for the alteration of the agreement under section 35 thereof,

the court shall have power to direct that the application made under the said section 31(6) or 36(1) shall be deemed to have been accompanied by an application for an order under section 2 of this Act.

APPENDIX 1

(2) Where the court gives a direction under subsection (1) above it shall have power, in the proceedings on the application under the said section 31(6) or 36(1), to make any order which the court would have had power to make under the provisions of this Act if the application under the said section 31(6) or 36(1), as the case may be, had been made jointly with an application for an order under the said section 2; and the court shall have power to give such consequential directions as may be necessary for enabling the court to exercise any of the powers available to the court under this Act in the case of an application for an order under section 2.

(3) Where an order made under section 15(1) of this Act is in force with respect to a party to a marriage, the court shall not give a direction under subsection (1) above with respect to any application made under the said section 31(6) or 36(1) by that party on the death of the other party.

18A Availability of court's powers under this Act in applications under paragraphs 60 and 73 of Schedule 5 to the Civil Partnership Act 2004

(1) Where –

(a) a person against whom a secured periodical payments order was made under Schedule 5 to the Civil Partnership Act 2004 has died and an application is made under paragraph 60 of that Schedule for the variation or discharge of that order or for the revival of the operation of any suspended provision of the order, or

(b) a party to a maintenance agreement within the meaning of Part 13 of that Schedule has died, the agreement being one which provides for the continuation of payments under the agreement after the death of one of the parties, and an application is made under paragraph 73 of that Schedule for the alteration of the agreement under paragraph 69 of that Schedule,

the court shall have power to direct that the application made under paragraph 60 or 73 of that Schedule shall be deemed to have been accompanied by an application for an order under section 2 of this Act.

(2) Where the court gives a direction under subsection (1) above it shall have power, in the proceedings on the application under paragraph 60 or 73 of that Schedule, to make any order which the court would have had power to make under the provisions of this Act if the application under that paragraph had been made jointly with an application for an order under section 2 of this Act; and the court shall have power to give such consequential directions as may be necessary for enabling the court to exercise any of the powers available to the court under this Act in the case of an application for an order under section 2.

(3) Where an order made under section 15ZA(1) of this Act is in force with respect to a civil partner, the court shall not give a direction under subsection (1) above with respect to any application made under paragraph 60 or 73 of that Schedule by that civil partner on the death of the other civil partner.

Miscellaneous and supplementary provisions

19 Effect, duration and form of orders

(1) Where an order is made under section 2 of this Act then for all purposes, including the purposes of the enactments relating to inheritance tax, the

will or the law relating to intestacy, or both the will and the law relating to intestacy, as the case may be, shall have effect and be deemed to have had effect as from the deceased's death subject to the provisions of the order.
(2) Any order made under section 2 or 5 of this Act in favour of –
- (a) an applicant who was the former spouse or former civil partner of the deceased, or
- (b) an applicant who was the husband or wife of the deceased in a case where the marriage with the deceased was the subject of a decree of judicial separation and at the date of death the decree was in force and the separation was continuing, or
- (c) an applicant who was the civil partner of the deceased in a case where, at the date of death, a separation order under Chapter 2 of Part 2 of the Civil Partnership Act 2004 was in force in relation to their civil partnership and the separation was continuing,

shall, in so far as it provides for the making of periodical payments, cease to have effect on the formation by the applicant of a subsequent marriage or civil partnership, except in relation to any arrears due under the order on the date of the formation of the subsequent marriage or civil partnership.
(3) A copy of every order made under this Act other than an order made under section 15(1) or 15ZA(1) of this Act shall be sent to the principal registry of the Family Division for entry and filing, and a memorandum of the order shall be endorsed on, or permanently annexed to, the probate or letters of administration under which the estate is being administered.

20 Provisions as to personal representatives

(1) The provisions of this Act shall not render the personal representative of a deceased person liable for having distributed any part of the estate of the deceased, after the end of the period of six months from the date on which representation with respect to the estate of the deceased is first taken out, on the ground that he ought to have taken into account the possibility –
- (a) that the court might permit the making of an application for an order under section 2 of this Act after the end of that period, or
- (b) that, where an order has been made under the said section 2, the court might exercise in relation thereto the powers conferred on it by section 6 of this Act,

but this subsection shall not prejudice any power to recover, by reason of the making of an order under this Act, any part of the estate so distributed.
(2) Where the personal representative of a deceased person pays any sum directed by an order under section 5 of this Act to be paid out of the deceased's net estate, he shall not be under any liability by reason of that estate not being sufficient to make the payment, unless at the time of making the payment he has reasonable cause to believe that the estate is not sufficient.
(3) Where a deceased person entered into a contract by which he agreed to leave by his will any sum of money or other property to any person or by which he agreed that a sum of money or other property would be paid or transferred to any person out of his estate, then, if the personal representative of the deceased has reason to believe that the deceased entered into the

contract with the intention of defeating an application for financial provision under this Act, he may, notwithstanding anything in that contract, postpone the payment of that sum of money or the transfer of that property until the expiration of the period of six months from the date on which representation with respect to the estate of the deceased is first taken out or, if during that period an application is made for an order under section 2 of this Act, until the determination of the proceedings on that application.

21 ...

22 ...

23 Determination of date on which representation was first taken out

In considering for the purposes of this Act when representation with respect to the estate of a deceased person was first taken out, a grant limited to settled land or to trust property shall be left out of account, and a grant limited to real estate or to personal estate shall be left out of account unless a grant limited to the remainder of the estate has previously been made or is made at the same time.

24 Effect of this Act on s 46(1)(vi) of Administration of Estates Act 1925

Section 46(1)(vi) of the Administration of Estates Act 1925, in so far as it provides for the devolution of property on the Crown, the Duchy of Lancaster or the Duke of Cornwall as bona vacantia, shall have effect subject to the provisions of this Act.

25 Interpretation

(1) In this Act –

'beneficiary', in relation to the estate of a deceased person, means –

(a) a person who under the will of the deceased or under the law relating to intestacy is beneficially interested in the estate or would be so interested if an order had not been made under this Act, and

(b) a person who has received any sum of money or other property which by virtue of section 8(1) or 8(2) of this Act is treated as part of the net estate of the deceased or would have received that sum or other property if an order had not been made under this Act;

'child' includes an illegitimate child and a child en ventre sa mere at the death of the deceased;

'the court' unless the context otherwise requires means the High Court, or where a county court has jurisdiction by virtue of section 22 of this Act, a county court;

'former civil partner' means a person whose civil partnership with the deceased was during the lifetime of the deceased either –

(a) dissolved or annulled by an order made under the law of any part of the British Islands, or

(b) dissolved or annulled in any country or territory outside the British Islands by a dissolution or annulment which is entitled to be recognised as valid by the law of England and Wales;

'former spouse' means a person whose marriage with the deceased was during the lifetime of the deceased either –

(a) dissolved or annulled by a decree of divorce or a decree of nullity of marriage granted under the law of any part of the British Islands, or

(b) dissolved or annulled in any country or territory outside the British Islands by a divorce or annulment which is entitled to be recognised as valid by the law of England and Wales;

'net estate', in relation to a deceased person, means –

(a) all property of which the deceased had power to dispose by his will (otherwise than by virtue of a special power of appointment) less the amount of his funeral, testamentary and administration expenses, debts and liabilities, including any inheritance tax payable out of his estate on his death;

(b) any property in respect of which the deceased held a general power of appointment (not being a power exercisable by will) which has not been exercised;

(c) any sum of money or other property which is treated for the purposes of this Act as part of the net estate of the deceased by virtue of section 8(1) or (2) of this Act;

(d) any property which is treated for the purposes of this Act as part of the net estate of the deceased by virtue of an order made under section 9 of the Act;

(e) any sum of money or other property which is, by reason of a disposition or contract made by the deceased, ordered under section 10 or 11 of this Act to be provided for the purpose of the making of financial provision under this Act;

'property' includes any chose in action;

'reasonable financial provision' has the meaning assigned to it by section 1 of this Act;

'valuable consideration' does not include marriage or a promise of marriage;

'will' includes codicil.

(2) For the purposes of paragraph (a) of the definition of 'net estate' in subsection (1) above a person who is not of full age and capacity shall be treated as having power to dispose by will of all property of which he would have had power to dispose by will if he had been of full age and capacity.

(3) Any reference in this Act to provision out of the net estate of a deceased person includes a reference to provision extending to the whole of that estate.

(4) For the purposes of this Act any reference to a spouse, wife or husband shall be treated as including a reference to a person who in good faith entered into a void marriage with the deceased unless either –

(a) the marriage of the deceased and that person was dissolved or annulled during the lifetime of the deceased and the dissolution or annulment is recognised by the law of England and Wales, or

(b) that person has during the lifetime of the deceased formed a subsequent marriage or civil partnership.

(4A) For the purposes of this Act any reference to a civil partner shall be treated as including a reference to a person who in good faith formed a void civil partnership with the deceased unless either –

(a) the civil partnership between the deceased and that person was dissolved or annulled during the lifetime of the deceased and the dissolution or annulment is recognised by the law of England and Wales, or

APPENDIX 1

(b) that person has during the lifetime of the deceased formed a subsequent civil partnership or marriage.

(5) Any reference in this Act to the formation of, or to a person who has formed, a subsequent marriage or civil partnership includes (as the case may be) a reference to the formation of, or to a person who has formed, a marriage or civil partnership which is by law void or voidable.

(5A) The formation of a marriage or civil partnership shall be treated for the purposes of this Act as the formation of a subsequent marriage or civil partnership, in relation to either of the spouses or civil partners, notwithstanding that the previous marriage or civil partnership of that spouse or civil partner was void or voidable.

(6) Any reference in this Act to an order or decree made under the Matrimonial Causes Act 1973 or under any section of that Act shall be construed as including a reference to an order or decree which is deemed to have been made under that Act or under that section thereof, as the case may be.

(6A) Any reference in this Act to an order made under, or under any provision of, the Civil Partnership Act 2004 shall be construed as including a reference to anything which is deemed to be an order made (as the case may be) under that Act or provision.

(7) Any reference in this Act to any enactment is a reference to that enactment as amended by or under any subsequent enactment.

26 Consequential amendments, repeals and transitional provisions

(1) Section 36 of the Matrimonial Causes Act 1973 (which provides for the alteration of maintenance agreements by the High Court or a county court after the death of one of the parties) shall have effect subject to the following amendments (being amendments consequential on this Act), that is to say –

(a) in subsection (3) for the words 'section 7 of the Family Provision Act 1966' there shall be substituted the words 'section 22 of the Inheritance (Provision for Family and Dependants) Act 1975', for the words from 'the Inheritance (Family Provision) Act' to 'net estate' there shall be substituted the words 'that Act if the value of the property mentioned in that section' and for the words 'section 26 of the Matrimonial Causes Act 1965 (application for maintenance out of deceased's estate by former spouse)' there shall be substituted the words 'section 2 of that Act';

(b) in subsection (7) for the words from 'section 7' to 'subsection (5)' there shall be substituted the words 'section 22 of the Inheritance (Provision for Family and Dependants) Act 1975 (which enables rules of court to provide for the transfer from a county court to the High Court or from the High Court to a county court of proceedings for an order under section 2 of that Act) and paragraphs (a) and (b) of subsection (4)' and for the words 'any such proceedings as are referred to in subsection (1) of that section' there shall be substituted the words 'proceedings for an order under section 2 of that Act'.

(2) Subject to the provisions of this section, the enactments specified in the Schedule to this Act are hereby repealed to the extent specified in the third column of the Schedule; and in paragraph 5(2) of Schedule 2 to the Matrimonial Causes Act 1973 for the words 'that Act' there shall be substituted the words 'the Matrimonial Causes Act 1965'.

(3) The repeal of the said enactments shall not affect their operation in relation to any application made thereunder (whether before or after the commencement of this Act) with reference to the death of any person who died before the commencement of this Act.

(4) Without prejudice to the provisions of section 38 of the Interpretation Act 1889 (which relates to the effect of repeals) nothing in any repeal made by this Act shall affect any order made or direction given under any enactment repealed by this Act, and, subject to the provisions of this Act, every such order or direction (other than an order made under section 4A of the Inheritance (Family Provision) Act 1938 or section 28A of the Matrimonial Causes Act 1965) shall, if it is in force at the commencement of this Act or is made by virtue of subsection (2) above, continue in force as if it had been made under section 2(1)(a) of this Act, and for the purposes of section 6(7) of this Act the court in exercising its powers under that section in relation to an order continued in force by this subsection shall be required to have regard to any change in any of the circumstances to which the court would have been required to have regard when making that order if the order had been made with reference to the death of any person who died after the commencement of this Act.

27 Short title, commencement and extent

(1) This Act may be cited as the Inheritance (Provision for Family and Dependants) Act 1975.

(2) This Act does not extend to Scotland or Northern Ireland.

(3) This Act shall come into force on 1st April 1976.

SCHEDULE ENACTMENTS REPEALED

Section 26

Chapter	Short Title	Extent of Repeal
1938 c 72	The Inheritance (Family Provision) Act 1938	The whole Act.
1952 c 64	The Intestates' Estates Act 1952	Section 7 and Schedule 3.
1965 c 72	The Matrimonial Causes Act 1965	Section 26 to 28(A) and section 25(4) and (5) as applied by section 28(2).
1966 c 35	The Family Provision Act 1966	The whole Act, except section 1 and subsections (1) and (3) of section 10.
1969 c 46	The Family Law Reform Act 1969	Sections 5(1) and 18.
1970 c 31	The Administration of Justice Act 1970	In Schedule 2, paragraph 16.
1970 c 33	The Law Reform (Miscellaneous Provisions) Act 1970	Section 6.

APPENDIX 1

1970 c 45	The Matrimonial Proceedings and Property Act 1970	Section 36.
1971 c 23	The Courts Act 1971	Section 45(1)(a).
1973 c 18	The Matrimonial Causes Act 1973	In section 50, in subsection (1)(a) the words from 'and sections 26' to the end of the paragraph, in subsection (1)(d) the words 'or sections 26 to 28A of the Matrimonial Causes Act 1965' and in subsection (2)(a) the words 'or under section 26 or 27 of the Matrimonial Causes Act 1965'.
		In Schedule 2, paragraph 5(1) and in paragraph 12 the words '(a) sections 26 to 28A of the Matrimonial Causes Act 1965'.
1975 c 7	The Finance Act 1975	In Schedule 12, paragraph 6.

APPENDIX 2

Matrimonial Causes Act 1973, Part II

PART II – FINANCIAL RELIEF FOR PARTIES TO MARRIAGE AND CHILDREN OF FAMILY

Financial provision and property adjustment orders

21 Financial provision and property adjustment orders

(1) The financial provision orders for the purposes of this Act are the orders for periodical or lump sum provision available (subject to the provisions of this Act) under section 23 below for the purpose of adjusting the financial position of the parties to a marriage and any children of the family in connection with proceedings for divorce, nullity of marriage or judicial separation and under section 27(6) below on proof of neglect by one party to a marriage to provide, or to make a proper contribution towards, reasonable maintenance for the other or a child of the family, that is to say –

  (a) any order for periodical payments in favour of a party to a marriage under section 23(1)(a) or 27(6)(a) or in favour of a child of the family under section 23(1)(d), (2) or (4) or 27(6)(d);

  (b) any order for secured periodical payments in favour of a party to a marriage under section 23(1)(b) or 27(6)(b) or in favour of a child of the family under section 23(1)(e), (2) or (4) or 27(6)(e); and

  (c) any order for lump sum provision in favour of a party to a marriage under section 23(1)(c) or 27(6)(c) or in favour of a child of the family under section 23(1)(f), (2) or (4) or 27(6)(f);

and references in this Act (except in paragraphs 17(1) and 23 of Schedule 1 below) to periodical payments orders, secured periodical payments orders, and orders for the payment of a lump sum are references to all or some of the financial provision orders requiring the sort of financial provision in question according as the context of each reference may require.

(2) The property adjustment orders for the purposes of this Act are the orders dealing with property rights available (subject to the provisions of this Act) under section 24 below for the purpose of adjusting the financial position of the parties to a marriage and any children of the family on or after the grant of a decree of divorce, nullity of marriage or judicial separation, that is to say –

  (a) any order under subsection (1)(a) of that section for a transfer of property;

  (b) any order under subsection (1)(b) of that section for a settlement of property; and

APPENDIX 2

(c) any order under subsection (1)(c) or (d) of that section for a variation of settlement.

21A Pension sharing orders

(1) For the purposes of this Act, a pension sharing order is an order which –

(a) provides that one party's –

(i) shareable rights under a specified pension arrangement, or
(ii) shareable state scheme rights,

be subject to pension sharing for the benefit of the other party, and

(b) specifies the percentage value to be transferred.

(2) In subsection (1) above –

(a) the reference to shareable rights under a pension arrangement is to rights in relation to which pension sharing is available under Chapter I of Part IV of the Welfare Reform and Pensions Act 1999, or under corresponding Northern Ireland legislation,
(b) the reference to shareable state scheme rights is to rights in relation to which pension sharing is available under Chapter II of Part IV of the Welfare Reform and Pensions Act 1999, or under corresponding Northern Ireland legislation, and
(c) 'party' means a party to a marriage.

Ancillary relief in connection with divorce proceedings, etc

22 Maintenance pending suit

On a petition for divorce, nullity of marriage or judicial separation, the court may make an order for maintenance pending suit, that is to say, an order requiring either party to the marriage to make to the other such periodical payments for his or her maintenance and for such term, being a term beginning not earlier than the date of the presentation of the petition and ending with the date of the determination of the suit, as the court thinks reasonable.

[22A Financial provision orders: divorce and separation[1]

(1) On an application made under this section, the court may at the appropriate time make one or more financial provision orders in favour of –

(a) a party to the marriage to which the application relates; or
(b) any of the children of the family.

(2) The 'appropriate time' is any time –

(a) after a statement of marital breakdown has been received by the court and before any application for a divorce order or for a separation order is made to the court by reference to that statement;
(b) when an application for a divorce order or separation order has been made under section 3 of the 1996 Act and has not been withdrawn;
(c) when an application for a divorce order has been made under section 4 of the 1996 Act and has not been withdrawn;
(d) after a divorce order has been made;
(e) when a separation order is in force.

(3) The court may make –
   (a) a combined order against the parties on one occasion,
   (b) separate orders on different occasions,
   (c) different orders in favour of different children,
   (d) different orders from time to time in favour of the same child,

   but may not make, in favour of the same party, more than one periodical payments order, or more than one order for payment of a lump sum, in relation to any marital proceedings, whether in the course of the proceedings or by reference to a divorce order or separation order made in the proceedings.

(4) If it would not otherwise be in a position to make a financial provision order in favour of a party or child of the family, the court may make an interim periodical payments order, an interim order for the payment of a lump sum or a series of such orders, in favour of that party or child.

(5) Any order for the payment of a lump sum made under this section may –
   (a) provide for the payment of the lump sum by instalments of such amounts as may be specified in the order; and
   (b) require the payment of the instalments to be secured to the satisfaction of the court.

(6) Nothing in subsection (5) above affects –
   (a) the power of the court under this section to make an order for the payment of a lump sum; or
   (b) the provisions of this Part of this Act as to the beginning of the term specified in any periodical payments order or secured periodical payments order.

(7) Subsection (8) below applies where the court –
   (a) makes an order under this section ('the main order') for the payment of a lump sum; and
   (b) directs –
      (i) that payment of that sum, or any part of it, is to be deferred; or
      (ii) that that sum, or any part of it, is to be paid by instalments.

(8) In such a case, the court may, on or at any time after making the main order, make an order ('the order for interest') for the amount deferred, or the instalments, to carry interest (at such rate as may be specified in the order for interest) –
   (a) from such date, not earlier than the date of the main order, as may be so specified;
   (b) until the date when the payment is due.

(9) This section is to be read subject to any restrictions imposed by this Act and to section 19 of the 1996 Act.]

[22B Restrictions affecting section 22A[2]

(1) No financial provision order, other than an interim order, may be made under section 22A above so as to take effect before the making of a divorce order or separation order in relation to the marriage, unless the court is satisfied –
   (a) that the circumstances of the case are exceptional; and
   (b) that it would be just and reasonable for the order to be so made.

APPENDIX 2

(2) Except in the case of an interim periodical payments order, the court may not make a financial provision order under section 22A above at any time while the period for reflection and consideration is interrupted under section 7(8) of the 1996 Act.

(3) No financial provision order may be made under section 22A above by reference to the making of a statement of marital breakdown if, by virtue of section 5(3) or 7(9) of the 1996 Act (lapse of divorce or separation process), it has ceased to be possible –

(a) for an application to be made by reference to that statement; or
(b) for an order to be made on such an application.

(4) No financial provision order may be made under section 22A after a divorce order has been made, or while a separation order is in force, except –

(a) in response to an application made before the divorce order or separation order was made; or
(b) on a subsequent application made with the leave of the court.

(5) In this section, 'period for reflection and consideration' means the period fixed by section 7 of the 1996 Act.]

23 Financial provision orders in connection with divorce proceedings, etc

(1) On granting a decree of divorce, a decree of nullity of marriage or a decree of judicial separation or at any time thereafter (whether, in the case of a decree of divorce or of nullity of marriage, before or after the decree is made absolute), the court may make any one or more of the following orders, that is to say –

(a) an order that either party to the marriage shall make to the other such periodical payments, for such term, as may be specified in the order;
(b) an order that either party to the marriage shall secure to the other to the satisfaction of the court such periodical payments, for such term, as may be so specified;
(c) an order that either party to the marriage shall pay to the other such lump sum or sums as may be so specified;
(d) an order that a party to the marriage shall make to such person as may be specified in the order for the benefit of a child of the family, or to such a child, such periodical payments, for such term, as may be so specified;
(e) an order that a party to the marriage shall secure to such person as may be so specified for the benefit of such a child, or to such a child, to the satisfaction of the court, such periodical payments, for such term, as may be so specified;
(f) an order that a party to the marriage shall pay to such person as may be so specified for the benefit of such a child, or to such a child, such lump sum as may be so specified;

subject, however, in the case of an order under paragraph (d), (e) or (f) above, to the restrictions imposed by section 29(1) and (3) below on the making of financial provision orders in favour of children who have attained the age of eighteen.

(2) The court may also, subject to those restrictions, make any one or more of the orders mentioned in subsection (1)(d), (e) and (f) above –

(a) in any proceedings for divorce, nullity of marriage or judicial separation, before granting a decree; and

(b) where any such proceedings are dismissed after the beginning of the trial, either forthwith or within a reasonable period after the dismissal.

(3) Without prejudice to the generality of subsection (1)(c) or (f) above –

    (a) an order under this section that a party to a marriage shall pay a lump sum to the other party may be made for the purpose of enabling that other party to meet any liabilities or expenses reasonably incurred by him or her in maintaining himself or herself or any child of the family before making an application for an order under this section in his or her favour;

    (b) an order under this section for the payment of a lump sum to or for the benefit of a child of the family may be made for the purpose of enabling any liabilities or expenses reasonably incurred by or for the benefit of that child before the making of an application for an order under this section in his favour to be met; and

    (c) an order under this section for the payment of a lump sum may provide for the payment of that sum by instalments of such amount as may be specified in the order and may require the payment of the instalments to be secured to the satisfaction of the court.

(4) The power of the court under subsection (1) or (2)(a) above to make an order in favour of a child of the family shall be exercisable from time to time; and where the court makes an order in favour of a child under subsection (2)(b) above, it may from time to time, subject to the restrictions mentioned in subsection (1) above, make a further order in his favour of any of the kinds mentioned in subsection (1)(d), (e) or (f) above.

(5) Without prejudice to the power to give a direction under section 30 below for the settlement of an instrument by conveyancing counsel, where an order is made under subsection (1)(a), (b) or (c) above on or after granting a decree of divorce or nullity of marriage, neither the order nor any settlement made in pursuance of the order shall take effect unless the decree has been made absolute.

(6) Where the court –

    (a) makes an order under this section for the payment of a lump of sum; and

    (b) directs –

        (i) that payment of that sum or any part of it shall be deferred; or

        (ii) that that sum or any part of it shall be paid by instalments,

the court may order that the amount deferred or the instalments shall carry interest at such rate as may be specified by the order from such date, not earlier than the date of the order, as may be so specified, until the date when payment of it is due.

[23 Financial provision orders: nullity[3]

(1) On or after granting a decree of nullity of marriage (whether before or after the decree is made absolute), the court may, on an application made under this section, make one or more financial provision orders in favour of –

    (a) either party to the marriage; or

    (b) any child of the family.

(2) Before granting a decree in any proceedings for nullity of marriage, the court may make against either or each of the parties to the marriage –

    (a) an interim ′periodical payments order, an interim order for the payment of a lump sum, or a series of such orders, in favour of the other party;

APPENDIX 2

    (b) an interim periodical payments order, an interim order for the payment of a lump sum, a series of such orders or any one or more other financial provision orders in favour of each child of the family.

(3) Where any such proceedings are dismissed, the court may (either immediately or within a reasonable period after the dismissal) make any one or more financial provision orders in favour of each child of the family.

(4) An order under this section that a party to a marriage must pay a lump sum to the other party may be made for the purpose of enabling that other party to meet any liabilities or expenses reasonably incurred by him or her in maintaining himself or herself or any child of the family before making an application for an order under this section in his or her favour.

(5) An order under this section for the payment of a lump sum to or for the benefit of a child of the family may be made for the purpose of enabling any liabilities or expenses reasonably incurred by or for the benefit of that child before the making of an application for an order under this section in his favour to be met.

(6) An order under this section for the payment of a lump sum may –

    (a) provide for the payment of that sum by instalments of such amount as may be specified in the order; and
    (b) require the payment of the instalments to be secured to the satisfaction of the court.

(7) Nothing in subsections (4) to (6) above affects –

    (a) the power under subsection (1) above to make an order for the payment of a lump sum; or
    (b) the provisions of this Act as to the beginning of the term specified in any periodical payments order or secured periodical payments order.

(8) The powers of the court under this section to make one or more financial provision orders are exercisable against each party to the marriage by the making of –

    (a) a combined order on one occasion, or
    (b) separate orders on different occasions,

but the court may not make more than one periodical payments order, or more than one order for payment of a lump sum, in favour of the same party.

(9) The powers of the court under this section so far as they consist in power to make one or more orders in favour of the children of the family –

    (a) may be exercised differently in favour of different children; and
    (b) except in the case of the power conferred by subsection (3) above, may be exercised from time to time in favour of the same child; and
    (c) in the case of the power conferred by that subsection, if it is exercised by the making of a financial provision order of any kind in favour of a child, shall include power to make, from time to time, further financial provision orders of that or any other kind in favour of that child.

(10) Where an order is made under subsection (1) above in favour of a party to the marriage on or after the granting of a decree of nullity of marriage, neither the order nor any settlement made in pursuance of the order takes effect unless the decree has been made absolute.

(11) Subsection (10) above does not affect the power to give a direction under section 30 below for the settlement of an instrument by conveyancing counsel.

(12) Where the court –
- (a) makes an order under this section ('the main order') for the payment of a lump sum; and
- (b) directs –
  - (i) that payment of that sum or any part of it is to be deferred; or
  - (ii) that that sum or any part of it is to be paid by instalments,

it may, on or at any time after making the main order, make an order ('the order for interest') for the amount deferred or the instalments to carry interest at such rate as may be specified by the order for interest from such date, not earlier than the date of the main order, as may be so specified, until the date when payment of it is due.

(13) This section is to be read subject to any restrictions imposed by this Act.]

[23A Property adjustment orders: divorce and separation[4]

(1) On an application made under this section, the court may, at any time mentioned in section 22A(2) above, make one or more property adjustment orders.

(2) If the court makes, in favour of the same party to the marriage, more than one property adjustment order in relation to any marital proceedings, whether in the course of the proceedings or by reference to a divorce order or separation order made in the proceedings, each order must fall within a different paragraph of section 21(2) above.

(3) The court shall exercise its powers under this section, so far as is practicable, by making on one occasion all such provision as can be made by way of one or more property adjustment orders in relation to the marriage as it thinks fit.

(4) Subsection (3) above does not affect section 31 or 31A below.

(5) This section is to be read subject to any restrictions imposed by this Act and to section 19 of the 1996 Act.]

[23B Restrictions affecting section 23A[5]

(1) No property adjustment order may be made under section 23A above so as to take effect before the making of a divorce order or separation order in relation to the marriage unless the court is satisfied –
- (a) that the circumstances of the case are exceptional; and
- (b) that it would be just and reasonable for the order to be so made.

(2) The court may not make a property adjustment order under section 23A above at any time while the period for reflection and consideration is interrupted under section 7(8) of the 1996 Act.

(3) No property adjustment order may be made under section 23A above by virtue of the making of a statement of marital breakdown if, by virtue of section 5(3) or 7(5) of the 1996 Act (lapse of divorce or separation process), it has ceased to be possible –
- (a) for an application to be made by reference to that statement; or
- (b) for an order to be made on such an application.

(4) No property adjustment order may be made under section 23A above after a divorce order has been made, or while a separation order is in force, except –
- (a) in response to an application made before the divorce order or separation order was made; or
- (b) on a subsequent application made with the leave of the court.

APPENDIX 2

(5) In this section, 'period for reflection and consideration' means the period fixed by section 7 of the 1996 Act.]

24 Property adjustment orders in connection with divorce proceedings, etc

(1) On granting a decree of divorce, a decree of nullity of marriage or a decree of judicial separation or at any time thereafter (whether, in the case of a decree of divorce or of nullity of marriage, before or after the decree is made absolute), the court may make any one or more of the following orders, that is to say –

(a) an order that a party to the marriage shall transfer to the other party, to any child of the family or to such person as may be specified in the order for the benefit of such a child such property as may be so specified, being property to which the first-mentioned party is entitled, either in possession or reversion;

(b) an order that a settlement of such property as may be so specified, being property to which a party to the marriage is so entitled, be made to the satisfaction of the court for the benefit of the other party to the marriage and of the children of the family or either or any of them;

(c) an order varying for the benefit of the parties to the marriage and of the children of the family or either or any of them any ante-nuptial or post-nuptial settlement (including such a settlement made by will or codicil) made on the parties to the marriage, other than one in the form of a pension arrangement (within the meaning of section 25D below);

(d) an order extinguishing or reducing the interest of either of the parties to the marriage under any such settlement, other than one in the form of a pension arrangement (within the meaning of section 25D below);

subject, however, in the case of an order under paragraph (a) above, to the restrictions imposed by section 29(1) and (3) below on the making of orders for a transfer of property in favour of children who have attained the age of eighteen.

(2) The court may make an order under subsection (1)(c) above notwithstanding that there are no children of the family.

(3) Without prejudice to the power to give a direction under section 30 below for the settlement of an instrument by conveyancing counsel, where an order is made under this section on or after granting a decree of divorce or nullity of marriage, neither the order nor any settlement made in pursuance of the order shall take effect unless the decree has been made absolute.

24A Orders for sale of property

(1) Where the court makes under section 23 or 24 of this Act a secured periodical payments order, an order for the payment of a lump sum or a property adjustment order, then, on making that order or at any time thereafter, the court may make a further order for the sale of such property as may be specified in the order, being property in which or in the proceeds of sale of which either or both of the parties to the marriage has or have a beneficial interest, either in possession or reversion.

(2) Any order made under subsection (1) above may contain such consequential or supplementary provisions as the court thinks fit and, without prejudice to the generality of the foregoing provision, may include –

(a) provision requiring the making of a payment out of the proceeds of sale of the property to which the order relates, and

(b) provision requiring any such property to be offered for sale to a person, or class of persons, specified in the order.

(3) Where an order is made under subsection (1) above on or after the grant of a decree of divorce or nullity of marriage, the order shall not take effect unless the decree has been made absolute.

(4) Where an order is made under subsection (1) above, the court may direct that the order, or such provision thereof as the court may specify, shall not take effect until the occurrence of an event specified by the court or the expiration of a period so specified.

(5) Where an order under subsection (1) above contains a provision requiring the proceeds of sale of the property to which the order relates to be used to secure periodical payments to a party to the marriage, the order shall cease to have effect on the death or re-marriage of, or formation of a civil partnership by, that person.

(6) Where a party to a marriage has a beneficial interest in any property, or in the proceeds of sale thereof, and some other person who is not a party to the marriage also has a beneficial interest in that property or in the proceeds of sale thereof, then, before deciding whether to make an order under this section in relation to that property, it shall be the duty of the court to give that other person an opportunity to make representations with respect to the order; and any representations made by that other person shall be included among the circumstances to which the court is required to have regard under section 25(1) below.

24B Pension sharing orders in connection with divorce proceedings etc

(1) On granting a decree of divorce or a decree of nullity of marriage or at any time thereafter (whether before or after the decree is made absolute), the court may, on an application made under this section, make one or more pension sharing orders in relation to the marriage.

(2) A pension sharing order under this section is not to take effect unless the decree on or after which it is made has been made absolute.

(3) A pension sharing order under this section may not be made in relation to a pension arrangement which –

(a) is the subject of a pension sharing order in relation to the marriage, or
(b) has been the subject of pension sharing between the parties to the marriage.

(4) A pension sharing order under this section may not be made in relation to shareable state scheme rights if –

(a) such rights are the subject of a pension sharing order in relation to the marriage, or
(b) such rights have been the subject of pension sharing between the parties to the marriage.

(5) A pension sharing order under this section may not be made in relation to the rights of a person under a pension arrangement if there is in force a requirement imposed by virtue of section 25B or 25C below which relates to benefits or future benefits to which he is entitled under the pension arrangement.

[24B Pension sharing orders: divorce[6]

(1) On an application made under this section, the court may at the appropriate time make one or more pension sharing orders.

APPENDIX 2

(2) The 'appropriate time' is any time –

   (a) after a statement of marital breakdown has been received by the court and before any application for a divorce order or for a separation order is made to the court by reference to that statement;
   (b) when an application for a divorce order has been made under section 3 of the 1996 Act and has not been withdrawn;
   (c) when an application for a divorce order has been made under section 4 of the 1996 Act and has not been withdrawn;
   (d) after a divorce order has been made.

(3) The court shall exercise its powers under this section, so far as is practicable, by making on one occasion all such provision as can be made by way of one or more pension sharing orders in relation to the marriage as it thinks fit.

(4) This section is to be read subject to any restrictions imposed by this Act and to section 19 of the 1996 Act.]

[24BA Restrictions affecting section 24B[7]

(1) No pension sharing order may be made under section 24B above so as to take effect before the making of a divorce order in relation to the marriage.

(2) The court may not make a pension sharing order under section 24B above at any time while the period for reflection and consideration is interrupted under section 7(8) of the 1996 Act.

(3) No pension sharing order may be made under section 24B above by virtue of a statement of marital breakdown if, by virtue of section 5(3) or 7(9) of the 1996 Act (lapse of divorce process), it has ceased to be possible –

   (a) for an application to be made by reference to that statement, or
   (b) for an order to be made on such an application.

(4) No pension sharing order may be made under section 24B above after a divorce order has been made, except –

   (a) in response to an application made before the divorce order was made, or
   (b) on a subsequent application made with the leave of the court.

(5) A pension sharing order under section 24B above may not be made in relation to a pension arrangement which –

   (a) is the subject of a pension sharing order in relation to the marriage, or
   (b) has been the subject of pension sharing between the parties to the marriage.

(6) A pension sharing order under section 24B above may not be made in relation to shareable state scheme rights if –

   (a) such rights are the subject of a pension sharing order in relation to the marriage, or
   (b) such rights have been the subject of pension sharing between the parties to the marriage.

(7) A pension sharing order under section 24B above may not be made in relation to the rights of a person under a pension arrangement if there is in force a requirement imposed by virtue of section 25B or 25C below which relates to benefits or future benefits to which he is entitled under the pension arrangement.

(8) In this section, 'period for reflection and consideration' means the period fixed by section 7 of the 1996 Act.]

MATRIMONIAL CAUSES ACT 1973

[24BB Pension sharing orders: nullity of marriage[8]

(1) On or after granting a decree of nullity of marriage (whether before or after the decree is made absolute), the court may, on an application made under this section, make one or more pension sharing orders in relation to the marriage.

(2) The court shall exercise its powers under this section, so far as is practicable, by making on one occasion all such provision as can be made by way of one or more pension sharing orders in relation to the marriage as it thinks fit.

(3) Where a pension sharing order is made under this section on or after the granting of a decree of nullity of marriage, the order is not to take effect unless the decree has been made absolute.

(4) This section is to be read subject to any restrictions imposed by this Act.]

[24BC Restrictions affecting section 24BB[9]

(1) A pension sharing order under section 24BB above may not be made in relation to a pension arrangement which –

    (a) is the subject of a pension sharing order in relation to the marriage, or
    (b) has been the subject of pension sharing between the parties to the marriage.

(2) A pension sharing order under section 24BB above may not be made in relation to shareable state scheme rights if –

    (a) such rights are the subject of a pension sharing order in relation to the marriage, or
    (b) such rights have been the subject of pension sharing between the parties to the marriage.

(3) A pension sharing order under section 24BB above may not be made in relation to the rights of a person under a pension arrangement if there is in force a requirement imposed by virtue of section 25B or 25C below which relates to benefits or future benefits to which he is entitled under the pension arrangement.]

24C Pension sharing orders: duty to stay

(1) No pension sharing order may be made so as to take effect before the end of such period after the making of the order as may be prescribed by regulations made by the Lord Chancellor.

(2) The power to make regulations under this section shall be exercisable by statutory instrument which shall be subject to annulment in pursuance of a resolution of either House of Parliament.

24D Pension sharing orders: apportionment of charges

If a pension sharing order relates to rights under a pension arrangement, the court may include in the order provision about the apportionment between the parties of any charge under section 41 of the Welfare Reform and Pensions Act 1999 (charges in respect of pension sharing costs), or under corresponding Northern Ireland legislation.

24E Pension compensation sharing orders in connection with divorce proceedings

(1) On granting a decree of divorce or a decree of nullity of marriage or at any time thereafter (whether before or after the decree is made absolute), the

APPENDIX 2

court may, on an application made under this section, make a pension compensation sharing order in relation to the marriage.

(2) A pension compensation sharing order under this section is not to take effect unless the decree on or after which it is made has been made absolute.

(3) A pension compensation sharing order under this section may not be made in relation to rights to PPF compensation that –

    (a) are the subject of pension attachment,
    (b) derive from rights under a pension scheme that were the subject of pension sharing between the parties to the marriage,
    (c) are the subject of pension compensation attachment, or
    (d) are or have been the subject of pension compensation sharing between the parties to the marriage.

(4) For the purposes of subsection (3)(a), rights to PPF compensation 'are the subject of pension attachment' if any of the following three conditions is met.

(5) The first condition is that –

    (a) the rights derive from rights under a pension scheme in relation to which an order was made under section 23 imposing a requirement by virtue of section 25B(4), and
    (b) that order, as modified under section 25E(3), remains in force.

(6) The second condition is that –

    (a) the rights derive from rights under a pension scheme in relation to which an order was made under section 23 imposing a requirement by virtue of section 25B(7), and
    (b) that order –

        (i) has been complied with, or
        (ii) has not been complied with and, as modified under section 25E(5), remains in force.

(7) The third condition is that –

    (a) the rights derive from rights under a pension scheme in relation to which an order was made under section 23 imposing a requirement by virtue of section 25C, and
    (b) that order remains in force.

(8) For the purposes of subsection (3)(b), rights under a pension scheme 'were the subject of pension sharing between the parties to the marriage' if the rights were at any time the subject of a pension sharing order in relation to the marriage or a previous marriage between the same parties.

(9) For the purposes of subsection (3)(c), rights to PPF compensation 'are the subject of pension compensation attachment' if there is in force a requirement imposed by virtue of section 25F relating to them.

(10) For the purposes of subsection (3)(d), rights to PPF compensation 'are or have been the subject of pension compensation sharing between the parties to the marriage' if they are or have ever been the subject of a pension compensation sharing order in relation to the marriage or a previous marriage between the same parties.

24F Pension compensation sharing orders: duty to stay

(1) No pension compensation sharing order may be made so as to take effect before the end of such period after the making of the order as may be prescribed by regulations made by the Lord Chancellor.

(2) The power to make regulations under this section shall be exercisable by statutory instrument which shall be subject to annulment in pursuance of a resolution of either House of Parliament.

24G Pension compensation sharing orders: apportionment of charges

The court may include in a pension compensation sharing order provision about the apportionment between the parties of any charge under section 117 of the Pensions Act 2008 (charges in respect of pension compensation sharing costs), or under corresponding Northern Ireland legislation.

25 Matters to which court is to have regard in deciding how to exercise its powers under ss 23, 24, 24A, 24B and 24E

(1) It shall be the duty of the court in deciding whether to exercise its powers under section 23, 24, 24A, 24B or 24E above and, if so, in what manner, to have regard to all the circumstances of the case, first consideration being given to the welfare while a minor of any child of the family who has not attained the age of eighteen.

(2) As regards the exercise of the powers of the court under section 23(1)(a), (b) or (c), 24, 24A, 24B or 24E above in relation to a party to the marriage, the court shall in particular have regard to the following matters –

   (a) the income, earning capacity, property and other financial resources which each of the parties to the marriage has or is likely to have in the foreseeable future, including in the case of earning capacity any increase in that capacity which it would in the opinion of the court be reasonable to expect a party to the marriage to take steps to acquire;

   (b) the financial needs, obligations and responsibilities which each of the parties to the marriage has or is likely to have in the foreseeable future;

   (c) the standard of living enjoyed by the family before the breakdown of the marriage;

   (d) the age of each party to the marriage and the duration of the marriage;

   (e) any physical or mental disability of either of the parties to the marriage;

   (f) the contributions which each of the parties has made or is likely in the foreseeable future to make to the welfare of the family, including any contribution by looking after the home or caring for the family;

   (g) the conduct of each of the parties, if that conduct is such that it would in the opinion of the court be inequitable to disregard it;

   (h) in the case of proceedings for divorce or nullity of marriage, the value to each of the parties to the marriage of any benefit which, by reason of the dissolution or annulment of the marriage, that party will lose the chance of acquiring.

(3) As regards the exercise of the powers of the court under section 23(1)(d), (e) or (f), (2) or (4), 24 or 24A above in relation to a child of the family, the court shall in particular have regard to the following matters –

   (a) the financial needs of the child;

APPENDIX 2

- (b) the income, earning capacity (if any), property and other financial resources of the child;
- (c) any physical or mental disability of the child;
- (d) the manner in which he was being and in which the parties to the marriage expected him to be educated or trained;
- (e) the considerations mentioned in relation to the parties to the marriage in paragraphs (a), (b), (c) and (e) of subsection (2) above.

(4) As regards the exercise of the powers of the court under section 23(1)(d), (e) or (f), (2) or (4), 24 or 24A above against a party to a marriage in favour of a child of the family who is not the child of that party, the court shall also have regard –

- (a) to whether that party assumed any responsibility for the child's maintenance, and, if so, to the extent to which, and the basis upon which, that party assumed such responsibility and to the length of time for which that party discharged such responsibility;
- (b) to whether in assuming and discharging such responsibility that party did so knowing that the child was not his or her own;
- (c) to the liability of any other person to maintain the child.

25A Exercise of court's powers in favour of party to marriage on decree of divorce or nullity of marriage

(1) Where on or after the grant of a decree of divorce or nullity of marriage the court decides to exercise its powers under section 23(1)(a), (b) or (c), 24, 24A, 24B or 24E above in favour of a party to the marriage, it shall be the duty of the court to consider whether it would be appropriate so to exercise those powers that the financial obligations of each party towards the other will be terminated as soon after the grant of a divorce order or decree of nullity as the court considers just and reasonable.

(2) Where the court decides in such a case to make a periodical payments or secured periodical payments order in favour of a party to the marriage, the court shall in particular consider whether it would be appropriate to require those payments to be made or secured only for such term as would in the opinion of the court be sufficient to enable the party in whose favour the order is made to adjust without undue hardship to the termination of his or her financial dependence on the other party.

(3) Where on or after the grant of a decree of divorce or nullity of marriage an application is made by a party to the marriage for a periodical payments or secured periodical payments order in his or her favour, then, if the court considers that no continuing obligation should be imposed on either party to make or secure periodical payments in favour of the other, the court may dismiss the application with a direction that the applicant shall not be entitled to make any future application in relation to that marriage for an order under section 23(1)(a) or (b) above.

25B Pensions

(1) The matters to which the court is to have regard under section 25(2) above include –

- (a) in the case of paragraph (a), any benefits under a pension arrangement which a party to the marriage has or is likely to have, and
- (b) in the case of paragraph (h), any benefits under a pension arrangement which, by reason of the dissolution or annulment of the marriage, a party to the marriage will lose the chance of acquiring,

and, accordingly, in relation to benefits under a pension arrangement, section 25(2)(a) above shall have effect as if 'in the foreseeable future' were omitted.

(2) ...

(3) The following provisions apply where, having regard to any benefits under a pension arrangement the court determines to make an order under section 23 above.

(4) To the extent to which the order is made having regard to any benefits under a pension arrangement, the order may require the person responsible for the pension arrangement in question, if at any time any payment in respect of any benefits under the arrangement becomes due to the party with pension rights, to make a payment for the benefit of the other party.

(5) The order must express the amount of any payment required to be made by virtue of subsection (4) above as a percentage of the payment which becomes due to the party with pension rights.

(6) Any such payment by the person responsible for the arrangement –

   (a) shall discharge so much of his liability to the party with pension rights as corresponds to the amount of the payment, and
   (b) shall be treated for all purposes as a payment made by the party with pension rights in or towards the discharge of his liability under the order.

(7) Where the party with pension rights has a right of commutation under the arrangement, the order may require him to exercise it to any extent; and this section applies to any payment due in consequence of commutation in pursuance of the order as it applies to other payments in respect of benefits under the arrangement.

(7A) The power conferred by subsection (7) above may not be exercised for the purpose of commuting a benefit payable to the party with pension rights to a benefit payable to the other party.

(7B) The power conferred by subsection (4) or (7) above may not be exercised in relation to a pension arrangement which –

   (a) is the subject of a pension sharing order in relation to the marriage, or
   (b) has been the subject of pension sharing between the parties to the marriage.

(7C) In subsection (1) above, references to benefits under a pension arrangement include any benefits by way of pension, whether under a pension arrangement or not.

25C Pensions: lump sums

(1) The power of the court under section 23 above to order a party to a marriage to pay a lump sum to the other party includes, where the benefits which the party with pension rights has or is likely to have under a pension arrangement include any lump sum payable in respect of his death, power to make any of the following provision by the order.

(2) The court may –

   (a) if the person responsible for the pension arrangement in question has power to determine the person to whom the sum, or any part of it, is to be paid, require him to pay the whole or part of that sum, when it becomes due, to the other party,
   (b) if the party with pension rights has power to nominate the person to whom the sum, or any part of it, is to be paid, require the party with

APPENDIX 2

pension rights to nominate the other party in respect of the whole or part of that sum,

(c) in any other case, require the person responsible for the pension arrangement in question to pay the whole or part of that sum, when it becomes due, for the benefit of the other party instead of to the person to whom, apart from the order, it would be paid.

(3) Any payment by the person responsible for the arrangement under an order made under section 23 above by virtue of this section shall discharge so much of his liability in respect of the party with pension rights as corresponds to the amount of the payment.

(4) The powers conferred by this section may not be exercised in relation to a pension arrangement which –

(a) is the subject of a pension sharing order in relation to the marriage, or
(b) has been the subject of pension sharing between the parties to the marriage.

25D Pensions: supplementary

(1) Where –

(a) an order made under section 23 above by virtue of section 25B or 25C above imposes any requirement on the person responsible for a pension arrangement ('the first arrangement') and the party with pension rights acquires rights under another pension arrangement ('the new arrangement') which are derived (directly or indirectly) from the whole of his rights under the first arrangement, and
(b) the person responsible for the new arrangement has been given notice in accordance with regulations made by the Lord Chancellor,

the order shall have effect as if it had been made instead in respect of the person responsible for the new arrangement.

(2) The Lord Chancellor may by regulations –

(a) in relation to any provision of sections 25B or 25C above which authorises the court making an order under section 23 above to require the person responsible for a pension arrangement to make a payment for the benefit of the other party, make provision as to the person to whom, and the terms on which, the payment is to be made,
(ab) make, in relation to payment under a mistaken belief as to the continuation in force of a provision included by virtue of section 25B or 25C above in an order under section 23 above, provision about the rights or liabilities of the payer, the payee or the person to whom the payment was due,
(b) require notices to be given in respect of changes of circumstances relevant to such orders which include provision made by virtue of sections 25B and 25C above,
(ba) make provision for the person responsible for a pension arrangement to be discharged in prescribed circumstances from a requirement imposed by virtue of section 25B or 25C above,
(c) . . .
(d) . . .
(e) make provision about calculation and verification in relation to the valuation of –

(i) benefits under a pension arrangement, or
(ii) shareable state scheme rights,

for the purposes of the court's functions in connection with the exercise of any of its powers under this Part of this Act.

(2A) Regulations under subsection (2)(e) above may include –

(a) provision for calculation or verification in accordance with guidance from time to time prepared by a prescribed person, and
(b) provision by reference to regulations under section 30 or 49(4) of the Welfare Reform and Pensions Act 1999.

(2B) Regulations under subsection (2) above may make different provision for different cases.

(2C) Power to make regulations under this section shall be exercisable by statutory instrument which shall be subject to annulment in pursuance of a resolution of either House of Parliament.

(3) In this section and sections 25B and 25C above –

'occupational pension scheme' has the same meaning as in the Pension Schemes Act 1993;

'the party with pension rights' means the party to the marriage who has or is likely to have benefits under a pension arrangement and 'the other party' means the other party to the marriage;

'pension arrangement' means –

(a) an occupational pension scheme,
(b) a personal pension scheme,
(c) a retirement annuity contract,
(d) an annuity or insurance policy purchased, or transferred, for the purpose of giving effect to rights under an occupational pension scheme or a personal pension scheme, and
(e) an annuity purchased, or entered into, for the purpose of discharging liability in respect of a pension credit under section 29(1)(b) of the Welfare Reform and Pensions Act 1999 or under corresponding Northern Ireland legislation;

'personal pension scheme' has the same meaning as in the Pension Schemes Act 1993;

'prescribed' means prescribed by regulations;

'retirement annuity contract' means a contract or scheme approved under Chapter III of Part XIV of the Income and Corporation Taxes Act 1988;

'shareable state scheme rights' has the same meaning as in section 21A(1) above; and

'trustees or managers', in relation to an occupational pension scheme or a personal pension scheme, means –

(a) in the case of a scheme established under a trust, the trustees of the scheme, and
(b) in any other case, the managers of the scheme.

(4) In this section and sections 25B and 25C above, references to the person responsible for a pension arrangement are –

(a) in the case of an occupational pension scheme or a personal pension scheme, to the trustees or managers of the scheme,
(b) in the case of a retirement annuity contract or an annuity falling within paragraph (d) or (e) of the definition of 'pension arrangement' above, the provider of the annuity, and

APPENDIX 2

    (c)   in the case of an insurance policy falling within paragraph (d) of the definition of that expression, the insurer.

25E   The Pension Protection Fund

(1) The matters to which the court is to have regard under section 25(2) include –

    (a)   in the case of paragraph (a), any PPF compensation to which a party to the marriage is or is likely to be entitled, and

    (b)   in the case of paragraph (h), any PPF compensation which, by reason of the dissolution or annulment of the marriage, a party to the marriage will lose the chance of acquiring entitlement to,

and, accordingly, in relation to PPF compensation, section 25(2)(a) shall have effect as if 'in the foreseeable future' were omitted.

(2) Subsection (3) applies in relation to an order under section 23 so far as it includes provision made by virtue of section 25B(4) which –

    (a)   imposed requirements on the trustees or managers of an occupational pension scheme for which the Board has assumed responsibility in accordance with Chapter 3 of Part 2 of the Pensions Act 2004 (pension protection) or any provision in force in Northern Ireland corresponding to that Chapter, and

    (b)   was made before the trustees or managers of the scheme received the transfer notice in relation to the scheme.

(3) The order is to have effect from the time when the trustees or managers of the scheme receive the transfer notice –

    (a)   as if, except in prescribed descriptions of case –

        (i)   references in the order to the trustees or managers of the scheme were references to the Board, and

        (ii)   references in the order to any pension or lump sum to which the party with pension rights is or may become entitled under the scheme were references to any PPF compensation to which that person is or may become entitled in respect of the pension or lump sum, and

    (b)   subject to such other modifications as may be prescribed.

(4) Subsection (5) applies to an order under section 23 if –

    (a)   it includes provision made by virtue of section 25B(7) which requires the party with pension rights to exercise his right of commutation under an occupational pension scheme to any extent, and

    (b)   before the requirement is complied with the Board has assumed responsibility for the scheme as mentioned in subsection (2)(a).

(5) From the time the trustees or managers of the scheme receive the transfer notice, the order is to have effect with such modifications as may be prescribed.

(6) Regulations may modify section 25C as it applies in relation to an occupational pension scheme at any time when there is an assessment period in relation to the scheme.

(7) Where the court makes a pension sharing order in respect of a person's shareable rights under an occupational pension scheme, or an order which

includes provision made by virtue of section 25B(4) or (7) in relation to such a scheme, the Board subsequently assuming responsibility for the scheme as mentioned in subsection (2)(a) does not affect –

    (a) the powers of the court under section 31 to vary or discharge the order or to suspend or revive any provision of it, or

    (b) on an appeal, the powers of the appeal court to affirm, reinstate, set aside or vary the order.

(8) Regulations may make such consequential modifications of any provision of, or made by virtue of, this Part as appear to the Lord Chancellor necessary or expedient to give effect to the provisions of this section.

(9) In this section –

'assessment period' means an assessment period within the meaning of Part 2 of the Pensions Act 2004 (pension protection) (see sections 132 and 159 of that Act) or an equivalent period under any provision in force in Northern Ireland corresponding to that Part;

'the Board' means the Board of the Pension Protection Fund;

'occupational pension scheme' has the same meaning as in the Pension Schemes Act 1993;

'prescribed' means prescribed by regulations;

'PPF compensation' means compensation payable under Chapter 3 of Part 2 of the Pensions Act 2004 (pension protection) or any provision in force in Northern Ireland corresponding to that Chapter;

'regulations' means regulations made by the Lord Chancellor;

'shareable rights' are rights in relation to which pension sharing is available under Chapter 1 of Part 4 of the Welfare Reform and Pensions Act 1999 or any provision in force in Northern Ireland corresponding to that Chapter;

'transfer notice' has the same meaning as in section 160 of the Pensions Act 2004 or any corresponding provision in force in Northern Ireland.

(10) Any power to make regulations under this section is exercisable by statutory instrument, which shall be subject to annulment in pursuance of a resolution of either House of Parliament.

25F Attachment of pension compensation

(1) This section applies where, having regard to any PPF compensation to which a party to the marriage is or is likely to be entitled, the court determines to make an order under section 23.

(2) To the extent to which the order is made having regard to such compensation, the order may require the Board of the Pension Protection Fund, if at any time any payment in respect of PPF compensation becomes due to the party with compensation rights, to make a payment for the benefit of the other party.

(3) The order must express the amount of any payment required to be made by virtue of subsection (2) as a percentage of the payment which becomes due to the party with compensation rights.

(4) Any such payment by the Board of the Pension Protection Fund –

    (a) shall discharge so much of its liability to the party with compensation rights as corresponds to the amount of the payment, and

(b) shall be treated for all purposes as a payment made by the party with compensation rights in or towards the discharge of that party's liability under the order.

(5) Where the party with compensation rights has a right to commute any PPF compensation, the order may require that party to exercise it to any extent; and this section applies to any payment due in consequence of commutation in pursuance of the order as it applies to other payments in respect of PPF compensation.

(6) The power conferred by subsection (5) may not be exercised for the purpose of commuting compensation payable to the party with compensation rights to compensation payable to the other party.

(7) The power conferred by subsection (2) or (5) may not be exercised in relation to rights to PPF compensation that –

(a) derive from rights under a pension scheme that were at any time the subject of a pension sharing order in relation to the marriage, or a previous marriage between the same parties, or

(b) are or have ever been the subject of a pension compensation sharing order in relation to the marriage or a previous marriage between the same parties.

25G Pension compensation: supplementary

(1) The Lord Chancellor may by regulations –

(a) make provision, in relation to any provision of section 25F which authorises the court making an order under section 23 to require the Board of the Pension Protection Fund to make a payment for the benefit of the other party, as to the person to whom, and the terms on which, the payment is to be made;

(b) make provision, in relation to payment under a mistaken belief as to the continuation in force of a provision included by virtue of section 25F in an order under section 23, about the rights or liabilities of the payer, the payee or the person to whom the payment was due;

(c) require notices to be given in respect of changes of circumstances relevant to orders under section 23 which include provision made by virtue of section 25F;

(d) make provision for the Board of the Pension Protection Fund to be discharged in prescribed circumstances from a requirement imposed by virtue of section 25F;

(e) make provision about calculation and verification in relation to the valuation of PPF compensation for the purposes of the court's functions in connection with the exercise of any of its powers under this Part.

(2) Regulations under subsection (1)(e) may include –

(a) provision for calculation or verification in accordance with guidance from time to time prepared by a prescribed person;

(b) provision by reference to regulations under section 112 of the Pensions Act 2008.

(3) Regulations under subsection (1) may make different provision for different cases.

(4) The power to make regulations under subsection (1) is exercisable by statutory instrument which shall be subject to annulment in pursuance of a resolution of either House of Parliament.
(5) In this section and section 25F –

'the party with compensation rights' means the party to the marriage who is or is likely to be entitled to PPF compensation, and 'the other party' means the other party to the marriage;

'prescribed' means prescribed by regulations.

26 Commencement of proceedings for ancillary relief, etc

(1) Where a petition for divorce, nullity of marriage or judicial separation has been presented, then, subject to subsection (2) below, proceedings for maintenance pending suit under section 22 above for a financial provision order under section 23 above, or for a property adjustment order may be begun, subject to and in accordance with rules of court, at any time after the presentation of the petition.
(2) Rules of court may provide, in such cases as may be prescribed by the rules –
   (a) that applications for any such relief as is mentioned in subsection (1) above shall be made in the petition or answer; and
   (b) that applications for any such relief which are not so made, or are not made until after the expiration of such period following the presentation of the petition or filing of the answer as may be so prescribed, shall be made only with the leave of the court.

Financial provision in case of neglect to maintain

27 Financial provision orders, etc, in case of neglect by party to marriage to maintain other party or child of the family

(1) Either party to a marriage may apply to the court for an order under this section on the ground that the other party to the marriage (in this section referred to as the respondent) –
   (a) has failed to provide reasonable maintenance for the applicant, or
   (b) has failed to provide, or to make a proper contribution towards, reasonable maintenance for any child of the family.
(2) The court shall not entertain an application under this section unless –
   (a) the applicant or the respondent is domiciled in England and Wales on the date of the application; or
   (b) the applicant has been habitually resident there throughout the period of one year ending with that date; or
   (c) the respondent is resident there on that date.
(3) Where an application under this section is made on the ground mentioned in subsection (1)(a) above, then, in deciding –
   (a) whether the respondent has failed to provide reasonable maintenance for the applicant, and
   (b) what order, if any, to make under this section in favour of the applicant,

APPENDIX 2

the court shall have regard to all the circumstances of the case including the matters mentioned in section 25(2) above, and where an application is also made under this section in respect of a child of the family who has not attained the age of eighteen, first consideration shall be given to the welfare of the child while a minor.

(3A) Where an application under this section is made on the ground mentioned in subsection (1)(b) above then, in deciding –

  (a) whether the respondent has failed to provide, or to make a proper contribution towards, reasonable maintenance for the child of the family to whom the application relates, and
  (b) what order, if any, to make under this section in favour of the child,

the court shall have regard to all the circumstances of the case including the matters mentioned in section 25(3)(a) to (e) above, and where the child of the family to whom the application relates is not the child of the respondent, including also the matters mentioned in section 25(4) above.

(3B) In relation to an application under this section on the ground mentioned in subsection (1)(a) above, section 25(2)(c) above shall have effect as if for the reference therein to the breakdown of the marriage there were substituted a reference to the failure to provide reasonable maintenance for the applicant, and in relation to an application under this section on the ground mentioned in subsection (1)(b) above, section 25(2)(c) above (as it applies by virtue of section 25(3)(e) above) shall have effect as if for the reference therein to the breakdown of the marriage there were substituted a reference to the failure to provide, or to make a proper contribution towards, reasonable maintenance for the child of the family to whom the application relates.

(5) Where on an application under this section it appears to the court that the applicant or any child of the family to whom the application relates is in immediate need of financial assistance, but it is not yet possible to determine what order, if any, should be made on the application, the court may make an interim order for maintenance, that is to say, an order requiring the respondent to make to the applicant until the determination of the application such periodical payments as the court thinks reasonable

(6) Where on an application under this section the applicant satisfies the court of any ground mentioned in subsection (1) above, the court may make any one or more of the following orders, that is to say –

  (a) an order that the respondent shall make to the applicant such periodical payments, for such term, as may be specified in the order;
  (b) an order that the respondent shall secure to the applicant, to the satisfaction of the court, such periodical payments, for such term, as may be so specified;
  (c) an order that the respondent shall pay to the applicant such lump sum as may be so specified;
  (d) an order that the respondent shall make to such person as may be specified in the order for the benefit of the child to whom the application relates, or to that child, such periodical payments, for such term, as may be so specified;
  (e) an order that the respondent shall secure to such person as may be so specified for the benefit of that child, or to that child, to the satisfaction of the court, such periodical payments, for such term, as may be so specified;

(f) an order that the respondent shall pay to such person as may be so specified for the benefit of that child, or to that child, such lump sum as may be so specified;

subject, however, in the case of an order under paragraph (d), (e) or (f) above, to the restrictions imposed by section 29(1) and (3) below on the making of financial provision orders in favour of children who have attained the age of eighteen.

(6A) An application for the variation under section 31 of this Act of a periodical payments order or secured periodical payments order made under this section in favour of a child may, if the child has attained the age of sixteen, be made by the child himself.

(6B) Where a periodical payments order made in favour of a child under this section ceases to have effect on the date on which the child attains the age of sixteen or at any time after that date but before or on the date on which he attains the age of eighteen, then if, on an application made to the court for an order under this subsection, it appears to the court that –

(a) the child is, will be or (if an order were made under this subsection) would be receiving instruction at an educational establishment or undergoing training for a trade, profession or vocation, whether or not he also is, will be or would be in gainful employment; or

(b) there are special circumstances which justify the making of an order under this subsection,

the court shall have power by order to revive the first mentioned order from such date as the court may specify, not being earlier than the date of the making of the application, and to exercise its power under section 31 of this Act in relation to any order so revived.

(7) Without prejudice to the generality of subsection (6)(c) or (f) above, an order under this section for the payment of a lump sum –

(a) may be made for the purpose of enabling any liabilities or expenses reasonably incurred in maintaining the applicant or any child of the family to whom the application relates before the making of the application to be met;

(b) may provide for the payment of that sum by instalments of such amount as may be specified in the order and may require the payment of the instalments to be secured to the satisfaction of the court.

(8) . . .

Additional provisions with respect to financial provision and property adjustment orders

28 Duration of continuing financial provision orders in favour of party to marriage, and effect of remarriage or formation of civil partnership

(1) Subject in the case of an order made on or after the grant of a decree of a divorce or nullity of marriage to the provisions of sections 25A(2) above and 31(7) below, the term to be specified in a periodical payments or secured periodical payments order in favour of a party to a marriage shall be such term as the court thinks fit, except that the term shall not begin before or extend beyond the following limits, that is to say –

(a) in the case of a periodical payments order, the term shall begin not earlier than the date of the making of an application for the order, and

APPENDIX 2

shall be so defined as not to extend beyond the death of either of the parties to the marriage or, where the order is made on or after the grant of a decree of divorce or nullity of marriage, the remarriage of, or formation of a civil partnership by, the party in whose favour the order is made; and

(b) in the case of a secured periodical payments order, the term shall begin not earlier than the date of the making of an application for the order, and shall be so defined as not to extend beyond the death or, where the order is made on or after the grant of such a decree, the remarriage of, or formation of a civil partnership by, the party in whose favour the order is made.

(1A) Where a periodical payments or secured periodical payments order in favour of a party to a marriage is made on or after the grant of a decree of divorce or nullity of marriage, the court may direct that that party shall not be entitled to apply under section 31 below for the extension of the term specified in the order.

(2) Where a periodical payments or secured periodical payments order in favour of a party to a marriage is made otherwise than on or after the grant of a decree of divorce or nullity of marriage, and the marriage in question is subsequently dissolved or annulled but the order continues in force, the order shall, notwithstanding anything in it, cease to have effect on the remarriage of, or formation of a civil partnership by, that party, except in relation to any arrears due under it on the date of the remarriage or formation of the civil partnership.

(3) If after the grant of a decree dissolving or annulling a marriage either party to that marriage remarries whether at any time before or after the commencement of this Act or forms a civil partnership, that party shall not be entitled to apply, by reference to the grant of that decree, for a financial provision order in his or her favour, or for a property adjustment order, against the other party to that marriage.

29 Duration of continuing financial provision orders in favour of children, and age limit on making certain orders in their favour

(1) Subject to subsection (3) below, no financial provision order and no order for a transfer of property under section 24(1)(a) above shall be made in favour of a child who has attained the age of eighteen.

(2) The term to be specified in a periodical payments or secured periodical payments order in favour of a child may begin with the date of the making of an application for the order in question or any later date or a date ascertained in accordance with subsection (5) or (6) below but –

(a) shall not in the first instance extend beyond the date of the birthday of the child next following his attaining the upper limit of the compulsory school age (construed in accordance with section 8 of the Education Act 1996) unless the court considers that in the circumstances of the case the welfare of the child requires that it should extend to a later date; and

(b) shall not in any event, subject to subsection (3) below, extend beyond the date of the child's eighteenth birthday.

(3) Subsection (1) above, and paragraph (b) of subsection (2), shall not apply in the case of a child, if it appears to the court that –

(a) the child is, or will be, or if an order were made without complying with either or both of those provisions would be, receiving instruction at an educational establishment or undergoing training for a trade, profession or vocation, whether or not he is also, or will also be, in gainful employment; or

(b) there are special circumstances which justify the making of an order without complying with either or both of those provisions.

(4) Any periodical payments order in favour of a child shall, notwithstanding anything in the order, cease to have effect on the death of the person liable to make payments under the order, except in relation to any arrears due under the order on the date of the death.

(5) Where –

(a) a maintenance calculation ('the current calculation') is in force with respect to a child; and
(b) an application is made under Part II of this Act for a periodical payments or secured periodical payments order in favour of that child –
  (i) in accordance with section 8 of the Child Support Act 1991, and
  (ii) before the end of the period of 6 months beginning with the making of the current calculation

the term to be specified in any such order made on that application may be expressed to begin on, or at any time after, the earliest permitted date.

(6) For the purposes of subsection (5) above, 'the earliest permitted date' is whichever is the later of –

(a) the date 6 months before the application is made; or
(b) the date on which the current calculation took effect or, where successive maintenance calculations have been continuously in force with respect to a child, on which the first of those calculations took effect.

(7) Where –

(a) a maintenance calculation ceases to have effect or is cancelled by or under any provision of the Child Support Act 1991; and
(b) an application is made, before the end of the period of 6 months beginning with the relevant date, for a periodical payments or secured periodical payments order in favour of a child with respect to whom that maintenance calculation was in force immediately before it ceased to have effect or was cancelled,

the term to be specified in any such order made on that application may begin with the date on which that maintenance calculation ceased to have effect or, as the case may be, the date with effect from which it was cancelled, or any later date.

(8) In subsection (7)(b) above –

(a) where the maintenance calculation ceased to have effect, the relevant date is the date on which it so ceased; and
(b) where the maintenance assessment was cancelled, the relevant date is the later of –
  (i) the date on which the person who cancelled it did so, and
  (ii) the date from which the cancellation first had effect.

APPENDIX 2

30 Direction for settlement of instrument for securing payments or effecting property adjustment

Where the court decides to make a financial provision order requiring any payments to be secured or a property adjustment order –

(a) it may direct that the matter be referred to one of the conveyancing counsel of the court for him to settle a proper instrument to be executed by all necessary parties; and
(b) where the order is to be made in proceedings for divorce, nullity of marriage or judicial separation it may, if it thinks fit, defer the grant of the decree in question until the instrument has been duly executed.

Variation, discharge and enforcement of certain orders, etc

31 Variation, discharge, etc, of certain orders for financial relief

(1) Where the court has made an order to which this section applies, then, subject to the provisions of this section and of section 28(1A) above, the court shall have power to vary or discharge the order or to suspend any provision thereof temporarily and to revive the operation of any provision so suspended.

(2) This section applies to the following orders, that is to say –

(a) any order for maintenance pending suit and any interim order for maintenance;
(b) any periodical payments order;
(c) any secured periodical payments order;
(d) any order made by virtue of section 23(3)(c) or 27(7)(b) above (provision for payment of a lump sum by instalments);
(dd) any deferred order made by virtue of section 23(1)(c) (lump sums) which includes provision made by virtue of –

  (i) section 25B(4), or
  (ii) section 25C,

  (provision in respect of pension rights)

(e) any order for a settlement of property under section 24(1)(b) or for a variation of settlement under section 24(1)(c) or (d) above, being an order made on or after the grant of a decree of judicial separation;
(f) any order made under section 24A(1) above for the sale of property;
(g) a pension sharing order under section 24B above which is made at a time before the decree has been made absolute.

(2A) Where the court has made an order referred to in subsection (2)(a), (b) or (c) above, then, subject to the provisions of this section, the court shall have power to remit the payment of any arrears due under the order or of any part thereof.

(2B) Where the court has made an order referred to in subsection (2)(dd)(ii) above, this section shall cease to apply to the order on the death of either of the parties to the marriage.

(3) The powers exercisable by the court under this section in relation to an order shall be exercisable also in relation to any instrument executed in pursuance of the order.

(4) The court shall not exercise the powers conferred by this section in relation to an order for a settlement under section 24(1)(b) or for a variation of

settlement under section 24(1)(c) or (d) above except on an application made in proceedings –

(a) for the rescission of the decree of judicial separation by reference to which the order was made, or
(b) for the dissolution of the marriage in question.

(4A) In relation to an order which falls within paragraph (g) of subsection (2) above ('the subsection (2) order') –

(a) the powers conferred by this section may be exercised –
 (i) only on an application made before the subsection (2) order has or, but for paragraph (b) below, would have taken effect; and
 (ii) only if, at the time when the application is made, the decree has not been made absolute; and
(b) an application made in accordance with paragraph (a) above prevents the subsection (2) order from taking effect before the application has been dealt with.

(4B) No variation of a pension sharing order shall be made so as to take effect before the decree is made absolute.

(4C) The variation of a pension sharing order prevents the order taking effect before the end of such period after the making of the variation as may be prescribed by regulations made by the Lord Chancellor.

(5) Subject to subsections (7A) to (7G) below and without prejudice to any power exercisable by virtue of subsection (2)(d), (dd), (e) or (g) above or otherwise than by virtue of this section, no property adjustment order or pension sharing order shall be made on an application for the variation of a periodical payments or secured periodical payments order made (whether in favour of a party to a marriage or in favour of a child of the family) under section 23 above, and no order for the payment of a lump sum shall be made on an application for the variation of a periodical payments or secured periodical payments order in favour of a party to a marriage (whether made under section 23 or under section 27 above).

(6) Where the person liable to make payments under a secured periodical payments order has died, an application under this section relating to that order (and to any order made under section 24A(1) above which requires the proceeds of sale of property to be used for securing those payments) may be made by the person entitled to payments under the periodical payments order or by the personal representatives of the deceased person, but no such application shall, except with the permission of the court, be made after the end of the period of six months from the date on which representation in regard to the estate of that person is first taken out.

(7) In exercising the powers conferred by this section the court shall have regard to all the circumstances of the case, first consideration being given to the welfare while a minor of any child of the family who has not attained the age of eighteen, and the circumstances of the case shall include any change in any of the matters to which the court was required to have regard when making the order to which the application relates, and –

(a) in the case of a periodical payments or secured periodical payments order made on or after the grant of a decree of divorce or nullity of marriage, the court shall consider whether in all the circumstances and after having regard to any such change it would be appropriate to

APPENDIX 2

vary the order so that payments under the order are required to be made or secured only for such further period as will in the opinion of the court be sufficient (in the light of any proposed exercise by the court, where the marriage has been dissolved, of its powers under subsection (7B) below) to enable the party in whose favour the order was made to adjust without undue hardship to the termination of those payments;

(b) in a case where the party against whom the order was made has died, the circumstances of the case shall also include the changed circumstances resulting from his or her death.

(7A) Subsection (7B) below applies where, after the dissolution of a marriage, the court –

(a) discharges a periodical payments order or secured periodical payments order made in favour of a party to the marriage; or
(b) varies such an order so that payments under the order are required to be made or secured only for such further period as is determined by the court.

(7B) The court has power, in addition to any power it has apart from this subsection, to make supplemental provision consisting of any of –

(a) an order for the payment of a lump sum in favour of a party to the marriage;
(b) one or more property adjustment orders in favour of a party to the marriage;
(ba) one or more pension sharing orders;
(c) a direction that the party in whose favour the original order discharged or varied was made is not entitled to make any further application for –

  (i) a periodical payments or secured periodical payments order, or
  (ii) an extension of the period to which the original order is limited by any variation made by the court.

(7C) An order for the payment of a lump sum made under subsection (7B) above may –

(a) provide for the payment of that sum by instalments of such amount as may be specified in the order; and
(b) require the payment of the instalments to be secured to the satisfaction of the court.

(7D) Section 23(6) above apply where the court makes an order for the payment of a lump sum under subsection (7B) above as they apply where it makes such an order under section 23 above.

(7E) If under subsection (7B) above the court makes more than one property adjustment order in favour of the same party to the marriage, each of those orders must fall within a different paragraph of section 21(2) above.

(7F) Sections 24A and 30 above apply where the court makes a property adjustment order under subsection (7B) above as they apply where it makes such an order under section 24 above.

(7G) Subsections (3) to (5) of section 24B above apply in relation to a pension sharing order under subsection (7B) above as they apply in relation to a pension sharing order under that section.

(8) The personal representatives of a deceased person against whom a secured periodical payments order was made shall not be liable for having distributed any part of the estate of the deceased after the expiration of the period of six months referred to in subsection (6) above on the ground that they ought to have taken into account the possibility that the court might permit an application under this section to be made after that period by the person entitled to payments under the order; but this subsection shall not prejudice any power to recover any part of the estate so distributed arising by virtue of the making of an order in pursuance of this section.

(9) In considering for the purposes of subsection (6) above the question when representation was first taken out, a grant limited to settled land or to trust property shall be left out of account and a grant limited to real estate or to personal estate shall be left out of account unless a grant limited to the remainder of the estate has previously been made or is made at the same time.

(10) Where the court, in exercise of its powers under this section, decides to vary or discharge a periodical payments or secured periodical payments order, then, subject to section 28(1) and (2) above, the court shall have power to direct that the variation or discharge shall not take effect until the expiration of such period as may be specified in the order.

(11) Where –

(a) a periodical payments or secured periodical payments order in favour of more than one child ('the order') is in force;

(b) the order requires payments specified in it to be made to or for the benefit of more than one child without apportioning those payments between them;

(c) a maintenance calculation ('the calculation') is made with respect to one or more, but not all, of the children with respect to whom those payments are to be made; and

(d) an application is made, before the end of the period of 6 months beginning with the date on which the calculation was made, for the variation or discharge of the order,

the court may, in exercise of its powers under this section to vary or discharge the order, direct that the variation or discharge shall take effect from the date on which the calculation took effect or any later date.

(12) Where –

(a) an order ('the child order') of a kind prescribed for the purposes of section 10(1) of the Child Support Act 1991 is affected by a maintenance calculation;

(b) on the date on which the child order became so affected there was in force a periodical payments or secured periodical payments order ('the spousal order') in favour of a party to a marriage having the care of the child in whose favour the child order was made; and

(c) an application is made, before the end of the period of 6 months beginning with the date on which the maintenance calculation was made, for the spousal order to be varied or discharged,

the court may, in exercise of its powers under this section to vary or discharge the spousal order, direct that the variation or discharge shall take effect from the date on which the child order became so affected or any later date.

APPENDIX 2

(13) For the purposes of subsection (12) above, an order is affected if it ceases to have effect or is modified by or under section 10 of the Child Support Act 1991.

(14) Subsections (11) and (12) above are without prejudice to any other power of the court to direct that the variation of discharge of an order under this section shall take effect from a date earlier than that on which the order for variation or discharge was made.

(15) The power to make regulations under subsection (4C) above shall be exercisable by statutory instrument which shall be subject to annulment in pursuance of a resolution of either House of Parliament.

[31A **Variation etc following reconciliations**[10]

(1) Where, at a time before the making of a divorce order –

    (a) an order ('a paragraph (a) order') for the payment of a lump sum has been made under section 22A above in favour of a party,

    (b) such an order has been made in favour of a child of the family but the payment has not yet been made, or

    (c) a property adjustment order ('a paragraph (c) order') has been made under section 23A above,

the court may, on an application made jointly by the parties to the marriage, vary or discharge the order.

(2) Where the court varies or discharges a paragraph (a) order, it may order the repayment of an amount equal to the whole or any part of the lump sum.

(3) Where the court varies or discharges a paragraph (c) order, it may (if the order has taken effect) –

    (a) order any person to whom property was transferred in pursuance of the paragraph (c) order to transfer –

        (i) the whole or any part of that property, or

        (ii) the whole or any part of any property appearing to the court to represent that property,

    in favour of a party to the marriage or a child of the family; or

    (b) vary any settlement to which the order relates in favour of any person or extinguish or reduce any person's interest under that settlement.

(4) Where the court acts under subsection (3) it may make such supplemental provision (including a further property adjustment order or an order for the payment of a lump sum) as it thinks appropriate in consequence of any transfer, variation, extinguishment or reduction to be made under paragraph (a) or (b) of that subsection.

(5) Sections 24A and 30 above apply for the purposes of this section as they apply where the court makes a property adjustment order under section 23A or 24 above.

(6) The court shall not make an order under subsection (2), (3) or (4) above unless it appears to it that there has been a reconciliation between the parties to the marriage.

(7) The court shall also not make an order under subsection (3) or (4) above unless it appears to it that the order will not prejudice the interests of –

    (a) any child of the family; or

    (b) any person who has acquired any right or interest in consequence of the paragraph (c) order and is not a party to the marriage or a child of the family.]

[31B Discharge of pension sharing orders on making of separation order[11]

Where, after the making of a pension sharing order under section 24B above in relation to a marriage, a separation order is made in relation to the marriage, the pension sharing order is discharged.]

32 Payment of certain arrears unenforceable without the leave of the court

(1) A person shall not be entitled to enforce through the High Court or any county court the payment of any arrears due under an order for maintenance pending suit, an interim order for maintenance or any financial provision order without the leave of that court if those arrears became due more than twelve months before proceedings to enforce the payment of them are begun.

(2) The court hearing an application for the grant of leave under this section may refuse leave, or may grant leave subject to such restrictions and conditions (including conditions as to the allowing of time for payment or the making of payment by instalments) as that court thinks proper, or may remit the payment of the arrears or of any part thereof.

(3) An application for the grant of leave under this section shall be made in such manner as may be prescribed by rules of court.

33 Orders for repayment in certain cases of sums paid under certain orders

(1) Where on an application made under this section in relation to an order to which this section applies it appears to the court that by reason of –

 (a) a change in the circumstances of the person entitled to, or liable to make, payments under the order since the order was made, or
 (b) the changed circumstances resulting from the death of the person so liable,

 the amount received by the person entitled to payments under the order in respect of a period after those circumstances changed or after the death of the person liable to make payments under the order, as the case may be, exceeds the amount which the person so liable or his or her personal representatives should have been required to pay, the court may order the respondent to the application to pay to the applicant such sum, not exceeding the amount of the excess, as the court thinks just.

(2) This section applies to the following orders, that is to say –

 (a) any order for maintenance pending suit and any interim order for maintenance;
 (b) any periodical payments order; and
 (c) any secured periodical payments order.

(3) An application under this section may be made by the person liable to make payments under an order to which this section applies or his or her personal representatives and may be made against the person entitled to payments under the order or her or his personal representatives.

(4) An application under this section may be made in proceedings in the High Court or a county court for –

 (a) the variation or discharge of the order to which this section applies, or
 (b) leave to enforce, or the enforcement of, the payment of arrears under that order;

APPENDIX 2

but when not made in such proceedings shall be made to a county court, and accordingly references in this section to the court are references to the High Court or a county court, as the circumstances require.

(5) The jurisdiction conferred on a county court by this section shall be exercisable notwithstanding that by reason of the amount claimed in the application the jurisdiction would not but for this subsection be exercisable by a county court.

(6) An order under this section for the payment of any sum may provide for the payment of that sum by instalments of such amount as may be specified in the order.

Consent orders

33A Consent orders for financial provision on property adjustment

(1) Notwithstanding anything in the preceding provisions of this Part of this Act, on an application for a consent order for financial relief the court may, unless it has reason to think that there are other circumstances into which it ought to inquire, make an order in the terms agreed on the basis only of the prescribed information furnished with the application.

(2) Subsection (1) above applies to an application for a consent order varying or discharging an order for financial relief as it applies to an application for an order for financial relief.

(3) In this section –

'consent order', in relation to an application for an order, means an order in the terms applied for to which the respondent agrees;

'order for financial relief' means an order under any of sections 23, 24, 24A, 24B or 27 above; and

'prescribed' means prescribed by rules of court.

Maintenance agreements

34 Validity of maintenance agreements

(1) If a maintenance agreement includes a provision purporting to restrict any right to apply to a court for an order containing financial arrangements, then –

  (a) that provision shall be void; but
  (b) any other financial arrangements contained in the agreement shall not thereby be rendered void or unenforceable and shall, unless they are void or unenforceable for any other reason (and subject to sections 35 and 36 below), be binding on the parties to the agreement.

(2) In this section and in section 35 below –

'maintenance agreement' means any agreement in writing made, whether before or after the commencement of this Act, between the parties to a marriage, being –

  (a) an agreement containing financial arrangements, whether made during the continuance or after the dissolution or annulment of the marriage; or
  (b) a separation agreement which contains no financial arrangements in a case where no other agreement in writing between the same parties contains such arrangements;

'financial arrangements' means provisions governing the rights and liabilities towards one another when living separately of the parties to a marriage (including a marriage which has been dissolved or annulled) in respect of the making or securing of payments or the disposition or use of any property, including such rights and liabilities with respect to the maintenance or education of any child, whether or not a child of the family.

35 Alteration of agreements by court during lives of parties

(1) Where a maintenance agreement is for the time being subsisting and each of the parties to the agreement is for the time being either domiciled or resident in England and Wales, then, subject to subsection (3) below, either party may apply to the court or to a magistrates' court for an order under this section.

(2) If the court to which the application is made is satisfied either –

(a) that by reason of a change in the circumstances in the light of which any financial arrangements contained in the agreement were made or, as the case may be, financial arrangements were omitted from it (including a change foreseen by the parties when making the agreement), the agreement should be altered so as to make different, or, as the case may be, so as to contain, financial arrangements, or

(b) that the agreement does not contain proper financial arrangements with respect to any child of the family,

then subject to subsections (3), (4) and (5) below, that court may by order make such alterations in the agreement –

(i) by varying or revoking any financial arrangements contained in it, or
(ii) by inserting in it financial arrangements for the benefit of one of the parties to the agreement or of a child of the family,

as may appear to that court to be just having regard to all the circumstances, including, if relevant, the matters mentioned in section 25(4) above; and the agreement shall have effect thereafter as if any alteration made by the order had been made by agreement between the parties and for valuable consideration.

(3) A magistrates' court shall not entertain an application under subsection (1) above unless both the parties to the agreement are resident in England and Wales and the court acts in, or is authorised by the Lord Chancellor to act for, a local justice area in which at least one of the parties is resident, and shall not have power to make any order on such an application except –

(a) in a case where the agreement includes no provision for periodical payments by either of the parties, an order inserting provision for the making by one of the parties of periodical payments for the maintenance of the other party or for the maintenance of any child of the family;

(b) in a case where the agreement includes provision for the making by one of the parties of periodical payments, an order increasing or reducing the rate of, or terminating, any of those payments.

(4) Where a court decides to alter, by order under this section, an agreement by inserting provision for the making or securing by one of the parties to the agreement of periodical payments for the maintenance of the other party or by increasing the rate of the periodical payments which the agreement provides shall be made by one of the parties for the maintenance of the other, the term for which the payments or, as the case may be, the additional

APPENDIX 2

payments attributable to the increase are to be made under the agreement as altered by the order shall be such term as the court may specify, subject to the following limits, that is to say –

(a) where the payments will not be secured, the term shall be so defined as not to extend beyond the death of either of the parties to the agreement or the remarriage of, or formation of a civil partnership by, the party to whom the payments are to be made;

(b) where the payments will be secured, the term shall be so defined as not to extend beyond the death or remarriage of, or formation of a civil partnership by, that party.

(5) Where a court decides to alter, by order under this section, an agreement by inserting provision for the making or securing by one of the parties to the agreement of periodical payments for the maintenance of a child of the family or by increasing the rate of the periodical payments which the agreement provides shall be made or secured by one of the parties for the maintenance of such a child, then, in deciding the term for which under the agreement as altered by the order the payments, or as the case may be, the additional payments attributable to the increase are to be made or secured for the benefit of the child, the court shall apply the provisions of section 29(2) and (3) above as to age limits as if the order in question were a periodical payments or secured periodical payments order in favour of the child.

(6) For the avoidance of doubt it is hereby declared that nothing in this section or in section 34 above affects any power of a court before which any proceedings between the parties to a maintenance agreement are brought under any other enactment (including a provision of this Act) to make an order containing financial arrangements or any right of either party to apply for such an order in such proceedings.

36 Alteration of agreements by court after death of one party

(1) Where a maintenance agreement within the meaning of section 34 above provides for the continuation of payments under the agreement after the death of one of the parties and that party dies domiciled in England and Wales, the surviving party or the personal representatives of the deceased party may, subject to subsections (2) and (3) below, apply to the High Court or a county court for an order under section 35 above.

(2) An application under this section shall not, except with the permission of the High Court or a county court, be made after the end of the period of six months from the date on which representation in regard to the estate of the deceased is first taken out.

(3) A county court shall not entertain an application under this section, or an application for permission to make an application under this section, unless it would have jurisdiction by virtue of section 22 of the Inheritance (Provision for Family and Dependants) Act 1975 (which confers jurisdiction on county courts in proceedings under that Act if the value of the property mentioned in that section does not exceed £5,000 or such larger sum as may be fixed by order of the Lord Chancellor) to hear and determine proceedings for an order under section 2 of that Act in relation to the deceased's estate.

(4) If a maintenance agreement is altered by a court on an application made in pursuance of subsection (1) above, the like consequences shall ensue as if the alteration had been made immediately before the death by agreement between the parties and for valuable consideration.

MATRIMONIAL CAUSES ACT 1973

(5) The provisions of this section shall not render the personal representatives of the deceased liable for having distributed any part of the estate of the deceased after the expiration of the period of six months referred to in subsection (2) above on the ground that they ought to have taken into account the possibility that a court might permit an application by virtue of this section to be made by the surviving party after that period; but this subsection shall not prejudice any power to recover any part of the estate so distributed arising by virtue of the making of an order in pursuance of this section.

(6) Section 31(9) above shall apply for the purposes of subsection (2) above as it applies for the purposes of subsection (6) of section 31.

(7) Subsection (3) of section 22 of the Inheritance (Provision for Family and Dependants) Act 1975 (which enables rules of court to provide for the transfer from a county court to the High Court or from the High Court to a county court of proceedings for an order under section 2 of that Act) and paragraphs (a) and (b) of subsection (4) of that section (provisions relating to proceedings commenced in county court before coming into force of order of the Lord Chancellor under that section) shall apply in relation to proceedings consisting of any such application as is referred to in subsection (3) above as they apply in relation to proceedings for an order under section 2 of that Act.

Miscellaneous and supplemental

37 Avoidance of transactions intended to prevent or reduce financial relief

(1) For the purposes of this section 'financial relief' means relief under any of the provisions of sections 22, 23, 24, 24B, 27, 31 (except subsection (6)) and 35 above, and any reference in this section to defeating a person's claim for financial relief is a reference to preventing financial relief from being granted to that person, or to that person for the benefit of a child of the family, or reducing the amount of any financial relief which might be so granted, or frustrating or impeding the enforcement of any order which might be or has been made at his instance under any of those provisions.

(2) Where proceedings for financial relief are brought by one person against another, the court may, on the application of the first-mentioned person –

(a) if it is satisfied that the other party to the proceedings is, with the intention of defeating the claim for financial relief, about to make any disposition or to transfer out of the jurisdiction or otherwise deal with any property, make such order as it thinks fit for restraining the other party from so doing or otherwise for protecting the claim;

(b) if it is satisfied that the other party has, with that intention, made a reviewable disposition and that if the disposition were set aside financial relief or different financial relief would be granted to the applicant, make an order setting aside the disposition;

(c) if it is satisfied, in a case where an order has been obtained under any of the provisions mentioned in subsection (1) above by the applicant against the other party, that the other party has, with that intention, made a reviewable disposition, make an order setting aside the disposition;

and an application for the purposes of paragraph (b) above shall be made in the proceedings for the financial relief in question.

(3) Where the court makes an order under subsection (2)(b) or (c) above setting aside a disposition it shall give such consequential directions as it thinks fit

for giving effect to the order (including directions requiring the making of any payments or the disposal of any property).

(4) Any disposition made by the other party to the proceedings for financial relief in question (whether before or after the commencement of those proceedings) is a reviewable disposition for the purposes of subsection (2)(b) and (c) above unless it was made for valuable consideration (other than marriage) to a person who, at the time of the disposition, acted in relation to it in good faith and without notice of any intention on the part of the other party to defeat the applicant's claim for financial relief.

(5) Where an application is made under this section with respect to a disposition which took place less than three years before the date of the application or with respect to a disposition or other dealing with property which is about to take place and the court is satisfied –

(a) in a case falling within subsection (2)(a) or (b) above, that the disposition or other dealing would (apart from this section) have the consequence, or

(b) in a case falling within subsection (2)(c) above, that the disposition has had the consequence,

of defeating the applicant's claim for financial relief, it shall be presumed, unless the contrary is shown, that the person who disposed of or is about to dispose of or deal with the property did so or, as the case may be, is about to do so, with the intention of defeating the applicant's claim for financial relief.

(6) In this section 'disposition' does not include any provision contained in a will or codicil but, with that exception, includes any conveyance, assurance or gift of property of any description, whether made by an instrument or otherwise.

(7) This section does not apply to a disposition made before 1st January 1968.

38 Orders for repayment in certain cases of sums paid after cessation of order by reason of remarriage or formation of civil partnership

(1) Where –

(a) a periodical payments or secured periodical payments order in favour of a party to a marriage (hereafter in this section referred to as 'a payments order') has ceased to have effect by reason of the remarriage of, or formation of a civil partnership by, that party, and

(b) the person liable to make payments under the order or his or her personal representatives made payments in accordance with it in respect of a period after the date of the remarriage or formation of the civil partnership in the mistaken belief that the order was still subsisting,

the person so liable or his or her personal representatives shall not be entitled to bring proceedings in respect of a cause of action arising out of the circumstances mentioned in paragraphs (a) and (b) above against the person entitled to payments under the order or her or his personal representatives, but may instead make an application against that person or her or his personal representatives under this section.

(2) On an application under this section the court may order the respondent to pay to the applicant a sum equal to the amount of the payments made in respect of the period mentioned in subsection (1)(b) above or, if it appears to the court that it would be unjust to make that order, it may either order the respondent to pay to the applicant such lesser sum as it thinks fit or dismiss the application.

(3) An application under this section may be made in proceedings in the High Court or a county court for leave to enforce, or the enforcement of, payment of arrears under the order in question, but when not made in such proceedings shall be made to a county court; and accordingly references in this section to the court are references to the High Court or a county court, as the circumstances require.

(4) The jurisdiction conferred on a county court by this section shall be exercisable notwithstanding that by reason of the amount claimed in the application the jurisdiction would not but for this subsection be exercisable by a county court.

(5) An order under this section for the payment of any sum may provide for the payment of that sum by instalments of such amount as may be specified in the order.

(6) The designated officer for a magistrates' court to whom any payments under a payments order are required to be made, and the collecting officer under an attachment of earnings order made to secure payments under a payments order, shall not be liable –

   (a) in the case of the designated officer, for any act done by him in pursuance of the payments order after the date on which that order ceased to have effect by reason of the remarriage of, or formation of a civil partnership by, the person entitled to payments under it, and
   (b) in the case of the collecting officer, for any act done by him after that date in accordance with any enactment or rule of court specifying how payments made to him in compliance with the attachment of earnings order are to be dealt with,

if, but only if, the act was one which he would have been under a duty to do had the payments order not so ceased to have effect and the act was done before notice in writing of the fact that the person so entitled had remarried or formed a civil partnership was given to him by or on behalf of that person, the person liable to make payments under the payments order or the personal representatives of either of those persons.

(7) In this section 'collecting officer', in relation to an attachment of earnings order, means the officer of the High Court, the registrar of a county court or the designated officer for a magistrates' court to whom a person makes payments in compliance with the order.

39 Settlement, etc, made in compliance with a property adjustment order may be avoided on bankruptcy of settlor

The fact that a settlement or transfer of property had to be made in order to comply with a property adjustment order shall not prevent that settlement or transfer from being a transaction in respect of which an order may be made under section 339 or 340 of the Insolvency Act 1986 (transfers at an undervalue and preferences).

40 Payments, etc, under order made in favour of person suffering from mental disorder

(1) Where the court makes an order under this Part of this Act requiring payments (including a lump sum payment) to be made, or property to be transferred, to a party to a marriage and the court is satisfied that the person in whose favour the order is made ('P') lacks capacity (within the meaning of the Mental Capacity Act 2005) in relation to the provisions of the order then, subject to any order, direction or authority made or given in relation to P under that Act, the court may order the payments to be made, or as the

APPENDIX 2

case may be, the property to be transferred, to such person ('D') as it may direct.

(2) In carrying out any functions of his in relation to an order made under subsection (1), D must act in P's best interests (within the meaning of that Act).

40A Appeals relating to pension sharing orders which have taken effect

(1) Subsections (2) and (3) below apply where an appeal against a pension sharing order is begun on or after the day on which the order takes effect.

(2) If the pension sharing order relates to a person's rights under a pension arrangement, the appeal court may not set aside or vary the order if the person responsible for the pension arrangement has acted to his detriment in reliance on the taking effect of the order.

(3) If the pension sharing order relates to a person's shareable state scheme rights, the appeal court may not set aside or vary the order if the Secretary of State has acted to his detriment in reliance on the taking effect of the order.

(4) In determining for the purposes of subsection (2) or (3) above whether a person has acted to his detriment in reliance on the taking effect of the order, the appeal court may disregard any detriment which in its opinion is insignificant.

(5) Where subsection (2) or (3) above applies, the appeal court may make such further orders (including one or more pension sharing orders) as it thinks fit for the purpose of putting the parties in the position it considers appropriate.

(6) Section 24C above only applies to a pension sharing order under this section if the decision of the appeal court can itself be the subject of an appeal.

(7) In subsection (2) above, the reference to the person responsible for the pension arrangement is to be read in accordance with section 25D(4) above.

NOTES

1. Section 22A prospectively inserted by the Family Law Act 1996, s.15, Sched.2, para.3.
2. Section 22B prospectively inserted by the Family Law Act 1996, s.15, Sched.2, para.3.
3. Section 23 prospectively substituted by the Family Law Act 1996, s.15, Sched.2, para.4.
4. Section 23A prospectively inserted by the Family Law Act 1996, s.15, Sched.2, para.5.
5. Section 23B prospectively inserted by the Family Law Act 1996, s.15, Sched.2, para.5.
6. Sections 24B–24BC prospectively substituted for s.24B by the Family Law Act 1996, s.15, Sched.2, para.6A.
7. Sections 24B–24BC prospectively substituted for s.24B by the Family Law Act 1996, s.15, Sched.2, para.6A.
8. Sections 24B–24BC prospectively substituted for s.24B by the Family Law Act 1996, s.15, Sched.2, para.6A.
9. Sections 24B–24BC prospectively substituted for s.24B by the Family Law Act 1996, s.15, Sched.2, para.6A.
10. Section 31A prospectively inserted by the Family Law Act 1996, s.15, Sched.2, para.8.
11. Section 31B prospectively inserted by the Family Law Act 1996, s.66(1), Sched.8, para.16A.

APPENDIX 3

Matrimonial and Family Proceedings Act 1984, Part III

PART III FINANCIAL RELIEF IN ENGLAND AND WALES AFTER OVERSEAS DIVORCE ETC

Applications for financial relief

12 Applications for financial relief after overseas divorce etc

(1) Where –
   (a) a marriage has been dissolved or annulled, or the parties to a marriage have been legally separated, by means of judicial or other proceedings in an overseas country, and
   (b) the divorce, annulment or legal separation is entitled to be recognised as valid in England and Wales,

   either party to the marriage may apply to the court in the manner prescribed by rules of court for an order for financial relief under this Part of this Act.

(2) If after a marriage has been dissolved or annulled in an overseas country one of the parties to the marriage forms a subsequent marriage or civil partnership, that party shall not be entitled to make an application in relation to that marriage.

(3) The reference in subsection (2) above to the forming of a subsequent marriage or civil partnership includes a reference to the forming of a marriage or civil partnership which is by law void or voidable.

(4) In this Part of this Act except sections 19, 23, and 24 'order for financial relief' means an order under section 17 or 22 below of a description referred to in that section.

13 Leave of the court required for applications for financial relief

(1) No application for an order for financial relief shall be made under this Part of this Act unless the leave of the court has been obtained in accordance with rules of court; and the court shall not grant leave unless it considers that there is substantial ground for the making of an application for such an order.

(2) The court may grant leave under this section notwithstanding that an order has been made by a court in a country outside England and Wales requiring the other party to the marriage to make any payment or transfer any property to the applicant or a child of the family.

(3) Leave under this section may be granted subject to such conditions as the court thinks fit.

APPENDIX 3

14 Interim orders for maintenance

(1) Where leave is granted under section 13 above for the making of an application for an order for financial relief and it appears to the court that the applicant or any child of the family is in immediate need of financial assistance, the court may make an interim order for maintenance, that is to say, an order requiring the other party to the marriage to make to the applicant or to the child such periodical payments, and for such term, being a term beginning not earlier than the date of the grant of leave and ending with the date of the determination of the application for an order for financial relief, as the court thinks reasonable.

(2) If it appears to the court that the court has jurisdiction to entertain the application for an order for financial relief by reason only of paragraph (c) of section 15(1) below the court shall not make an interim order under this section.

(3) An interim order under subsection (1) above may be made subject to such conditions as the court thinks fit.

15 Jurisdiction of the court

(1) Subject to subsection (2) below, the court shall have jurisdiction to entertain an application for an order for financial relief if any of the following jurisdictional requirements are satisfied, that is to say –

(a) either of the parties to the marriage was domiciled in England and Wales on the date of the application for leave under section 13 above or was so domiciled on the date on which the divorce, annulment or legal separation obtained in the overseas country took effect in that country; or

(b) either of the parties to the marriage was habitually resident in England and Wales throughout the period of one year ending with the date of the application for leave or was so resident throughout the period of one year ending with the date on which the divorce, annulment or legal separation obtained in the overseas country took effect in that country; or

(c) either or both of the parties to the marriage had at the date of the application for leave a beneficial interest in possession in a dwelling-house situated in England or Wales which was at some time during the marriage a matrimonial home of the parties to the marriage.

(2) Where the jurisdiction of the court to entertain proceedings under this Part of this Act would fall to be determined by reference to the jurisdictional requirements imposed by virtue of Part I of the Civil Jurisdiction and Judgments Act 1982 (implementation of certain European conventions) or by virtue of Council Regulation (EC) No 44/2001 of 22nd December 2000 on jurisdiction and the recognition and enforcement of judgments in civil and commercial matters, as amended from time to time and as applied by the Agreement made on 19th October 2005 between the European Community and the Kingdom of Denmark on jurisdiction and the recognition and enforcement of judgments in civil and commercial matters (OJ No L 299 16.11.2005 at p 62) then –

(a) satisfaction of the requirements of subsection (1) above shall not obviate the need to satisfy the requirements imposed by virtue of that Regulation or Part I of that Act; and

(b) satisfaction of the requirements imposed by virtue of that Regulation or Part I of that Act shall obviate the need to satisfy the requirements of subsection (1) above;

and the court shall entertain or not entertain the proceedings accordingly.

MATRIMONIAL AND FAMILY PROCEEDINGS ACT 1984

16 Duty of the court to consider whether England and Wales is appropriate venue for application

(1) Before making an order for financial relief the court shall consider whether in all the circumstances of the case it would be appropriate for such an order to be made by a court in England and Wales, and if the court is not satisfied that it would be appropriate, the court shall dismiss the application.

(2) The court shall in particular have regard to the following matters –

(a) the connection which the parties to the marriage have with England and Wales;

(b) the connection which those parties have with the country in which the marriage was dissolved or annulled or in which they were legally separated;

(c) the connection which those parties have with any other country outside England and Wales;

(d) any financial benefit which the applicant or a child of the family has received, or is likely to receive, in consequence of the divorce, annulment or legal separation, by virtue of any agreement or the operation of the law of a country outside England and Wales;

(e) in a case where an order has been made by a court in a country outside England and Wales requiring the other party to the marriage to make any payment or transfer any property for the benefit of the applicant or a child of the family, the financial relief given by the order and the extent to which the order has been complied with or is likely to be complied with;

(f) any right which the applicant has, or has had, to apply for financial relief from the other party to the marriage under the law of any country outside England and Wales and if the applicant has omitted to exercise that right the reason for that omission;

(g) the availability in England and Wales of any property in respect of which an order under this Part of this Act in favour of the applicant could be made;

(h) the extent to which any order made under this Part of this Act is likely to be enforceable;

(i) the length of time which has elapsed since the date of the divorce, annulment or legal separation.

Orders for financial provision and property adjustment

17 Orders for financial provision and property adjustment

(1) Subject to section 20 below, on an application by a party to a marriage for an order for financial relief under this section, the court may –

(a) make any one or more of the orders which it could make under Part II of the 1973 Act if a decree of divorce, a decree of nullity of marriage or a decree of judicial separation in respect of the marriage had been granted in England and Wales, that is to say –

(i) any order mentioned in section 23(1) of the 1973 Act (financial provision orders); and

(ii) any order mentioned in section 24(1) of that Act (property adjustment orders);

APPENDIX 3

  (b) if the marriage has been dissolved or annulled, make one or more orders each of which would, within the meaning of that Part of that Act, be a pension sharing order in relation to the marriage;

(2) Subject to section 20 below, where the court makes a secured periodical payments order, an order for the payment of a lump sum or a property adjustment order under subsection (1) above, then, on making that order or at any time thereafter, the court may make any order mentioned in section 24A(1) of the 1973 Act (orders for sale of property) which the court would have power to make if the order under subsection (1) above had been made under Part II of the 1973 Act.

18 Matters to which the court is to have regard in exercising its powers under s 17

(1) In deciding whether to exercise its powers under section 17 above and, if so, in what manner the court shall act in accordance with this section.

(2) The court shall have regard to all the circumstances of the case, first consideration being given to the welfare while a minor of any child of the family who has not attained the age of eighteen.

(3) As regards the exercise of those powers in relation to a party to the marriage, the court shall in particular have regard to the matters mentioned in section 25(2)(a) to (h) of the 1973 Act and shall be under duties corresponding with those imposed by section 25A(1) and (2) of the 1973 Act where it decides to exercise under section 17 above powers corresponding with the powers referred to in those subsections.

(3A) The matters to which the court is to have regard under subsection (3) above –

  (a) so far as relating to paragraph (a) of section 25(2) of the 1973 Act, include any benefits under a pension arrangement which a party to the marriage has or is likely to have and any PPF compensation to which a party to the marriage is or is likely to be entitled, (whether or not in the foreseeable future), and

  (b) so far as relating to paragraph (h) of that provision, include –

   (i) any benefits under a pension arrangement which, by reason of the dissolution or annulment of the marriage, a party to the marriage will lose the chance of acquiring, and

   (ii) any PPF compensation which, by reason of the dissolution or annulment of the marriage, a party to the marriage will lose the chance of acquiring entitlement to.

(4) As regards the exercise of those powers in relation to a child of the family, the court shall in particular have regard to the matters mentioned in section 25(3)(a) to (e) of the 1973 Act.

(5) As regards the exercise of those powers against a party to the marriage in favour of a child of the family who is not the child of that party, the court shall also have regard to the matters mentioned in section 25(4)(a) to (c) of the 1973 Act.

(6) Where an order has been made by a court outside England and Wales for the making of payments or the transfer of property by a party to the marriage, the court in considering in accordance with this section the financial resources of the other party to the marriage or a child of the family shall have regard to the extent to which that order has been complied with or is likely to be complied with.

(7) In this section –

(a) 'pension arrangement' has the meaning given by section 25D(3) of the 1973 Act, and
(b) references to benefits under a pension arrangement include any benefits by way of pension, whether under a pension arrangement or not, and
(c) 'PPF compensation' means compensation payable under Chapter 3 of Part 2 of the Pensions Act 2004 (pension protection) or any provision in force in Northern Ireland corresponding to that Chapter.

19 Consent orders for financial provision or property adjustment

(1) Notwithstanding anything in section 18 above, on an application for a consent order for financial relief the court may, unless it has reason to think that there are other circumstances into which it ought to inquire, make an order in the terms agreed on the basis only of the prescribed information furnished with the application.
(2) Subsection (1) above applies to an application for a consent order varying or discharging an order for financial relief as it applies to an application for an order for financial relief.
(3) In this section –

'consent order', in relation to an application for an order, means an order in the terms applied for to which the respondent agrees;

'order for financial relief' means an order under section 17 above; and

'prescribed' means prescribed by rules of court.

20 Restriction of powers of court where jurisdiction depends on matrimonial home in England or Wales

(1) Where the court has jurisdiction to entertain an application for an order for financial relief by reason only of the situation in England or Wales of a dwelling-house which was a matrimonial home of the parties, the court may make under section 17 above any one or more of the following orders (but no other) –

(a) an order that either party to the marriage shall pay to the other such lump sum as may be specified in the order;
(b) an order that a party to the marriage shall pay to such person as may be so specified for the benefit of a child of the family, or to such a child, such lump sum as may be so specified;
(c) an order that a party to the marriage shall transfer to the other party, to any child of the family or to such person as may be so specified for the benefit of such a child, the interest of the first-mentioned party in the dwelling-house, or such part of that interest as may be so specified;
(d) an order that a settlement of the interest of a party to the marriage in the dwelling-house, or such part of that interest as may be so specified, be made to the satisfaction of the court for the benefit of the other party to the marriage and of the children of the family or either or any of them;
(e) an order varying for the benefit of the parties to the marriage and of the children of the family or either or any of them any ante-nuptial or post-nuptial settlement (including such a settlement made by will or codicil) made on the parties to the marriage so far as that settlement relates to an interest in the dwelling-house;
(f) an order extinguishing or reducing the interest of either of the parties to the marriage under any such settlement so far as that interest is an interest in the dwelling-house;

APPENDIX 3

(g) an order for the sale of the interest of a party to the marriage in the dwelling-house.

(2) Where, in the circumstances mentioned in subsection (1) above, the court makes an order for the payment of a lump sum by a party to the marriage, the amount of the lump sum shall not exceed, or where more than one such order is made the total amount of the lump sums shall not exceed in aggregate, the following amount, that is to say –

(a) if the interest of that party in the dwelling-house is sold in pursuance of an order made under subsection (1)(g) above, the amount of the proceeds of the sale of that interest after deducting therefrom any costs incurred in the sale thereof;

(b) if the interest of that party is not so sold, the amount which in the opinion of the court represents the value of that interest.

(3) Where the interest of a party to the marriage in the dwelling-house is held jointly or in common with any other person or persons –

(a) the reference in subsection (1)(g) above to the interest of a party to the marriage shall be construed as including a reference to the interest of that other person, or the interest of those other persons, in the dwelling-house, and

(b) the reference in subsection (2)(a) above to the amount of the proceeds of a sale ordered under subsection (1)(g) above shall be construed as a reference to that part of those proceeds which is attributable to the interest of that party to the marriage in the dwelling-house.

21 Application to orders under ss 14 and 17 of certain provisions of Part II of Matrimonial Causes Act 1973

(1) The following provisions of Part II of the 1973 Act (financial relief for parties to marriage and children of family) shall apply in relation to an order under section 14 or 17 above as they apply in relation to a like order under that Part of that Act, that is to say –

(a) section 23(3) (provisions as to lump sums);
(b) section 24A(2), (4), (5) and (6) (provisions as to orders for sale);
(ba) section 24B(3) to (5) (provisions about pension sharing orders in relation to divorce and nullity);
(bb) section 24C (duty to stay pension sharing orders);
(bc) section 24D (apportionment of pension sharing charges);
(bd) section 25B(3) to (7B) (power, by financial provision order, to attach payments under a pension arrangement, or to require the exercise of a right of commutation under such an arrangement);
(be) section 25C (extension of lump sum powers in relation to death benefits under a pension arrangement);
(bf) section 25E(2) to (10) (the Pension Protection Fund);
(c) section 28(1) and (2) (duration of continuing financial provision orders in favour of party to marriage);
(d) section 29 (duration of continuing financial provision orders in favour of children, and age limit on making certain orders in their favour);
(e) section 30 (direction for settlement of instrument for securing payments or effecting property adjustment), except paragraph (b);

(f) section 31 variation, discharge etc of certain orders for financial relief), except subsection (2)(e) and subsection (4);
(g) section 32 (payment of certain arrears unenforceable without the leave of the court);
(h) section 33 (orders for repayment of sums paid under certain orders);
(i) section 38 (orders for repayment of sums paid after cessation of order by reason of remarriage);
(j) section 39 (settlements etc made in compliance with a property adjustment order may be avoided on bankruptcy of settlor); and
(k) section 40 (payments etc under order made in favour of person suffering from mental disorder);
(l) section 40A (appeals relating to pension sharing orders which have taken effect).

(2) Subsection (1)(bd) and (be) above shall not apply where the court has jurisdiction to entertain an application for an order for financial relief by reason only of the situation in England or Wales of a dwelling-house which was a matrimonial home of the parties.

(3) Section 25D(1) of the 1973 Act (effect of transfers on orders relating to rights under a pension arrangement) shall apply in relation to an order made under section 17 above by virtue of subsection (1)(bd) or (be) above as it applies in relation to an order made under section 23 of that Act by virtue of section 25B or 25C of the 1973 Act.

(4) The Lord Chancellor may by regulations make for the purposes of this Part of this Act provision corresponding to any provision which may be made by him under subsections (2) to (2B) of section 25D of the 1973 Act.

(5) Power to make regulations under this section shall be exercisable by statutory instrument which shall be subject to annulment in pursuance of a resolution of either House of Parliament.

Orders for transfer of tenancies

22 Powers of court in relation to certain tenancies of dwelling-houses

(1) This section applies if –

(a) an application is made by a party to a marriage for an order for financial relief; and
(b) one of the parties is entitled, either in his own right or jointly with the other party, to occupy a dwelling-house situated in England or Wales by virtue of a tenancy which is a relevant tenancy within the meaning of Schedule 7 to the Family Law Act 1996 (certain statutory tenancies).

(2) The court may make in relation to that dwelling-house any order which it could make under Part II of that Schedule if –

(a) a divorce order,
(b) a separation order, or
(c) a decree of nullity of marriage,

had been made or granted in England and Wales in respect of the marriage.

(3) The provisions of paragraphs 10, 11 and 14(1) in Part III of that Schedule apply in relation to any order under this section as they apply to any order under Part II of that Schedule.

APPENDIX 3

Avoidance of transactions intended to prevent or reduce financial relief

23 Avoidance of transactions intended to defeat applications for financial relief

(1) For the purposes of this section 'financial relief' means relief under section 14 or 17 above and any reference to defeating a claim by a party to a marriage for financial relief is a reference to preventing financial relief from being granted or reducing the amount of relief which might be granted, or frustrating or impeding the enforcement of any order which might be or has been made under either of those provisions at the instance of that party.

(2) Where leave is granted under section 13 above for the making by a party to a marriage of an application for an order for financial relief under section 17 above, the court may, on an application by that party –

　(a) if it is satisfied that the other party to the marriage is, with the intention of defeating the claim for financial relief, about to make any disposition or to transfer out of the jurisdiction or otherwise deal with any property, make such order as it thinks fit for restraining the other party from so doing or otherwise for protecting the claim;

　(b) if it is satisfied that the other party has, with that intention, made a reviewable disposition and that if the disposition were set aside financial relief or different financial relief would be granted to the applicant, make an order setting aside the disposition.

(3) Where an order for financial relief under section 14 or 17 above has been made by the court at the instance of a party to a marriage, then, on an application made by that party, the court may, if it is satisfied that the other party to the marriage has, with the intention of defeating the claim for financial relief, made a reviewable disposition, make an order setting aside the disposition.

(4) Where the court has jurisdiction to entertain the application for an order for financial relief by reason only of paragraph (c) of section 15(1) above, it shall not make any order under subsection (2) or (3) above in respect of any property other than the dwelling-house concerned.

(5) Where the court makes an order under subsection (2)(b) or (3) above setting aside a disposition it shall give such consequential directions as it thinks fit for giving effect to the order (including directions requiring the making of any payments or the disposal of any property).

(6) Any disposition made by the other party to the marriage (whether before or after the commencement of the application) is a reviewable disposition for the purposes of subsections (2)(b) and (3) above unless it was made for valuable consideration (other than marriage) to a person who, at the time of the disposition, acted in relation to it in good faith and without notice of any intention on the part of the other party to defeat the applicant's claim for financial relief.

(7) Where an application is made under subsection (2) or (3) above with respect to a disposition which took place less than three years before the date of the application or with respect to a disposition or other dealing with property which is about to take place and the court is satisfied –

　(a) in a case falling within subsection(2)(a) or (b) above, that the disposition or other dealing would (apart from this section) have the consequence, or

　(b) in a case falling within subsection (3) above, that the disposition has had the consequence,

MATRIMONIAL AND FAMILY PROCEEDINGS ACT 1984

of defeating a claim by the applicant for financial relief, it shall be presumed, unless the contrary is shown, that the person who disposed of or is about to dispose of or deal with the property did so or, as the case may be, is about to do so, with the intention of defeating the applicant's claim for financial relief.

(8) In this section 'disposition' does not include any provision contained in a will or codicil but, with that exception, includes any conveyance, assurance or gift of property of any description, whether made by an instrument or otherwise.

(9) The preceding provisions of this section are without prejudice to any power of the High Court to grant injunctions under section 37 of the Senior Courts Act 1981.

24 Prevention of transactions intended to defeat prospective applications for financial relief

(1) Where, on an application by a party to a marriage, it appears to the court –

   (a) that the marriage has been dissolved or annulled, or that the parties to the marriage have been legally separated, by means of judicial or other proceedings in an overseas country; and

   (b) that the applicant intends to apply for leave to make an application for an order for financial relief under section 17 above as soon as he or she has been habitually resident in England and Wales for a period of one year; and

   (c) that the other party to the marriage is, with the intention of defeating a claim for financial relief, about to make any disposition or to transfer out of the jurisdiction or otherwise deal with any property,

the court may make such order as it thinks fit for restraining the other party from taking such action as is mentioned in paragraph (c) above.

(2) For the purposes of an application under subsection (1) above –

   (a) the reference to defeating a claim for financial relief shall be construed in accordance with subsection (1) of section 23 above (omitting the reference to any order which has been made); and

   (b) subsections (7) and (8) of section 23 above shall apply for the purposes of an application under that section.

(3) The preceding provisions of this section are without prejudice to any power of the High Court to grant injunctions under section 37 of the Senior Courts Act 1981.

Financial provision out of estate of deceased party to marriage

25 Extension of powers under Inheritance (Provision for Family and Dependants) Act 1975 in respect of former spouses

(1) The Inheritance (Provision for Family and Dependants) Act 1975 shall have effect with the following amendments, being amendments designed to give to persons whose marriages are dissolved or annulled overseas the same rights to apply for provision under that Act (as amended by section 8 of this Act) as persons whose marriages are dissolved or annulled under the 1973 Act.

(2) In section 25(1), for the definition of 'former wife' and 'former husband' there shall be substituted the following definition –

APPENDIX 3

'"former wife" or "former husband" means a person whose marriage with the deceased was during the lifetime of the deceased either –

(a) dissolved or annulled by a decree of divorce or a decree of nullity of marriage granted under the law of any part of the British Islands, or
(b) dissolved or annulled in any country or territory outside the British Islands by a divorce or annulment which is entitled to be recognised as valid by the law of England and Wales;'.

(3) After section 15 (restriction in divorce proceedings etc. of applications under the Act) there shall be inserted the following section –

'15A Restriction imposed in proceedings under Matrimonial and Family Proceedings Act 1984 on application under this Act

(1) On making an order under section 17 of the Matrimonial and Family Proceedings Act 1984 (orders for financial provision and property adjustment following overseas divorces, etc.) the court, if it considers it just to do so, may, on the application of either party to the marriage, order that the other party to the marriage shall not on the death of the applicant be entitled to apply for an order under section 2 of this Act.

In this subsection "the court" means the High Court or, where a county court has jurisdiction by virtue of Part V of the Matrimonial and Family Proceedings Act 1984, a county court.

(2) Where an order under subsection (1) above has been made with respect to a party to a marriage which has been dissolved or annulled, then, on the death of the other party to that marriage, the court shall not entertain an application under section 2 of this Act made by the first-mentioned party.

(3) Where an order under subsection (1) above has been made with respect to a party to a marriage the parties to which have been legally separated, then, if the other party to the marriage dies while the legal separation is in force, the court shall not entertain an application under section 2 of this Act made by the first-mentioned party.'

26 ...

Interpretation

27 Interpretation of Part III

In this Part of this Act –

'the 1973 Act' means the Matrimonial Causes Act 1973;

'child of the family' has the meaning as in section 52(1) of the 1973 Act;

'the court' means the High Court or, where a county court has jurisdiction by virtue of Part V of this Act, a county court;

'dwelling-house' includes any building or part thereof which is occupied as a dwelling, and any yard, garden, garage or outhouse belonging to the dwelling-house and occupied therewith;

'order for financial relief' has the meaning given by section 12(4) above;

'overseas country' means a country or territory outside the British Islands;

'possession' includes receipt of, or the right to receive, rents and profits;

'property adjustment order' means such an order as is specified in section 24(1)(a), (b), (c) or (d) of the 1973 Act;

'rent' does not include mortgage interest;

'secured periodical payments order' means such an order as is specified in section 23(1)(b) or (e) of the 1973 Act.

APPENDIX 4

Children Act 1989, extracts

PART II ORDERS WITH RESPECT TO CHILDREN IN FAMILY PROCEEDINGS

[. . .]

Financial relief

15 Orders for financial relief with respect to children

(1) Schedule 1 (which consists primarily of the re-enactment, with consequential amendments and minor modifications, of provisions of section 6 of the Family Law Reform Act 1969 the Guardianship of Minors Acts 1971 and 1973, the Children Act 1975 and of sections 15 and 16 of the Family Law Reform Act 1987) makes provision in relation to financial relief for children.

(2) The powers of a magistrates' court under section 60 of the Magistrates' Courts Act 1980 to revoke, revive or vary an order for the periodical payment of money and the power of the clerk of a magistrates' court to vary such an order shall not apply in relation to an order made under Schedule 1.

[. . .]

SCHEDULE 1 FINANCIAL PROVISION FOR CHILDREN

Section 15(1)

Orders for financial relief against parents

1 (1) On an application made by a parent, guardian or special guardian of a child, or by any person in whose favour a residence order is in force with respect to a child, the court may –

    (a) in the case of an application to the High Court or a county court, make one or more of the orders mentioned in sub-paragraph (2);

    (b) in the case of an application to a magistrates' court, make one or both of the orders mentioned in paragraphs (a) and (c) of that sub-paragraph.

(2) The orders referred to in sub-paragraph (1) are –

CHILDREN ACT 1989

    (a) an order requiring either or both parents of a child –

        (i) to make to the applicant for the benefit of the child; or
        (ii) to make to the child himself,

    such periodical payments, for such term, as may be specified in the order;

    (b) an order requiring either or both parents of a child –

        (i) to secure to the applicant for the benefit of the child; or
        (ii) to secure to the child himself,

    such periodical payments, for such term, as may be so specified;

    (c) an order requiring either or both parents of a child –

        (i) to pay to the applicant for the benefit of the child; or
        (ii) to pay to the child himself,

    such lump sum as may be so specified;

    (d) an order requiring a settlement to be made for the benefit of the child, and to the satisfaction of the court, of property –

        (i) to which either parent is entitled (either in possession or in reversion); and
        (ii) which is specified in the order;

    (e) an order requiring either or both parents of a child –

        (i) to transfer to the applicant, for the benefit of the child; or
        (ii) to transfer to the child himself,

    such property to which the parent is, or the parents are, entitled (either in possession or in reversion) as may be specified in the order.

(3) The powers conferred by this paragraph may be exercised at any time.

(4) An order under sub-paragraph (2)(a) or (b) may be varied or discharged by a subsequent order made on the application of any person by or to whom payments were required to be made under the previous order.

(5) Where a court makes an order under this paragraph –

    (a) it may at any time make a further such order under sub-paragraph (2)(a), (b) or (c) with respect to the child concerned if he has not reached the age of eighteen;

    (b) it may not make more than one order under sub-paragraph (2)(d) or (e) against the same person in respect of the same child.

(6) On making, varying or discharging a residence order or a special guardianship order the court may exercise any of its powers under this Schedule even though no application has been made to it under this Schedule.

(7) Where a child is a ward of court, the court may exercise any of its powers under this Schedule even though no application has been made to it.

Orders for financial relief for persons over eighteen

2   (1) If, on an application by a person who has reached the age of eighteen, it appears to the court –

    (a) that the applicant is, will be or (if an order were made under this paragraph) would be receiving instruction at an educational

APPENDIX 4

establishment or undergoing training for a trade, profession or vocation, whether or not while in gainful employment; or

(b) that there are special circumstances which justify the making of an order under this paragraph,

the court may make one or both of the orders mentioned in sub-paragraph (2).

(2) The orders are –

(a) an order requiring either or both of the applicant's parents to pay to the applicant such periodical payments, for such term, as may be specified in the order;

(b) an order requiring either or both of the applicant's parents to pay to the applicant such lump sum as may be so specified.

(3) An application may not be made under this paragraph by any person if, immediately before he reached the age of sixteen, a periodical payments order was in force with respect to him.

(4) No order shall be made under this paragraph at a time when the parents of the applicant are living with each other in the same household.

(5) An order under sub-paragraph (2)(a) may be varied or discharged by a subsequent order made on the application of any person by or to whom payments were required to be made under the previous order.

(6) In sub-paragraph (3) 'periodical payments order' means an order made under –

(a) this Schedule;
(b) . . .
(c) section 23 or 27 of the Matrimonial Causes Act 1973;
(d) Part I of the Domestic Proceedings and Magistrates' Courts Act 1978;
(e) Part 1 or 9 of Schedule 5 to the Civil Partnership Act 2004 (financial relief in the High Court or a county court etc);
(f) Schedule 6 to the 2004 Act (financial relief in the magistrates' courts etc),

for the making or securing of periodical payments.

(7) The powers conferred by this paragraph shall be exercisable at any time.

(8) Where the court makes an order under this paragraph it may from time to time while that order remains in force make a further such order.

Duration of orders for financial relief

3 (1) The term to be specified in an order for periodical payments made under paragraph 1(2)(a) or (b) in favour of a child may begin with the date of the making of an application for the order in question or any later date or a date ascertained in accordance with sub-paragraph (5) or (6) but –

(a) shall not in the first instance extend beyond the child's seventeenth birthday unless the court thinks it right in the circumstances of the case to specify a later date; and

(b) shall not in any event extend beyond the child's eighteenth birthday.

(2) Paragraph (b) of sub-paragraph (1) shall not apply in the case of a child if it appears to the court that –

CHILDREN ACT 1989

(a) the child is, or will be or (if an order were made without complying with that paragraph) would be receiving instruction at an educational establishment or undergoing training for a trade, profession or vocation, whether or not while in gainful employment; or
(b) there are special circumstances which justify the making of an order without complying with that paragraph.

(3) An order for periodical payments made under paragraph 1(2)(a) or 2(2)(a) shall, notwithstanding anything in the order, cease to have effect on the death of the person liable to make payments under the order.

(4) Where an order is made under paragraph 1(2)(a) or (b) requiring periodical payments to be made or secured to the parent of a child, the order shall cease to have effect if –

(a) any parent making or securing the payments; and
(b) any parent to whom the payments are made or secured,

live together for a period of more than six months.

(5) Where –

(a) a maintenance calculation ('the current calculation') is in force with respect to a child; and
(b) an application is made for an order under paragraph 1(2)(a) or (b) of this Schedule for periodical payments in favour of that child –

(i) in accordance with section 8 of the Child Support Act 1991; and
(ii) before the end of the period of 6 months beginning with the making of the current calculation,

the term to be specified in any such order made on that application may be expressed to begin on, or at any time after, the earliest permitted date.

(6) For the purposes of subsection (5) above, 'the earliest permitted date' is whichever is the later of –

(a) the date 6 months before the application is made; or
(b) the date on which the current calculation took effect or, where successive maintenance calculations have been continuously in force with respect to a child, on which the first of those calculations took effect.

(7) Where –

(a) a maintenance calculation ceases to have effect by or under any provision of the Child Support Act 1991, and
(b) an application is made, before the end of the period of 6 months beginning with the relevant date, for an order for periodical payments under paragraph 1(2)(a) or (b) in favour of a child with respect to whom that maintenance calculation was in force immediately before it ceased to have effect,

the term to be specified in any such order, or in any interim order under paragraph 9, made on that application may begin with the date on which that maintenance calculation ceased to have effect, or any later date.

(8) In sub-paragraph (7)(b) –

(a) where the maintenance calculation ceased to have effect, the relevant date is the date on which it so ceased.

221

APPENDIX 4

Matters to which court is to have regard in making orders for financial relief

4   (1)   In deciding whether to exercise its powers under paragraph 1 or 2, and if so in what manner, the court shall have regard to all the circumstances including –

   (a)   the income, earning capacity, property and other financial resources which each person mentioned in sub-paragraph (4) has or is likely to have in the foreseeable future;
   (b)   the financial needs, obligations and responsibilities which each person mentioned in sub-paragraph (4) has or is likely to have in the foreseeable future;
   (c)   the financial needs of the child;
   (d)   the income, earning capacity (if any), property and other financial resources of the child;
   (e)   any physical or mental disability of the child;
   (f)   the manner in which the child was being, or was expected to be, educated or trained.

   (2)   In deciding whether to exercise its powers under paragraph 1 against a person who is not the mother or father of the child, and if so in what manner, the court shall in addition have regard to –

   (a)   whether that person has assumed responsibility for the maintenance of the child and, if so, the extent to which and basis on which he assumed that responsibility and the length of the period during which he met that responsibility;
   (b)   whether he did so knowing that the child was not his child;
   (c)   the liability of any other person to maintain the child.

   (3)   Where the court makes an order under paragraph 1 against a person who is not the father of the child, it shall record in the order that the order is made on the basis that the person against whom the order is made is not the child's father.

   (4)   The persons mentioned in sub-paragraph (1) are –

   (a)   in relation to a decision whether to exercise its powers under paragraph 1, any parent of the child;
   (b)   in relation to a decision whether to exercise its powers under paragraph 2, the mother and father of the child;
   (c)   the applicant for the order;
   (d)   any other person in whose favour the court proposes to make the order.

   (5)   In the case of a child who has a parent by virtue of section 42 or 43 of the Human Fertilisation and Embryology Act 2008, any reference in sub-paragraph (2), (3) or (4) to the child's father is a reference to the woman who is a parent of the child by virtue of that section.

Provisions relating to lump sums

5   (1)   Without prejudice to the generality of paragraph 1, an order under that paragraph for the payment of a lump sum may be made for the purpose of enabling any liabilities or expenses –

(a) incurred in connection with the birth of the child or in maintaining the child; and
(b) reasonably incurred before the making of the order,

to be met.
(2) The amount of any lump sum required to be paid by an order made by a magistrates' court under paragraph 1 or 2 shall not exceed £1000 or such larger amount as the Lord Chancellor may, after consulting the Lord Chief Justice, from time to time by order fix for the purposes of this sub-paragraph.
(3) The power of the court under paragraph 1 or 2 to vary or discharge an order for the making or securing of periodical payments by a parent shall include power to make an order under that provision for the payment of a lump sum by that parent.
(4) The amount of any lump sum which a person may be required to pay by virtue of sub-paragraph (3) shall not, in the case of an order made by a magistrates' court, exceed the maximum amount that may at the time of the making of the order be required to be paid under sub-paragraph (2), but a magistrates' court may make an order for the payment of a lump sum not exceeding that amount even though the parent was required to pay a lump sum by a previous order under this Act.
(5) An order made under paragraph 1 or 2 for the payment of a lump sum may provide for the payment of that sum by instalments.
(6) Where the court provides for the payment of a lump sum by instalments the court, on an application made either by the person liable to pay or the person entitled to receive that sum, shall have power to vary that order by varying –

(a) the number of instalments payable;
(b) the amount of any instalment payable;
(c) the date on which any instalment becomes payable.

(7) The Lord Chief Justice may nominate a judicial office holder (as defined in section 109(4) of the Constitutional Reform Act 2005) to exercise his functions under this paragraph.

Variation etc of orders for periodical payments

6 (1) In exercising its powers under paragraph 1 or 2 to vary or discharge an order for the making or securing of periodical payments the court shall have regard to all the circumstances of the case, including any change in any of the matters to which the court was required to have regard when making the order.
(2) The power of the court under paragraph 1 or 2 to vary an order for the making or securing of periodical payments shall include power to suspend any provision of the order temporarily and to revive any provision so suspended.
(3) Where on an application under paragraph 1 or 2 for the variation or discharge of an order for the making or securing of periodical payments the court varies the payments required to be made under that order, the court may provide that the payments as so varied shall be made from such date as the court may specify, except that, subject to sub-paragraph (9), the date shall not be earlier than the date of the making of the application.

APPENDIX 4

(4) An application for the variation of an order made under paragraph 1 for the making or securing of periodical payments to or for the benefit of a child may, if the child has reached the age of sixteen, be made by the child himself.

(5) Where an order for the making or securing of periodical payments made under paragraph 1 ceases to have effect on the date on which the child reaches the age of sixteen, or at any time after that date but before or on the date on which he reaches the age of eighteen, the child may apply to the court which made the order for an order for its revival.

(6) If on such an application it appears to the court that –

(a) the child is, will be or (if an order were made under this sub-paragraph) would be receiving instruction at an educational establishment or undergoing training for a trade, profession or vocation, whether or not while in gainful employment; or

(b) there are special circumstances which justify the making of an order under this paragraph,

the court shall have power by order to revive the order from such date as the court may specify, not being earlier than the date of the making of the application.

(7) Any order which is revived by an order under sub-paragraph (5) may be varied or discharged under that provision, on the application of any person by whom or to whom payments are required to be made under the revived order.

(8) An order for the making or securing of periodical payments made under paragraph 1 may be varied or discharged, after the death of either parent, on the application of a guardian or special guardian of the child concerned.

(9) Where –

(a) an order under paragraph 1(2)(a) or (b) for the making or securing of periodical payments in favour of more than one child ('the order') is in force;

(b) the order requires payments specified in it to be made to or for the benefit of more than one child without apportioning those payments between them;

(c) a maintenance calculation ('the calculation') is made with respect to one or more, but not all, of the children with respect to whom those payments are to be made; and

(d) an application is made, before the end of the period of 6 months beginning with the date on which the calculation was made, for the variation or discharge of the order,

the court may, in exercise of its powers under paragraph 1 to vary or discharge the order, direct that the variation or discharge shall take effect from the date on which the calculation took effect or any later date.

Variation of orders for periodical payments etc made by magistrates' courts

6A (1) Subject to sub-paragraphs (7) and (8), the power of a magistrates' court –

(a) under paragraph 1 or 2 to vary an order for the making of periodical payments, or

(b) under paragraph 5(6) to vary an order for the payment of a lump sum by instalments, shall include power, if the court is satisfied that payment has not been made in accordance with the order, to exercise one of its powers under paragraphs (a) to (d) of section 59(3) of the Magistrates' Courts Act 1980.

(2) In any case where –

(a) a magistrates' court has made an order under this Schedule for the making of periodical payments or for the payment of a lump sum by instalments, and

(b) payments under the order are required to be made by any method of payment falling within section 59(6) of the Magistrates' Courts Act 1980 (standing order, etc),

any person entitled to make an application under this Schedule for the variation of the order (in this paragraph referred to as 'the applicant') may apply to a magistrates' court acting in the same local justice area as the court which made the order for the order to be varied as mentioned in sub-paragraph (3).

(3) Subject to sub-paragraph (5), where an application is made under sub-paragraph (2), a justices' clerk, after giving written notice (by post or otherwise) of the application to any interested party and allowing that party, within the period of 14 days beginning with the date of the giving of that notice, an opportunity to make written representations, may vary the order to provide that payments under the order shall be made to the designated officer for the court.

(4) The clerk may proceed with an application under sub-paragraph (2) notwithstanding that any such interested party as is referred to in sub-paragraph (3) has not received written notice of the application.

(5) Where an application has been made under sub-paragraph (2), the clerk may, if he considers it inappropriate to exercise his power under sub-paragraph (3), refer the matter to the court which, subject to sub-paragraphs (7) and (8), may vary the order by exercising one of its powers under paragraphs (a) to (d) of section 59(3) of the Magistrates' Courts Act 1980.

(6) Subsection (4) of section 59 of the Magistrates' Courts Act 1980 (power of court to order that account be opened) shall apply for the purposes of sub-paragraphs (1) and (5) as it applies for the purposes of that section.

(7) Before varying the order by exercising one of its powers under paragraphs (a) to (d) of section 59(3) of the Magistrates' Courts Act 1980, the court shall have regard to any representations made by the parties to the application.

(8) If the court does not propose to exercise its power under paragraph (c), (cc) or (d) of subsection (3) of section 59 of the Magistrates' Courts Act 1980, the court shall, unless upon representations expressly made in that behalf by the applicant for the order it is satisfied that it is undesirable to do so, exercise its power under paragraph (b) of that subsection.

(9) None of the powers of the court, or of a justices' clerk, conferred by this paragraph shall be exercisable in relation to an order under this Schedule for the making of periodical payments, or for the payment of a lump sum by instalments, which is not a qualifying maintenance order (within the meaning of section 59 of the Magistrates' Courts Act 1980).

(10) In sub-paragraphs (3) and (4) 'interested party', in relation to an application made by the applicant under sub-paragraph (2), means a person who would be entitled to be a party to an application for the variation of

APPENDIX 4

the order made by the applicant under any other provision of this Schedule if such an application were made.

Variation of orders for secured periodical payments after death of parent

7 (1) Where the parent liable to make payments under a secured periodical payments order has died, the persons who may apply for the variation or discharge of the order shall include the personal representatives of the deceased parent.
   (2) No application for the variation of the order shall, except with the permission of the court, be made after the end of the period of six months from the date on which representation in regard to the estate of that parent is first taken out.
   (3) The personal representatives of a deceased person against whom a secured periodical payments order was made shall not be liable for having distributed any part of the estate of the deceased after the end of the period of six months referred to in sub-paragraph (2) on the ground that they ought to have taken into account the possibility that the court might permit an application for variation to be made after that period by the person entitled to payments under the order.
   (4) Sub-paragraph (3) shall not prejudice any power to recover any part of the estate so distributed arising by virtue of the variation of an order in accordance with this paragraph.
   (5) Where an application to vary a secured periodical payments order is made after the death of the parent liable to make payments under the order, the circumstances to which the court is required to have regard under paragraph 6(1) shall include the changed circumstances resulting from the death of the parent.
   (6) In considering for the purposes of sub-paragraph (2) the question when representation was first taken out, a grant limited to settled land or to trust property shall be left out of account and a grant limited to real estate or to personal estate shall be left out of account unless a grant limited to the remainder of the estate has previously been made or is made at the same time.
   (7) In this paragraph 'secured periodical payments order' means an order for secured periodical payments under paragraph 1(2)(b).

Financial relief under other enactments

8 (1) This paragraph applies where a residence order or a special guardianship order is made with respect to a child at a time when there is in force an order ('the financial relief order') made under any enactment other than this Act and requiring a person to contribute to the child's maintenance.
   (2) Where this paragraph applies, the court may, on the application of –
       (a) any person required by the financial relief order to contribute to the child's maintenance; or
       (b) any person in whose favour a residence order or a special guardianship order with respect to the child is in force,
       make an order revoking the financial relief order, or varying it by altering the amount of any sum payable under the order or by substituting the applicant for the person to whom any such sum is otherwise payable under that order.

CHILDREN ACT 1989

Interim orders

9 (1) Where an application is made under paragraph 1 or 2 the court may, at any time before it disposes of the application, make an interim order –

(a) requiring either or both parents to make such periodical payments, at such times and for such term as the court thinks fit; and

(b) giving any direction which the court thinks fit.

(2) An interim order made under this paragraph may provide for payments to be made from such date as the court may specify, except that, subject to paragraph 3(5) and (6), the date shall not be earlier than the date of the making of the application under paragraph 1 or 2.

(3) An interim order made under this paragraph shall cease to have effect when the application is disposed of or, if earlier, on the date specified for the purposes of this paragraph in the interim order.

(4) An interim order in which a date has been specified for the purposes of sub-paragraph (3) may be varied by substituting a later date.

Alteration of maintenance agreements

10 (1) In this paragraph and in paragraph 11 'maintenance agreement' means any agreement in writing made with respect to a child, whether before or after the commencement of this paragraph, which –

(a) is or was made between the father and mother of the child; and

(b) contains provision with respect to the making or securing of payments, or the disposition or use of any property, for the maintenance or education of the child,

and any such provisions are in this paragraph, and paragraph 11, referred to as 'financial arrangements'.

(2) Where a maintenance agreement is for the time being subsisting and each of the parties to the agreement is for the time being either domiciled or resident in England and Wales, then, either party may apply to the court for an order under this paragraph.

(3) If the court to which the application is made is satisfied either –

(a) that, by reason of a change in the circumstances in the light of which any financial arrangements contained in the agreement were made (including a change foreseen by the parties when making the agreement), the agreement should be altered so as to make different financial arrangements; or

(b) that the agreement does not contain proper financial arrangements with respect to the child,

then that court may by order make such alterations in the agreement by varying or revoking any financial arrangements contained in it as may appear to it to be just having regard to all the circumstances.

(4) If the maintenance agreement is altered by an order under this paragraph, the agreement shall have effect thereafter as if the alteration had been made by agreement between the parties and for valuable consideration.

(5) Where a court decides to make an order under this paragraph altering the maintenance agreement –

APPENDIX 4

    (a) by inserting provision for the making or securing by one of the parties to the agreement of periodical payments for the maintenance of the child; or

    (b) by increasing the rate of periodical payments required to be made or secured by one of the parties for the maintenance of the child,

then, in deciding the term for which under the agreement as altered by the order the payments or (as the case may be) the additional payments attributable to the increase are to be made or secured for the benefit of the child, the court shall apply the provisions of sub-paragraphs (1) and (2) of paragraph 3 as if the order were an order under paragraph 1(2)(a) or (b).

(6) A magistrates' court shall not entertain an application under sub-paragraph (2) unless both the parties to the agreement are resident in England and Wales and the court acts in, or is authorised by the Lord Chancellor to act for, a local justice area in which at least one of the parties is resident, and shall not have power to make any order on such an application except –

    (a) in a case where the agreement contains no provision for periodical payments by either of the parties, an order inserting provision for the making by one of the parties of periodical payments for the maintenance of the child;

    (b) in a case where the agreement includes provision for the making by one of the parties of periodical payments, an order increasing or reducing the rate of, or terminating, any of those payments.

(7) For the avoidance of doubt it is hereby declared that nothing in this paragraph affects any power of a court before which any proceedings between the parties to a maintenance agreement are brought under any other enactment to make an order containing financial arrangements or any right of either party to apply for such an order in such proceedings.

(8) In the case of a child who has a parent by virtue of section 42 or 43 of the Human Fertilisation and Embryology Act 2008, the reference in sub-paragraph (1)(a) to the child's father is a reference to the woman who is a parent of the child by virtue of that section.

11 (1) Where a maintenance agreement provides for the continuation, after the death of one of the parties, of payments for the maintenance of a child and that party dies domiciled in England and Wales, the surviving party or the personal representatives of the deceased party may apply to the High Court or a county court for an order under paragraph 10.

(2) If a maintenance agreement is altered by a court on an application under this paragraph, the agreement shall have effect thereafter as if the alteration had been made, immediately before the death, by agreement between the parties and for valuable consideration.

(3) An application under this paragraph shall not, except with leave of the High Court or a county court, be made after the end of the period of six months beginning with the day on which representation in regard to the estate of the deceased is first taken out.

(4) In considering for the purposes of sub-paragraph (3) the question when representation was first taken out, a grant limited to settled land or to trust property shall be left out of account and a grant limited to real estate or to personal estate shall be left out of account unless a grant limited to the remainder of the estate has previously been made or is made at the same time.

(5) A county court shall not entertain an application under this paragraph, or an application for leave to make an application under this paragraph, unless it would have jurisdiction to hear and determine proceedings for an order under section 2 of the Inheritance (Provision for Family and Dependants) Act 1975 in relation to the deceased's estate by virtue of section 25 of the County Courts Act 1984 (jurisdiction under the Act of 1975).

(6) The provisions of this paragraph shall not render the personal representatives of the deceased liable for having distributed any part of the estate of the deceased after the expiry of the period of six months referred to in sub-paragraph (3) on the ground that they ought to have taken into account the possibility that a court might grant leave for an application by virtue of this paragraph to be made by the surviving party after that period.

(7) Sub-paragraph (6) shall not prejudice any power to recover any part of the estate so distributed arising by virtue of the making of an order in pursuance of this paragraph.

Enforcement of orders for maintenance

12 (1) Any person for the time being under an obligation to make payments in pursuance of any order for the payment of money made by a magistrates' court under this Act shall give notice of any change of address to such person (if any) as may be specified in the order.

(2) Any person failing without reasonable excuse to give such a notice shall be guilty of an offence and liable on summary conviction to a fine not exceeding level 2 on the standard scale.

(3) An order for the payment of money made by a magistrates' court under this Act shall be enforceable as a magistrates' court maintenance order within the meaning of section 150(1) of the Magistrates' Courts Act 1980.

Direction for settlement of instrument by conveyancing counsel

13 Where the High Court or a county court decides to make an order under this Act for the securing of periodical payments or for the transfer or settlement of property, it may direct that the matter be referred to one of the conveyancing counsel of the court to settle a proper instrument to be executed by all necessary parties.

Financial provision for child resident in country outside England and Wales

14 (1) Where one parent of a child lives in England and Wales and the child lives outside England and Wales with –

(a) another parent of his;
(b) a guardian or special guardian of his; or
(c) a person in whose favour a residence order is in force with respect to the child,

the court shall have power, on an application made by any of the persons mentioned in paragraphs (a) to (c), to make one or both of the orders mentioned in paragraph 1(2)(a) and (b) against the parent living in England and Wales.

(2) Any reference in this Act to the powers of the court under paragraph 1(2) or to an order made under paragraph 1(2) shall include a reference to the powers which the court has by virtue of sub-paragraph (1) or (as the case may be) to an order made by virtue of sub-paragraph (1).

APPENDIX 4

Local authority contribution to child's maintenance

15 (1) Where a child lives, or is to live, with a person as the result of a residence order, a local authority may make contributions to that person towards the cost of the accommodation and maintenance of the child.

     (2) Sub-paragraph (1) does not apply where the person with whom the child lives, or is to live, is a parent of the child or the husband or wife or civil partner of a parent of the child.

Interpretation

16 (1) In this Schedule 'child' includes, in any case where an application is made under paragraph 2 or 6 in relation to a person who has reached the age of eighteen, that person.

     (2) In this Schedule, except paragraphs 2 and 15, 'parent' includes –

(a) any party to a marriage (whether or not subsisting) in relation to whom the child concerned is a child of the family, and
(b) any civil partner in a civil partnership (whether or not subsisting) in relation to whom the child concerned is a child of the family;

and for this purpose any reference to either parent or both parents shall be read as a reference to any parent of his and to all of his parents.

     (3) In this Schedule, 'maintenance calculation' has the same meaning as it has in the Child Support Act 1991 by virtue of section 54 of that Act as read with any regulations in force under that section.

APPENDIX 5

Civil Partnership Act 2004, Part 2, Chapters 3–5

PART 2 CIVIL PARTNERSHIP: ENGLAND AND WALES

CHAPTER 3

Property and Financial Arrangements

65 Contribution by civil partner to property improvement

(1) This section applies if –

  (a) a civil partner contributes in money or money's worth to the improvement of real or personal property in which or in the proceeds of sale of which either or both of the civil partners has or have a beneficial interest, and

  (b) the contribution is of a substantial nature.

(2) The contributing partner is to be treated as having acquired by virtue of the contribution a share or an enlarged share (as the case may be) in the beneficial interest of such an extent –

  (a) as may have been then agreed, or

  (b) in default of such agreement, as may seem in all the circumstances just to any court before which the question of the existence or extent of the beneficial interest of either of the civil partners arises (whether in proceedings between them or in any other proceedings).

(3) Subsection (2) is subject to any agreement (express or implied) between the civil partners to the contrary.

66 Disputes between civil partners about property

(1) In any question between the civil partners in a civil partnership as to title to or possession of property, either civil partner may apply to –

  (a) the High Court, or

  (b) such county court as may be prescribed by rules of court.

(2) On such an application, the court may make such order with respect to the property as it thinks fit (including an order for the sale of the property).

APPENDIX 5

(3) Rules of court made for the purposes of this section may confer jurisdiction on county courts whatever the situation or value of the property in dispute.

67 Applications under section 66 where property not in possession etc

(1) The right of a civil partner ('A') to make an application under section 66 includes the right to make such an application where A claims that the other civil partner ('B') has had in his possession or under his control –

   (a) money to which, or to a share of which, A was beneficially entitled, or
   (b) property (other than money) to which, or to an interest in which, A was beneficially entitled,

and that either the money or other property has ceased to be in B's possession or under B's control or that A does not know whether it is still in B's possession or under B's control.

(2) For the purposes of subsection (1)(a) it does not matter whether A is beneficially entitled to the money or share –

   (a) because it represents the proceeds of property to which, or to an interest in which, A was beneficially entitled, or
   (b) for any other reason.

(3) Subsections (4) and (5) apply if, on such an application being made, the court is satisfied that B –

   (a) has had in his possession or under his control money or other property as mentioned in subsection (1)(a) or (b), and
   (b) has not made to A, in respect of that money or other property, such payment or disposition as would have been appropriate in the circumstances.

(4) The power of the court to make orders under section 66 includes power to order B to pay to A –

   (a) in a case falling within subsection (1)(a), such sum in respect of the money to which the application relates, or A's s share of it, as the court considers appropriate, or
   (b) in a case falling within subsection (1)(b), such sum in respect of the value of the property to which the application relates, or A's interest in it, as the court considers appropriate.

(5) If it appears to the court that there is any property which –

   (a) represents the whole or part of the money or property, and
   (b) is property in respect of which an order could (apart from this section) have been made under section 66,

the court may (either instead of or as well as making an order in accordance with subsection (4)) make any order which it could (apart from this section) have made under section 66.

(6) Any power of the court which is exercisable on an application under section 66 is exercisable in relation to an application made under that section as extended by this section.

68 Applications under section 66 by former civil partners

(1) This section applies where a civil partnership has been dissolved or annulled.
(2) Subject to subsection (3), an application may be made under section 66 (including that section as extended by section 67) by either former civil part-

ner despite the dissolution or annulment (and references in those sections to a civil partner are to be read accordingly).

(3) The application must be made within the period of 3 years beginning with the date of the dissolution or annulment.

69 Actions in tort between civil partners

(1) This section applies if an action in tort is brought by one civil partner against the other during the subsistence of the civil partnership.

(2) The court may stay the proceedings if it appears –

   (a) that no substantial benefit would accrue to either civil partner from the continuation of the proceedings, or

   (b) that the question or questions in issue could more conveniently be disposed of on an application under section 66.

(3) Without prejudice to subsection (2)(b), the court may in such an action –

   (a) exercise any power which could be exercised on an application under section 66, or

   (b) give such directions as it thinks fit for the disposal under that section of any question arising in the proceedings.

70 Assurance policy by civil partner for benefit of other civil partner etc

Section 11 of the Married Women's Property Act 1882 (c 75) (money payable under policy of assurance not to form part of the estate of the insured) applies in relation to a policy of assurance –

   (a) effected by a civil partner on his own life, and

   (b) expressed to be for the benefit of his civil partner, or of his children, or of his civil partner and children, or any of them,

as it applies in relation to a policy of assurance effected by a husband and expressed to be for the benefit of his wife, or of his children, or of his wife and children, or of any of them.

71 Wills, administration of estates and family provision

Schedule 4 amends enactments relating to wills, administration of estates and family provision so that they apply in relation to civil partnerships as they apply in relation to marriage.

72 Financial relief for civil partners and children of family

(1) Schedule 5 makes provision for financial relief in connection with civil partnerships that corresponds to provision made for financial relief in connection with marriages by Part 2 of the Matrimonial Causes Act 1973 (c 18).

(2) Any rule of law under which any provision of Part 2 of the 1973 Act is interpreted as applying to dissolution of a marriage on the ground of presumed death is to be treated as applying (with any necessary modifications) in relation to the corresponding provision of Schedule 5.

(3) Schedule 6 makes provision for financial relief in connection with civil partnerships that corresponds to provision made for financial relief in connection with marriages by the Domestic Proceedings and Magistrates' Courts Act 1978 (c 22).

APPENDIX 5

(4) Schedule 7 makes provision for financial relief in England and Wales after a civil partnership has been dissolved or annulled, or civil partners have been legally separated, in a country outside the British Islands.

CHAPTER 4

Civil Partnership Agreements

73 Civil partnership agreements unenforceable

(1) A civil partnership agreement does not under the law of England and Wales have effect as a contract giving rise to legal rights.

(2) No action lies in England and Wales for breach of a civil partnership agreement, whatever the law applicable to the agreement.

(3) In this section and section 74 'civil partnership agreement' means an agreement between two people –

  (a) to register as civil partners of each other –

   (i) in England and Wales (under this Part),
   (ii) in Scotland (under Part 3),
   (iii) in Northern Ireland (under Part 4), or
   (iv) outside the United Kingdom under an Order in Council made under Chapter 1 of Part 5 (registration at British consulates etc or by armed forces personnel), or

  (b) to enter into an overseas relationship.

(4) This section applies in relation to civil partnership agreements whether entered into before or after this section comes into force, but does not affect any action commenced before it comes into force.

74 Property where civil partnership agreement is terminated

(1) This section applies if a civil partnership agreement is terminated.

(2) Section 65 (contributions by civil partner to property improvement) applies, in relation to any property in which either or both of the parties to the agreement had a beneficial interest while the agreement was in force, as it applies in relation to property in which a civil partner has a beneficial interest.

(3) Sections 66 and 67 (disputes between civil partners about property) apply to any dispute between or claim by one of the parties in relation to property in which either or both had a beneficial interest while the agreement was in force, as if the parties were civil partners of each other.

(4) An application made under section 66 or 67 by virtue of subsection (3) must be made within 3 years of the termination of the agreement.

(5) A party to a civil partnership agreement who makes a gift of property to the other party on the condition (express or implied) that it is to be returned if the agreement is terminated is not prevented from recovering the property merely because of his having terminated the agreement.

CHAPTER 5

Children

75 Parental responsibility, children of the family and relatives

(1) Amend the Children Act 1989 (c 41) ('the 1989 Act') as follows.
(2) In section 4A(1) (acquisition of parental responsibility by step-parent) after 'is married to' insert ', or a civil partner of,'.
(3) In section 105(1) (interpretation), for the definition of 'child of the family' (in relation to the parties to a marriage) substitute –

' "child of the family", in relation to parties to a marriage, or to two people who are civil partners of each other, means –

   (a) a child of both of them, and
   (b) any other child, other than a child placed with them as foster parents by a local authority or voluntary organisation, who has been treated by both of them as a child of their family.'

(4) In the definition of 'relative' in section 105(1), for 'by affinity)' substitute 'by marriage or civil partnership)'.

76 Guardianship

In section 6 of the 1989 Act (guardians: revocation and disclaimer) after subsection (3A) insert –

'(3B) An appointment under section 5(3) or (4) (including one made in an unrevoked will or codicil) is revoked if the person appointed is the civil partner of the person who made the appointment and either –

   (a) an order of a court of civil jurisdiction in England and Wales dissolves or annuls the civil partnership, or
   (b) the civil partnership is dissolved or annulled and the dissolution or annulment is entitled to recognition in England and Wales by virtue of Chapter 3 of Part 5 of the Civil Partnership Act 2004,

unless a contrary intention appears by the appointment.'

77 Entitlement to apply for residence or contact order

In section 10(5) of the 1989 Act (persons entitled to apply for residence or contact order) after paragraph (a) insert –

'(aa) any civil partner in a civil partnership (whether or not subsisting) in relation to whom the child is a child of the family;'.

78 Financial provision for children

(1) Amend Schedule 1 to the 1989 Act (financial provision for children) as follows.
(2) In paragraph 2(6) (meaning of 'periodical payments order') after paragraph (d) insert –

'(e) Part 1 or 9 of Schedule 5 to the Civil Partnership Act 2004 (financial relief in the High Court or a county court etc);

APPENDIX 5

    (f)   Schedule 6 to the 2004 Act (financial relief in the magistrates' courts etc),'.

(3) In paragraph 15(2) (person with whom a child lives or is to live) after 'husband or wife' insert 'or civil partner'.

(4) For paragraph 16(2) (extended meaning of 'parent') substitute –

'(2)   In this Schedule, except paragraphs 2 and 15, "parent" includes –

(a) any party to a marriage (whether or not subsisting) in relation to whom the child concerned is a child of the family, and

(b) any civil partner in a civil partnership (whether or not subsisting) in relation to whom the child concerned is a child of the family;

and for this purpose any reference to either parent or both parents shall be read as a reference to any parent of his and to all of his parents.'

APPENDIX 6

Form CG34 – Post-transaction valuation checks for capital gains

Application for post transaction valuation check

Please complete all relevant items and send the application to your HMRC Office (**not** to any of the Valuation Offices)

Taxpayer details

Name

Address

Postcode

Reference

National Insurance number *(where appropriate)*

Agent's name

Reference

Address

Postcode

Details of disposal

Date of disposal / /

Name and address of purchaser

Name

Address

Postcode

Reason for valuation

√ *as appropriate*

☐ Rebasing to 31 March 1982

☐ Market value disposal (disposal to a connected person or a bargain not at arm's length)

☐ Negligible value claim

☐ Other - *please specify*

Valuation required

Description of asset to be valued	Valuation date	Valuation offered

Shares — The description should include the name of the company, the registration number (if known), the class and the number of shares to be valued. Enter in the table your valuation **per share** and not the total value of your holding.

Goodwill — The description should provide sufficient information to identify the asset. If an incorporation is involved the details provided should identify the name and nature of the business from which the transfer has been made and also, the name and company registration number of the recipient company together with the registered office address.

Land — The description should provide sufficient information to identify the property, with details of your interest in the property and details of any tenancies existing at the valuation date. The term 'land' includes both land and buildings.

Other — The description should provide sufficient information to identify the asset.

Please turn over

CG34

HMRC 06/06

APPENDIX 6

You should also provide

√ to show items enclosed

☐ A capital gains computation for the disposal with an estimate of your capital gains tax liability for the tax year in which you made the disposal, or for companies the corporation tax liability on chargeable gains, or for partnership disposals, estimates of the liabilities of the individual partners

☐ Details of any reliefs due or to be claimed in respect of the disposal

☐ A copy of any valuation report obtained

☐ If available, the cost and date of acquisition of the asset and details of any improvements made

☐ For **share** valuations - full accounts for the three years up to the valuation date

☐ For **goodwill** valuations - full accounts for the three years up to the valuation date

☐ For **land** valuations -

  • if you held a leasehold interest, a copy of the lease applying at the valuation date

  • if the land was let at the valuation date, a copy of any tenancy agreement applying at that date

  • a plan showing the location of the land if the valuation is of undeveloped land

☐ Any other papers you feel may be relevant

Use this space to provide any other information that you consider is relevant to your valuation

FORM CG34 – POST-TRANSACTION VALUATION CHECKS FOR CAPITAL GAINS

HM Revenue & Customs

Post-transaction valuation checks for capital gains

Introduction

When working out your Capital Gains Tax liability, or in the case of companies, your Corporation Tax liability on chargeable gains, you sometimes have to value assets. If you use such valuations, we offer a free service to help you complete your Tax Return. You can ask your HMRC office to check valuations after you have made the disposal, including a deemed disposal following a claim that an asset has become of negligible value, but before you make your Return. Our service is available to all taxpayers, individuals, trustees and companies.

If we agree your valuations we will not challenge your use of those valuations in your Return unless there are any important facts affecting the valuations that you have not told us about. Agreement to your valuations does not necessarily mean that we agree the gain or loss. We will not consider the other figures you have used until you make your Return.

If we cannot agree your valuations we will suggest alternatives. We use specialist valuers to value some assets, mainly shares, land, goodwill and works of art. You will also be able to discuss your valuations with our valuers. You must file your Return by the filing date printed on it even if we have not been able to agree your valuations or suggest alternatives. Your Return must also tell us about any valuations that we have checked but been unable to agree.

If, after discussion, we cannot reach agreement on any valuations you use in your Return, you will be able to appeal to an independent tribunal.

How to get your valuations checked

If you want us to check your valuations, ask your HMRC office or any HMRC Enquiry Centre for one copy of form CG34 for each valuation you want us to check. Return the completed form(s) to us together with the information and documents requested on the form. You can also attach any other information that will help us understand your valuations.

If you do not provide all the information requested on the form, we may be unable to check your valuations. If you have difficulty getting all of this information, or you are not sure how to prepare a Capital Gains computation, ask us for help.

How long it will take

Your HMRC office, or our specialist valuers, will contact you as soon as possible after you make your application. Valuation is an exercise of judgement that can sometimes be a difficult and lengthy process, particularly if discussion is necessary.

The sooner you contact us after you have made a disposal, the more likely we will be able to reach agreement with you before you make your Return.

We expect that it will take a minimum of 56 days to agree your valuations or to provide you with an alternative. In more complex cases it may take longer. In a few very complex cases we may not be able to provide you with any alternative valuation before the filing date for your Return. If you want to use our service to have valuations checked before you submit your Return you should send any forms CG34 to your HMRC office at least two months before you need to make your Return.

Further information

We can give you further information about this scheme at your HMRC office or from your nearest HMRC Enquiry Centre.

APPENDIX 7

Form E

FINANCIAL STATEMENT OF	In the *[High/County Court] *[Principal Registry of the Family Division]
	Case No. *Always quote this*
	Petitioner's Solicitor's reference
	Respondent's Solicitor's reference

*Husband/*Wife/*Civil partner

(*delete as apprpriate)

Between

[ ] and [ ]

Who is the *husband/*wife/*civil partner *Petitioner/*Respondent in the *divorce/*dissolution suit

Applicant in this matter

Who is the *husband/*wife/*civil partner *Petitioner/*Respondent in the *divorce/*dissolution suit

Respondent in this matter

Please fill in this form fully and accurately. Where any box is not applicable, write 'N/A'.

You have a duty to the court to give a full, frank and clear disclosure of all your financial and other relevant circumstances.

A failure to give full and accurate disclosure may result in any order the court makes being set aside.

If you are found to have been deliberately untruthful, criminal proceedings for perjury may be taken against you.

You must attach documents to the form where they are specifically sought and you may attach other documents where it is necessary to explain or clarify any of the information that you give.

Essential documents that must accompany this statement are detailed in the form.

If there is not enough room on the form for any particular piece of information, you may continue on an attached sheet of paper.

> If you are in doubt about how to complete any part of this form you should seek legal advice.
>
> This Statement must be sworn before a solicitor, a commissioner for oaths or an Officer of the Court or, if abroad, a notary or duly authorised official, before it is filed with the Court or sent to the other party (see last page).

This statement is filed by

Name and address of solicitor

Form E Financial Statement (12.05)　　　　　　　　　　　　　　　　　　　　　　　HMCS

FORM E

1 General Information

1.1	Full name								
1.2	Date of birth	Date	Month	Year	1.3 Date of the marriage/civil partnership	Date	Month	Year
1.4	Occupation								

See **3.4.2** — 1.5 Date of the separation | Date | Month | Year | Tick here if not applicable ☐

1.6 Date of the

	Petition	Decree nisi/Decree of judicial separation Conditional order/ Separation order	Decree absolute/ Final order (if applicable)
	Date / Month / Year	Date / Month / Year	Date / Month / Year

1.7 If you have subsequently married or formed a civil partnership, or will do so, state the date | Date | Month | Year

1.8 Are you co-habiting? Yes ☐ No ☐

1.9 Do you intend to co-habit within the next six months? Yes ☐ No ☐

1.10 Details of any children of the family

Full names	Date of birth (Date / Month / Year)	With whom does the child live?

1.11 Details of the state of health of yourself and the children if you think this should be taken into account

Yourself	Children

APPENDIX 7

1.12 Details of the present and proposed future educational arrangements for the children.

Present arrangements	Future arrangements

See **Chapter 5** — **1.13** Details of any child support maintenance calculation or any maintenance order or agreement made in respect of any children of the family. If no calculation, order or agreement has been made, give an estimate of the liability of the non-resident parent in respect of the children of the family under the Child Support Act 1991.

1.14 If this application is to vary an order, attach a copy of the order and give details of the part that is to be varied and the changes sought. You may need to continue on a separate sheet.

1.15 Details of any other court cases between you and your spouse/civil partner, whether in relation to money, property, children or anything else.

Case No	Court

1.16 Your present residence and the occupants of it and on what terms you occupy it (e.g. tenant, owner-occupier).

Address	Occupants	Terms of occupation

FORM E

2 Financial Details *Part 1 Real Property and Personal Assets*

2.1 Complete this section in respect of the family home (the last family home occupied by you and your spouse/civil partner) if it remains unsold.

Documentation required for attachment to this section:
a) A copy of any valuation of the property obtained within the last six months. If you cannot provide this document, please give your own realistic estimate of the current market value
b) A recent mortgage statement confirming the sum outstanding on **each** mortgage

Property name and address	
Land Registry title number	
Mortgage company name(s) and address(es) and account number(s)	
Type of mortgage	
Details of who owns the property and the extent of your legal and beneficial interest in it (i.e. state if it is owned by you solely or jointly owned with your spouse/civil partner or with others)	
If you consider that the legal ownership as recorded at the Land Registry does not reflect the true position, state why	
Current market value of the property	
Balance outstanding on any mortgage(s)	
If a sale at this stage would result in penalties payable under the mortgage, state amount	
Estimate the costs of sale of the property	
Total equity in the property (i.e. market value less outstanding mortgage(s), penalties if any and the costs of sale)	

See **6.1.1, 6.1.2** and **6.1.3**

TOTAL value of your interest in the family home:
Total A £

APPENDIX 7

2.2 Details of your interest in any other property, land or buildings. Complete one page for each property you have an interest in. ——— See **6.3**

Documentation required for attachment to this section:
a) A copy of any valuation of the property obtained within the last six months. If you cannot provide this document, please give your own realistic estimate of the current market value
b) A recent mortgage statement confirming the sum outstanding on each mortgage

Property name and address	
Land Registry title number	
Mortgage company name(s) and address(es) and account number(s)	
Type of mortgage	
Details of who owns the property and the extent of your legal and beneficial interest in it (i.e. state if it is owned by you solely or jointly owned with your spouse/civil partner or with others)	
If you consider that the legal ownership as recorded at the Land Registry does not reflect the true position, state why	
Current market value of the property	
Balance outstanding on any mortgage(s)	
If a sale at this stage would result in penalties payable under the mortgage, state amount	
Estimate the costs of sale of the property	
Total equity in the property (i.e. market value less outstanding mortgage(s), penalties if any and the costs of sale)	
Total value of your interest in this property	

TOTAL value of your interest in ALL other property:
Total B £

FORM E

2.3 Details of all personal bank, building society and National Savings Accounts that you hold or have held at any time in the last twelve months and which are or were either in your own name or in which you have or have had any interest. This applies whether any such account is in credit or in debit. For joint accounts give your interest and the name of the other account holder. If the account is overdrawn, show a minus figure.

Documentation required for attachment to this section:
For each account listed, all statements covering the last 12 months.

Name of bank or building society, including branch name	Type of account (*e.g. current*)	Account number	Name of other account holder (*if applicable*)	Balance at the date of this statement	Total current value of your interest

TOTAL value of your interest in ALL accounts: (C1) £ 0.00

Consider CGT position of the assets listed. Many may be exempt – see **2.1.6**

2.4 Details of all investments, including shares, PEPs, ISAs, TESSAs, National Savings Investments (other than already shown above), bonds, stocks, unit trusts, investment trusts, gilts and other quoted securities that you hold or have an interest in. (Do not include dividend income as this will be dealt with separately later on.)

Documentation required for attachment to this section:
Latest statement or dividend counterfoil relating to each investment.

Name	Type of Investment	Size of Holding	Current value	Name of any other account holder (*if applicable*)	Total current value of your interest

TOTAL value of your interest in ALL holdings: (C2) £ 0.00

APPENDIX 7

2.5 Details of all life insurance policies including endowment policies that you hold or have an interest in. ———See **8.2**
Include those that do not have a surrender value. Complete one page for each policy.

Documentation required for attachment to this section:
A surrender valuation of each policy that has a surrender value.

Name of company	
Policy type	
Policy number	
If policy is assigned, state in whose favour and amount of charge	
Name of any other owner and the extent of your interest in the policy	

Maturity date *(if applicable)*	Date	Month	Year

Current surrender value *(if applicable)*	
If policy includes life insurance, the amount of the insurance and the name of the person whose life is insured	
Total current surrender value of your interest in this policy	
TOTAL value of your interest in ALL policies: (C3)	£

2.6 Details of all monies that are OWED TO YOU. Do not include sums owed in director's or partnership accounts which should be included at section 2.11.

Brief description of money owed and by whom	Balance outstanding	Total current value of your interest
TOTAL value of your interest in ALL debts owed to you: (C4)	£	0.00

7

246

FORM E

See **2.1.6**. Sterling is exempt from CGT. Foreign currency may be a chargeable asset for CGT unless included under exemption.

2.7 Details of all cash sums held in excess of £500. You must state where it is held and the currency it is held in.

Where held	Amount	Currency	Total current value of your interest

TOTAL value of your interest in ALL cash sums: (C5) £ 0.00

Many assets will be chattels. See **2.1.7** for CGT position.

2.8 Details of personal belongings individually worth more than £500.

INCLUDE:
- Cars (gross value)
- Collections, pictures and jewellery
- Furniture and house contents

Brief description of item	Total current value of your interest

TOTAL value of your interest in ALL personal belongings: (C6) £

Add together all the figures in boxes C1 to C6 to give the TOTAL current value of your interest in personal assets: TOTAL C £ 0.00

8

APPENDIX 7

2 Financial Details *Part 2 Capital: Liabilities and Capital Gains Tax*

2.9 Details of any liabilities you have.

EXCLUDE liabilities already shown such as:
- Mortgages
- Any overdrawn bank, building society or National Savings accounts

INCLUDE:
- Money owed on credit cards and store cards
- Bank loans
- Hire purchase agreements

List all credit and store cards held including those with a nil or positive balance. Where the liability is not solely your own, give the name(s) of the other account holder(s) and the amount of your share of the liability.

Liability	Name(s) of other account holder(s) *(if applicable)*	Total liability	Total current value of your interest in the liability

TOTAL value of your interest in ALL liabilities: (D1) £

See **2.1.4.** All assets should be reviewed to see if they are within charge to CGT and if there is an allowance/ exemption or relief that should be used/claimed.

2.10 If any Capital Gains Tax would be payable on the disposal now of any of your real property or personal assets, give your estimate of the tax liability.

Asset	Total Capital Gains Tax liability

TOTAL value of ALL your potential Capital Gains Tax liabilities: (D2) £

Add together D1 and D2 to give the TOTAL value of your liabilities: TOTAL D £ 0.00

FORM E

2 Financial Details *Part 3 Capital: Business assets and directorships*

2.11 Details of all your business interests. Complete one page for each business you have an interest in.

Documentation required for attachment to this section:
a) Copies of the business accounts for the last two financial years
b) Any documentation, if available at this stage, upon which you have based your estimate of the current value of your interest in this business, for example a letter from an accountant or a formal valuation. It is not essential to obtain a formal valuation at this stage

Name of the business	
Briefly describe the nature of the business	
Are you *(Please delete all those that are not applicable)*	a) Sole trader — See **8.3.1** b) Partner in a partnership with others c) Shareholder in a limited company — See **8.4** and **8.5**
If you are a partner or a shareholder, state the extent of your interest in the business (i.e. partnership share or the extent of your shareholding compared to the overall shares issued)	
State when your next set of accounts will be available	
If any of the figures in the last accounts are not an accurate reflection of the current position, state why. For example, if there has been a material change since the last accounts, or if the valuations of the assets are not a true reflection of their value (e.g. because property or other assets have not been re-valued in recent years or because they are shown at a book value)	
Total amount of any sums owed to you by the business by way of a director's loan account, partnership capital or current accounts or the like. Identify where these appear in the business accounts	
Your estimate of the current value of your business interest. Explain briefly the basis upon which you have reached that figure	— See **Chapter 10**
Your estimate of any Capital Gains Tax that would be payable if you were to dispose of your business now	
Net value of your interest in this business after any Capital Gains Tax liability	
TOTAL value of ALL your interests in business assets: TOTAL E	£

10

APPENDIX 7

2.12 List any directorships you hold or have held in the last 12 months (other than those already disclosed in Section 2.11).

FORM E

2 Financial Details *Part 4 Capital: Pensions*

2.13 Give details of all your pension rights. Complete a separate page for each pension.

EXCLUDE:
- Basic State Pension

INCLUDE (complete a separate page for each one):
- Additional State Pension (SERPS and State Second Pension (S2P))
- Free Standing Additional Voluntary Contribution Schemes (FSAVC) separate from the scheme of your employer
- Membership of ALL pension plans or schemes

Documentation required for attachment to this section:
a) A recent statement showing the cash equivalent transfer value (CETV) provided by the trustees or managers of each pension arrangement (or, in the case of the additional state pension, a valuation of these rights)
b) If any valuation is not available, give the estimated date when it will be available and attach a copy of your letter to the pension company or administrators from whom the information was sought and/or state the date on which an application for a valuation of a State Earnings Related Pension Scheme was submitted to the Department of Work and Pensions

See **8.1** — Name and address of pension arrangement

Your National Insurance Number

Number of pension arrangement or reference number

Type of scheme
e.g. occupational or personal, final salary, money purchase, additional state pension or other (if other, please give details)

Date the CETV was calculated

Is the pension in payment or drawdown or deferment? *(Please answer Yes or No)*

State the cash equivalent transfer value (CETV) quotation, or in the additional state pension, the valuation of those rights

If the arrangement is an occupational pension arrangement that is paying reduced CETVs, please quote what the CETV would have been if not reduced. If this is not possible, please indicate if the CETV quoted is a reduced CETV

TOTAL value of ALL your pension assets: TOTAL F £

APPENDIX 7

2 Financial Details *Part 5 Capital: Other assets*

2.14 Give details of any other assets not listed in Parts 1 to 4 above.

INCLUDE (the following list is not exhaustive):
- Any personal or business assets not yet disclosed
- Unrealisable assets
- Share option schemes, stating the estimated net sale proceeds of the shares if the options were capable of exercise now, and whether Capital Gains Tax or income tax would be payable
- Business expansion schemes
- Futures
- Commodities
- Trust interests (including interests under a discretionary trust), stating your estimate of the value of the interest and when it is likely to become realisable. If you say it will never be realisable, or has no value, give your reasons
- Any asset that is likely to be received in the foreseeable future
- Any asset held on your behalf by a third party
- Any asset not disclosed elsewhere on this form even if held outside England and Wales

You are reminded of your obligation to disclose all your financial assets and interests of ANY nature.

Type of asset	Value	Total NET value of your interest

TOTAL value of ALL your other assets: TOTAL G £

FORM E

2 Financial Details *Part 6 Income: Earned income from employment*

2.15 Details of earned income from employment. Complete one page for each employment.

Documentation required for attachment to this section:
a) P60 for the last financial year (you should have received this from your employer shortly after the last 5th April)
b) Your last three payslips
c) Your last Form P11D if you have been issued with one

Name and address of your employer	
Job title and brief details of the type of work you do	
Hours worked per week in this employment	
How long have you been with this employer?	
Explain the basis of your income i.e. state whether it is based on an annual salary or an hourly rate of pay and whether it includes commissions or bonuses	
Gross income for the last financial year as shown on your P60	
Net income for the last financial year i.e. gross income less income tax and national insurance	
Average net income for the last three months i.e. total income less income tax and national insurance divided by three	
Briefly explain any other entries on the attached payslips other than basic income, income tax and national insurance	
If the payslips attached for the last three months are not an accurate reflection of your normal income briefly explain why	
Details and value of any bonuses or other occasional payments that you receive from this employment not otherwise already shown, including the basis upon which they are paid	
Details and value of any benefits in kind, perks or other remuneration received from this employer in the last year (e.g. provision of a car, payment of travel, accommodation, meal expenses, etc.)	
Your estimate of your net income from this employment for the next 12 months. If this differs significantly from your current income explain why in box 4.1.2	

Estimated TOTAL of ALL net earned income from employment for the next 12 months: TOTAL H £

14

APPENDIX 7

2 Financial Details *Part 7 Income: Income from self-employment or partnership*

2.16 You will have already given details of your business and provided the last two years accounts at section 2.11. Complete this section giving details of your income from your business. Complete one page for each business.

Documentation required for attachment to this section:
a) A copy of your last tax assessment or, if that is not available, a letter from your accountant confirming your tax liability
b) If net income from the last financial year and estimated net income for the next 12 months is significantly different, a copy of management accounts for the period since your last account

Name of the business	
Date to which your last accounts were completed	
Your share of gross business profit from the last completed accounts	
Income tax and national insurance payable on your share of gross business profit above	
Net income for that year (using the two figures directly above, gross business profit less income tax and national insurance payable)	
Details and value of any benefits in kind, perks or other remuneration received from this business in the last year e.g. provision of a car, payment of travel, accommodation, meal expenses, etc.	
Amount of any regular monthly or other drawings that you take from this business	
If the estimated figure directly below is different from the net income as at the end date of the last completed accounts, briefly explain the reason(s)	
Your estimate of your net annual income for the next 12 months	

Estimated TOTAL of ALL net income from self-employment or partnership for the next 12 months: TOTAL I £

15

FORM E

2 Financial Details *Part 8 Income: Income from investments*
e.g. dividends, interest or rental income

2.17 Details of income received in the last financial year (the year ended last 5th April), and your estimate of your income for the current financial year. Indicate whether the income was paid gross or net of income tax. You are not required to calculate any tax payable that may arise.

Nature of income and the asset from which it derived	Paid gross or net	Income received in the last financial year	Estimated income for the next 12 months

Estimated TOTAL investment income for the next 12 months: **TOTAL J** £

APPENDIX 7

2 Financial Details Part 9 Income: *Income from state benefits (including state pension and child benefit)*

See **5.4** — 2.18 Details of all state benefits that you are currently receiving.

Name of benefit	Amount paid	Frequency of payment	Estimated income for the next 12 months

Estimated TOTAL benefit income for the next 12 months: TOTAL K £ _____

FORM E

2 Financial Details *Part 10 Income: Any other income*

2.19 Details of any other income not disclosed above.

INCLUDE:
- Any source from which income has been received during the last 12 months (even if it has now ceased)
- Any source from which income is likely to be received during the next 12 months

You are reminded of your obligation to give full disclosure of your financial circumstances.

Nature of income	Paid gross or net	Income received in the last financial year	Estimated income for the next 12 months

Estimated TOTAL other income for the next 12 months: TOTAL L £

APPENDIX 7

2 Financial Details *Summaries*

2.20 Summary of your capital (Parts 1 to 5).

Description	Reference of the section on this statement	Value
Current value of your interest in the family home	A	
Current value of your interest in all other property	B	
Current value of your interest in personal assets	C	
Current value of your liabilities	D	
Current value of your interest in business assets	E	
Current value of your pension assets	F	
Current value of all your other assets	G	
TOTAL value of your assets (Totals A to G less D):	£	0.00

2.21 Summary of your estimated income for the next 12 months (Parts 6 to 10).

Description	Reference of the section on this statement	Value
Estimated net total of income from employment	H	
Estimated net total of income from self-employment or partnership	I	
Estimated net total of investment income	J	
Estimated state benefit receipts	K	
Estimated net total of all other income	L	
Estimated TOTAL income for the next 12 months (Totals H to L):	£	0.00

FORM E

3 Financial Requirements *Part 1 Income needs*

3.1 Income needs for yourself and for any children living with you or provided for by you. ALL figures should be annual, monthly or weekly (state which). You *must not* use a combination of these periods. State your current income needs and, if these are likely to change in the near future, explain the anticipated change and give an estimate of the future cost.

The income needs below are: *(delete those not applicable)*	Weekly	Monthly	Annual
I anticipate my income needs are going to change because			

3.1.1 Income needs for yourself.

INCLUDE:
- All income needs for yourself
- Income needs for any children living with you or provided for by you only if these form part of your total income needs (e.g. housing, fuel, car expenses, holidays, etc)

Item	Current cost	Estimated future cost
SUB-TOTAL your income needs:	£	

3.1.2 Income needs for children living with you or provided for by you.

INCLUDE:
- Only those income needs that are different to those of your household shown above

Item	Current cost	Estimated future cost
SUB-TOTAL children's income needs:	£	
TOTAL of ALL income needs:	£	0.00

APPENDIX 7

3 Financial Requirements *Part 2 Capital needs*

3.2 Set out below the reasonable future capital needs for yourself and for any children living with you or provided for by you.

3.2.1 Capital needs for yourself.

INCLUDE:
- All capital needs for yourself
- Capital needs for any children living with you or provided for by you only if these form part of your total capital needs (e.g. housing, car, etc.)

Item	Cost
SUB-TOTAL your capital needs:	£

3.2.2 Capital needs for children living with you or provided for by you.

INCLUDE:
- Only those capital needs that are different to those of your household shown above

Item	Cost
SUB-TOTAL your children's capital needs:	£
TOTAL of ALL capital needs:	£ 0.00

FORM E

4 Other Information

4.1 Details of any significant changes in your assets or income.

At both sections 4.1.1 and 4.1.2, INCLUDE:
- ALL assets held both within and outside England and Wales
- The disposal of any asset

4.1.1 Significant changes in assets or income during the LAST 12 months.

4.1.2 Significant changes in assets or income likely to occur during the NEXT 12 months.

4.2 Brief details of the standard of living enjoyed by you and your spouse/civil partner during the marriage/civil partnership.

APPENDIX 7

4.3 Are there any particular contributions to the family property and assets or outgoings, or to family life, or the welfare of the family that have been made by you, your partner or anyone else that you think should be taken into account? If there are any such items, briefly describe the contribution and state the amount, when it was made and by whom.

INCLUDE:
- Contributions already made
- Contributions that will be made in the foreseeable future

4.4 Bad behaviour or conduct by the other party will only be taken into account in very exceptional circumstances when deciding how assets should be shared after divorce/dissolution. If you feel it should be taken into account in your case, identify the nature of the behaviour or conduct below.

4.5 Give details of any other circumstances that you consider could significantly affect the extent of the financial provision to be made by or for you or any child of the family.

INCLUDE (the following list is not exhaustive):
- Earning capacity
- Disability
- Inheritance prospects
- Redundancy
- Retirement
- Any plans to marry, form a civil partnership or cohabit
- Any contingent liabilities

FORM E

4.6 If you have subsequently married or formed a civil partnership (or intend to) or are living with another person (or intend to), give brief details, so far as they are known to you, of his or her income, assets and liabilities.

Annual Income		Assets and Liabilities	
Nature of income	Value (if known, state whether gross or net))	Item	Value (if known)
Total income:	£	Total assets/liabilities:	£

APPENDIX 7

5 Order Sought

5.1 If you are able at this stage, specify what kind of orders you are asking the court to make. Even if you cannot be specific at this stage, if you are able to do so, indicate:
   a) If the family home is still owned, whether you are asking for it to be transferred to yourself or your spouse/civil partner or whether you are saying it should be sold
   b) Whether you consider this is a case for continuing spousal maintenance/maintenance for your civil partner or whether you see the case as being appropriate for a "clean break". *(A 'clean break' means a settlement or order which provides amongst other things, that neither you nor your spouse/civil partner will have any further claim against the income or capital of the other party. A 'clean break' does not terminate the responsibility of a parent to a child.)*
   c) Whether you are seeking a pension sharing or pension attachment order
   d) If you are seeking a transfer or settlement of any property or assets, identify the property or assets in question

5.2 If you are seeking a variation of an ante-nuptial or post-nuptial settlement or a relevant settlement made during, or in anticipation of, a civil partnership, identify the settlement, by whom it was made, its trustees and beneficiaries and state why you allege it is a settlement which the court can vary.

5.3 If you are seeking an avoidance of disposition order, or if you have already applied for such an order, identify the property to which the disposition relates and the person or body in whose favour the disposition is alleged to have been made.

FORM E

Sworn confirmation of the information

I _____ *(the above-named Applicant/Respondent)*

of _____ MAKE OATH and confirm that the information given above is a full, frank, clear and accurate disclosure of my financial and other relevant circumstances.

Sworn by the above named

at)
)
)
)
this   day of   20   ) ....

Before me, ...

A solicitor, commissioner for oaths, an Officer of the Court appointed by the Judge to take affidavits, a notary or duly authorised official.

Address all communications to the Court Manager of the Court and quote the case number. If you do not quote this number, your correspondence may be returned.

APPENDIX 7

SCHEDULE OF DOCUMENTS TO ACCOMPANY FORM E

The following list shows the documents you must attach to your Form E if applicable. You may attach other documents where it is necessary to explain or clarify any of the information that you give in the Form E.

Form E paragraph	Document	Attached	Not applicable	To follow
1.14	**Application to vary an order:** if applicable, attach a copy of the relevant order.			
2.1	**Matrimonial home valuation:** a copy of any valuation relating to the matrimonial home that has been obtained in the last six months.			
2.1	**Matrimonial home mortgage(s):** a recent mortgage statement in respect of each mortgage on the matrimonial home confirming the amount outstanding.			
2.2	**Any other property:** a copy of any valuation relating to each other property disclosed that has been obtained in the last six months.			
2.2	**Any other property:** a recent mortgage statement in respect of each mortgage on each other property disclosed confirming the amount outstanding.			
2.3	**Personal bank, building society and National Savings accounts:** copies of statements for the last 12 months for each account that has been held in the last twelve months, either in your own name or in which you have or have had any interest.			
2.4	**Other investments:** the latest statement or dividend counterfoil relating to each investment as disclosed in paragraph 2.4.			
2.5	**Life insurance (including endowment) policies:** a surrender valuation for each policy that has a surrender value as disclosed under paragraph 2.5.			
2.11	**Business interests:** a copy of the business accounts for the last two financial years for each business interest disclosed.			
2.11	**Business interests:** any documentation that is available to confirm the estimate of the current value of the business, for example, a letter from an accountant or formal valuation if that has been obtained.			
2.13	**Pension rights:** a recent statement showing the cash equivalent transfer value (CETV) provided by the trustees or managers of each pension arrangement that you have disclosed (or, in the case of the additional state pension, a valuation of these rights). If not yet available, attach a copy of the letter sent to the pension company or administrators requesting the information.			
2.15	**Employment income:** your P60 for the last financial year in respect of each employment that you have.			
2.15	**Employment income:** your last three payslips in respect of each employment that you have.			
2.15	**Employment income:** your last form P11D if you have been issued with one.			
2.16	**Self-employment or partnership income:** a copy of your last tax assessment or if that is not available, a letter from your accountant confirming your tax liability.			
2.16	**Self-employment or partnership income:** if net income from the last financial year and the estimated income for the next twelve months is significantly different, a copy of the management accounts for the period since your last accounts.			
State relevant Form E paragraph	Description of other documents attached:			

FORM E

Case no.

*Delete as appropriate

In the

*[High/County Court]
*[Principal Registry of the Family Division]

In the marriage/Civil Partnership between

who is the husband/wife/civil partner

and

who is the husband/wife/civil partner

Financial Statement on behalf of

who is the husband/wife/civil partner
and the Petitioner/Respondent in the
divorce/dissolution suit

This statement is filed by

who are solicitors for the husband/wife/civil partner

Form E Financial Statement (12.05)   HMCS

APPENDIX 8

Form E Notes for guidance

Form E
(Financial Statement in Ancillary Relief Proceedings)
Notes for guidance

About these notes:
- They explain some of the terms used in Form E that may be unfamiliar to you.
- The most important notes are in **bold**. Please do not ignore them.
- There is also a checklist in Form E to tell you which documents you will need to attach to the form.

These notes are only a guide to help you complete Form E. If you require further help you should speak to a solicitor, Citizens Advice Bureau, legal advice centre or law centre. Public funding of your legal costs may be available from the Community Legal Service Fund.

Please note, while court staff will help on procedural matters, they cannot offer any legal advice.

Introduction

If you or your spouse/ civil partner apply to the court for a financial order, both you and the other person **must** complete a separate Form E. The purpose of the form is to enable you to provide the court with full details of your financial arrangements.

You must send your completed Form E to the court and a copy to the other party, no later than 35 days before the date of the First Appointment. The date of the First Appointment can be found on Form C (Notice of a first appointment) which will be sent to you by the court.

You should be aware that the court might make an order for costs against you if you do not follow the deadlines for filing Form E.

If you and the other person have agreed about the financial matters there is no need for either of you to complete a Form E. Your agreement (sometimes known as a consent application) should be submitted to the Court prior to the First Appointment.

You should ensure that any documents relevant to this application are attached to Form E.

FORM E NOTES FOR GUIDANCE

1 General Information

Section 1.6: The court can provide you with these dates if you are unsure. Please quote your case number when asking for details.

Section 1.11: You only need to provide details if you or your child(ren) are suffering from any form of physical or mental disability. The court does not need to know about minor ailments.

Section 1.13: You need to supply details of any Child Support Agency assessments, agreements or court orders in respect of child support.

Also, if an application has been made to the Child Support Agency but not decided let the court know the result of the application, when it has been decided. If you need help to complete this section you can contact the National Enquiry Line of the Child Support Agency (Telephone 0845 7133133).

Section 1.15: You should give details of any other previous or current court cases between you and the other person. (It would also help the court if you provided brief details about the nature of these proceedings e.g. residence/contact in respect of the children.)

2 Financial Details

Section 2.1: You need to tell the court if you own or part own the family home (or any other property) and how much you think it is currently worth.

Details of the Land Registry title number and of the balance outstanding on any mortgage can be obtained by contacting the company with whom you have your mortgage. You can also obtain your Land Registry Title number from HM Land Registry, Lincoln's Inn Fields, London, WC2A 3PH (Telephone 020 7917 8888).

Section 2.3: Overdrawn bank accounts should be included in this section and not in section 2.9.

Section 2.10: For further information about Capital Gains Tax you can contact the HM Revenue and Customs who produce a free booklet called "Capital Gains Tax - an introduction". (Reference number - CGT1). Telephone 0845 9000404. You may want to seek legal and/or financial advice to answer this question.

Section 2.13: You will need to provide the court with details of all your pension rights, including those relating to your present and/or a previous job and/or resulting from membership of a personal (i.e. privately arranged) pension scheme.

If you have been provided with a valuation of your pension rights or benefits by the person responsible for your pension scheme you must attach a copy of it to Form E. (You may only use a valuation if it will not be more than a year old at the date of the first appointment). If you do not have this information, or the valuation you have will be more than a year old, you should write to the person responsible for your pension scheme and ask them to provide you with an up to date valuation. If the valuation is not available a copy of your letter requesting the valuation should be attached to Form E together with any reply from the pension scheme letting you know when this information will be available. If you have more than one pension plan or scheme you must provide this information for each one.

APPENDIX 8

The administrators of your scheme will be able to provide the information requested. **It may help to send the administrators a copy of section 2.13 of Form E.**

If you have an occupational pension scheme your employer will be able to provide you with the name and address of your pension administrators.

If you have a personal pension scheme (i.e. privately arranged) you should contact the administrators directly. If you are unsure of the details of your pension scheme you can contact:

The Pensions Schemes Registry
PO Box 1NN
Newcastle Upon Tyne
NE99 1NN

You should obtain a valuation of your additional state pension by requesting form BR20 from the address or telephone number below. You may also find it useful to request a forecast of the benefit to be paid by filling in form BR19 which you can also get from the address or phone number below or from any social security office.

Future Pensions Centre
The Pension Service
Tyneview Park
Whitley Road
Newcastle upon Tyne
NE98 1BA

Telephone number: 0845 3000168

> **Note:** Please make certain that you provide the court with your National Insurance Number. If the Form E that you are using does not include a box for this, please write this information in below the 'Name and Address of your pension scheme, plan or policy').

Section 2.14: "unrealisable assets" are those which cannot be easily converted into cash.

A solicitor will be able to advise you whether an asset is realisable or not. If in doubt, the asset should be mentioned in this section and the judge will decide.

Section 2.20 and 2.21: This is a summary of the information you have provided previously in Parts 1-10 of Form E. To complete it, you will need to refer back to each section again and only note the figure in the box with an alphabetical reference number next to it. For example, you will find the figure for (A) on page 4, in section 2.1.

3 Financial Requirements

Section 3.1: In the box headed "Income needs of yourself" you need to add the weekly, monthly or annual cost of each item. It should include, for example, finance payments where a car or household goods are being purchased on credit. *(If you run out of space when completing this section, please continue on a separate sheet of paper and attach to Form E, clearly numbering the section they refer to e.g. section 2.3 cont.)*

Section 3.2: You should also include in this section details of any items you hope to buy in the near future. For example, the reasonable cost of buying a new car or house.

Page 3

270

FORM E NOTES FOR GUIDANCE

4 Other Information

Section 4.2: The term "standard of living" invites you to express your own view or opinion. Try to give details of the kind of lifestyle you and the family enjoyed during your marriage or civil partnership. For example, the number of holidays you took over the course of a year.

Section 4.3: The term "contribution" does not refer solely to financial contributions and you can include the fact that you looked after the family home and cared for the family unit.

Section 4.6: If you have remarried or subsequently formed a civil partnership (or intend to) or are living with another person (or intend to) you will need to complete this section. It is important that the court making the decision has as complete a picture of the available finances as possible.

5 Order sought

You may wish to seek legal advice to answer the questions in this part of Form E. Public funding of your legal costs may be available from the Community Legal Service Fund.

Section 5.3: An 'Avoidance of Disposition Order' is an order that the court can make to set aside or overturn a transaction that has already taken place (or that you believe is about to take place) e.g. a sale/mortgage of land or other asset. You might consider this transaction to be a step intended by the other party to deprive you of the benefit of sharing in it, or may have the effect of reducing the assets available for distribution between you.

Schedule of Documents to Accompany Form E

Now that you have completed Form E please ensure that copies of the items listed in the checklist, relevant to your application, are attached.

You should not attach original documents but keep them available for inspection by the other party and the Court.

If you are unable to attach any copy documents to Form E when you file it you *must* add a short note to Form E explaining why you were unable to attach the copy document.

Please note – any copy documents that you wish to attach to Form E will need to be sworn as an exhibit or attachment to Form E.

Sworn confirmation of the information you have provided in Form E is true

This section must be completed. You have to confirm either by swearing on oath or by affirming that the information you have provided is a **full, frank, clear and accurate disclosure** of your financial and other relevant circumstances. You can do this either before a member of the court staff (this is free) or before a solicitor or commissioner for oaths (there will be a fee for this).

Index

accumulation and maintenance (A&M) settlements 4.1.5
agricultural property relief (APR) 4.1.5, 4.3.1
  50 per cent relief 4.3.3
  100 per cent relief 4.3.3
  agricultural value 4.3.1
  business property relief and 4.3.1
  clawback 4.3.5
  conditions to be satisfied 4.3.2
  farmhouses 4.3.4
  hold over relief 2.2.4
  rate 4.3.3
  replacement property 4.3.5
Alternative Investment Market (AIM) shares
  capital gains tax 2.4, 10.2.4
  gifts of 2.2.4
  market value 10.2.4
animals
  capital gains tax 2.1.7
anti-avoidance rules
  capital gains tax
    non-UK resident companies 9.5.2
    non-UK resident trusts 9.5.2
  income tax
    settlements 9.5.1
    shadow director problems 9.5.1
    transfers abroad 9.5.1
  inheritance tax 9.5.3
antiques
  capital gains tax 2.1.6, 2.1.7

betting winnings
  capital gains tax 2.1.6
boats
  capital gains tax 2.1.6

business asset taper relief (BATR) 2.3.1
business property relief (BPR) 4.1.5, 4.2.1
  50 per cent relief 4.2.1
  100 per cent relief 4.2.1
  agricultural property relief and 4.3.1
  clawback 4.2.4
  investment businesses 4.2.2
  non-business assets 4.2.3
  rates 4.2.1
  replacement property 4.2.5
buy-to-let investment property 6.5

capital gains tax 2
  allowable losses 2.1.1
  animals and livestock 2.1.7
  annual exemption 2.1.1, 2.1.3, 2.1.8, 3.3.3
  anti-avoidance rules
    non-UK resident companies 9.5.2
    non-UK resident trusts 9.5.2
  antiques 2.1.6, 2.1.7
  asset 2
    capital sum derived from 2
    disposals 2
    loss, destruction etc 2
    transfers *see* transfers of assets
  betting winnings 2.1.6
  boats 2.1.6
  business asset taper relief (BATR) 2.3.1
  buy-to-let investment properties 6.5
  capital losses 2.1.1, 2.1.8
  capital sum derived from asset 2
  cars 2.1.6, 2.1.7
  cash 2.1.6
  chattels 2.1.7
    wasting assets 2.1.7
  choses in action 3.4.6

INDEX

civil partners 2.1.5
clogged losses 2.1.8, 3.2.3
cohabitees 2.1.5
    entrepreneurs' relief 2.3.5
    postponement/deferral of chargeable gains 2.1.9
    reliefs 2.1.10
    transfers between 1.1, 2.1.5, 2.1.8, 3.5
companies resident in UK 2.1.1
computation 2, 2.1.4
corporate bonds or options 2.1.6, 2.4
    entrepreneurs' relief 2.3.4
court orders for payments of lump sums 2.1.11
death 2
debentures 2.1.6
debt, disposal of 2.1.6
deferral of chargeable gains 2.1.9
deferred annuities 2.1.6
disposal
    meaning 2
    otherwise than by way of bargain at arm's length 2.1.5, 2.2.2
enterprise investment schemes (EISs) 2.1.6, 2.4
entrepreneurs' relief 2.1.10, 2.2.5, 2.3
    application to company takeovers, etc. 2.3.4
    associated disposals 2.3.3
    availability 2.3.2
    civil partners 2.3.5
    cohabitees 2.3.5
    hold over relief and 2.3.6
    holiday homes 6.5
    spouses 2.3.5
    trading business 2.3.2
exempt assets 2.1.6
family companies *see* family companies
family home 2.1.6, 6.1.1
    asset transfers and deferred consideration 3.4.6
    beneficial ownership 6.1.1
    deferred charges 2, 3.4.9, 3.4.7, 6.2.4
    establishing ownership 6.1.1
    Mesher orders 6.2.2
    principal private residence relief 2.1.10, 6.1.5, 6.3.1

farmhouses
    hold over relief 6.1.5
    as main residence and business asset 6.1.5
fine wines and spirits 2.1.6
foreign currency 2, 2.1.6
general principles 2.1
gifts otherwise than by way of a bargain at arm's length 2.1.5
gilt-edged securities 2.1.6
government non-marketable securities 2.1.6
hold over relief 2.2.1, 10.2.7
    calculation of gain 2.2.5
    choses in action 3.4.6
    claims under TCGA 1992 2.2.3
    entrepreneurs' relief and 2.3.6
    farmhouse, transfer of 6.1.5
    gifts of business assets 2.2.4
    Haines v. *Hill and another* 2.2.9
    making claims 2.2.8
    nature 2.2.2
    reductions in held over gain 2.2.6
    transfers made on divorce 2.2.7
    valuation of assets 2.2.8
holiday homes
    entrepreneurs' relief 6.5
    offshore company owns foreign holiday property 9.7.2
indexation 2.1.1
individual savings account investments 2.1.6, 2.4
individuals 2.1.1
investment bonds 8.2.1
investment portfolio 2.4
land and property
    buy-to-let investment property 6.5
    exchange of interests in *see* land and property
    family home *see* family home
    holiday homes 6.5
life assurance policies 2.1.6, 8.2.1
loan stock 2.1.6
lottery winnings 2.1.6
lump sum payments, court orders for 2.1.11
maintenance payments 5.2.2

273

INDEX

market value 2.2.5, 5.3.2, 6.1, 9.1.2, 10.2
    AIM shares 10.2.4
    assets generally 10.2.1
    HMRC agreement 10.2.7
    hold over relief 2.2.8
    imputation 2.1.5
    listed securities 10.2.2
    Mesher orders 6.2.2
    offshore structures 9.7.1
    transactions between connected parties 10.2.5
    transactions between unconnected persons 10.2.6
    transfers below market price 2.1.5
    transfers at less than 2.1
    unit trusts 10.2.3
    unquoted securities 10.2.4
medals 2.1.6
Mesher orders 6.2.2
motor cars 2.1.6, 2.1.7
offset of losses 2.1.1, 2.1.8
offshore funds 2.4
offshore structures and anti-avoidance legislation 9.5.2
personal equity plan shares 2.1.6
personal injury winnings and damages 2.1.6
personalised number plate 2.1.7
persons liable 2.1.1
pianos 2.1.6
postponement of chargeable gains 2.1.9
premium bonds 2.1.6
racehorses 2.1.6
rate 2.1.2, 2.3.1, 4.1.9
reliefs 2.1.10
remittance basis and 2.1.3, 2.1.8
residence 2.1.1, 2.1.8
    companies resident in UK 2.1.1
    individuals 2.1.1
    non-UK resident companies 9.5.2
    non-UK resident individuals 2.1.1, 2.1.8
    offshore structures and anti-avoidance legislation 9.5.2
    temporary non-residents 2.1.1
    trusts 2.1.1, 9.5.2
    UK resident companies 2.1.1
    UK resident trusts 2.1.1

savings certificates 2.1.6
secured maintenance orders 5.3.2
settlement, definition 4.1.7
shares
    AIM shares, valuation 10.2.4
    enterprise investment scheme private company 2.1.6
    personal equity plan shares 2.1.6
    unquoted shares 2.1.8
ships 2.1.7
shotguns 2.1.6, 2.1.7
stamp collection 2.1.7
tangible moveable property 2.1.6
temporary non-residents 2.1.1
territorial scope 9.1.2
transfers of assets *see* transfers of assets
Treasury gilts 2.4
trusts 4.1.12
    disposals 2
    former spouse/civil partner 4.1.9
    minor children 4.1.9
    non-UK resident trusts 9.5.2
    residence 2.1.1, 9.5.2
    UK resident trusts 2.1.1, 2.1.3
unquoted shares 2.1.8
venture capital trusts, shares in 2.4
wasting assets 2.1.7
wines and spirits 2.1.6
yachts 2.1.7

cars *see* motor cars
cash
    capital gains tax 2.1.6
chattels
    capital gains tax 2.1.7
    definition 2.1.7
    wasting assets 2.1.7
child tax credit 5.4.1, 5.4.3
children
    capital gains tax and 4.1.9
    court orders for maintenance 4.1.8
    income tax and 4.1.9
    inheritance tax and 4.1.5, 4.1.8, 4.1.10
    lifetime transfers to minor children 4.1.5
    settlements made under Children Act 1989 4.1.10
    transfers for children and grandchildren 9.6.2
    trusts for minor children 4.1.9

INDEX

civil partnership 1.1
cohabitees 1.1
    capital gains tax 2.1.5
        entrepreneurs' relief 2.3.5
        postponement/deferral of
            chargeable gains 2.1.9
        reliefs 2.1.10
        transfers between 1.1, 2.1.5,
            2.1.8, 3.5
collaborative legal process 1.2
corporate bonds or options
    capital gains tax 2.1.6, 2.4
        entrepreneurs' relief 2.3.4
corporation tax 2.1.1, 8.4.5, 8.4.4, 8.4.1
    contingent 10.10
currency *see* foreign currency

death
    capital gains tax 2
    inheritance tax 4.1, 4.1.1, 4.1.6
debentures
    capital gains tax 2.1.6
debt, disposal of
    capital gains tax 2.1.6
domicile 9.2.3
    of choice 9.2.3
    inheritance tax 4.1, 4.1.5, 9.1.3
    jurisdiction and 9.2.3
    of origin 9.2.3
    see also remittance basis of
        taxation; residence

enterprise investment schemes (EISs)
    capital gains tax 2.1.6, 2.4
entrepreneurs' relief (ER) 2.1.10,
    2.2.5, 2.3.1
    application to company takeovers,
        etc. 2.3.4
    associated disposals 2.3.3
    availability 2.3.2
    civil partners 2.3.5
    cohabitees 2.3.5
    hold over relief and 2.3.6
    holiday homes 6.5
    spouses 2.3.5
    trading business 2.3.2

family companies 8.4
    acquiring separated spouse's/civil
        partner's shares in company 8.4.5
        buy-back of shares 8.4.5
        formation of new company to
            acquire one share 8.4.5

        options used as part of
            deferred or structured
            share purchase 8.4.5
        splitting up company
            currently owned by both
            spouses 8.4.5
        transfer or sale of shares 8.4.5
        transfer of trade between
            companies 8.4.5
    close companies 8.4.1
    jointly held shares 8.4.3
    tax on extraction of funds 8.4.4
        beneficial loan followed by
            dividend 8.4.4
        bonus or increased
            remuneration 8.4.4
        dividend 8.4.4
        share repurchase by the
            company 8.4.4
        withdrawal of director's loan
            to company 8.4.4
    taxation of sums received 8.4.2
    valuation, in court
        proceedings 10.7
family home 6.1
    absence of owner due to
        employment 6.1.5
    business use 6.1.5
    capital gains tax 2.1.6, 6.1.1
        asset transfers and deferred
            consideration 3.4.6
        beneficial ownership 6.1.1
        deferred charges 2, 3.4.9,
            3.4.7, 6.2.4
        establishing ownership 6.1.1
        Mesher orders 6.2.2
        principal private residence
            relief 2.1.10, 6.1.5, 6.3.1
    division of assets 6.1.4
    farmhouses
        agricultural property relief
            4.3.4
        hold over relief 6.1.5
        inheritance tax 4.3.4
    hold over relief 6.1.5
    inheritance tax
        farmhouses 4.3.4
        Mesher orders 4.1.5, 6.2.3
    jurisdiction 6.1
    letting 6.1.5
    Mesher orders 6.2.3, 6.2.1
        capital gains tax 6.2.2
        inheritance tax 4.1.5, 6.2.3

INDEX

principal private residence
  relief 6.2.2
more than one property 6.3
  final period of exemption 6.3.2
  nomination of principal
    private residence 6.3.1,
    6.3.3, 6.5
  planning point 6.3.2
ownership
  establishing for CGT
    purposes 6.1.1
  joint tenants 6.1.2
  practical effects of beneficial
    ownership 6.1.3
  tenants in common 6.1.2
principal private residence relief
  (PPR) 2.1.10, 6.3.1
  choses in action 3.4.6
  HMRC view 6.1.5
  joint but unrelated
    owner-occupiers 6.1.5
  last 36 months of ownership
    6.1.5
  Mesher orders 6.2.2
  non-occupation relief 6.1.5
  occupation by non-owning
    spouse 6.1.5
  purpose 6.1.5
  qualifying residence 6.1.5
  restrictions 6.1.5
  transfer as part of financial
    settlement 6.1.5
sales between former spouses/civil
  partners after
  divorce/dissolution 6.2.5
stamp duty land tax exemption 6.4
transfer of property subject to a
  deferred charge 6.2.4
farmhouses
  agricultural property relief 4.3.4
  capital gains tax 6.1.5
  hold over relief 6.1.5
  inheritance tax 4.3.4
  as main residence and business
    asset 6.1.5
  market value 4.3.4
fine wines and spirits
  capital gains tax 2.1.6
foreign currency
  capital gains tax 2, 2.1.6
foreign tax 9.1.4
Form E 1.2, App 7

capital gains tax 1.2, 2.1.6, 2.2.1
  exempt assets 2.1.6
net values 10.1
notes for guidance 1.2, App 8

gifts with reservation of benefit (GROB)
  inheritance tax 4.4.1
gilt-edged securities
  capital gains tax 2.1.6
government non-marketable securities
  capital gains tax 2.1.6

hold over relief *see* capital gains tax
holiday homes
  capital gains tax 6.5, 9.7.2
  entrepreneurs' relief 6.5
  offshore company owns foreign
    holiday property 9.7.2

income tax
  anti-avoidance rules
    settlements 9.5.1
    shadow director problems 9.5.1
    transfers abroad 9.5.1
  family companies *see* family
    companies
  investment bonds 8.2.2
  life assurance policies 8.2.2
  maintenance payments 5.2.1
  married couples 1.1
  offshore structures and anti-
    avoidance rules 9.5
  secured maintenance orders 5.3.1
  settlement, definition 4.1.7
  territorial scope 9.1.1
  trusts 4.1.12
    former spouse/civil partner
      4.1.9, 9.6.4
    minor children 4.1.9
indexation 2.1.1, 2.1.8
individual savings account investments
  capital gains tax 2.1.6, 2.4
inheritance tax 4.1
  accumulation and maintenance
    (A&M) settlements 4.1.5
  agricultural property relief 4.3.1
    50 per cent relief 4.3.3
    100 per cent relief 4.3.3
    agricultural value 4.3.1
    business property relief
      and 4.3.1
    clawback 4.3.5

276

INDEX

conditions to be satisfied 4.3.2
farmhouses 4.3.4
rate 4.3.3
replacement property 4.3.5
anti-avoidance rules 9.5.3
business property relief 4.1.5, 4.2.1
50 per cent relief 4.2.1
100 per cent relief 4.2.1
agricultural property relief and 4.3.1
clawback 4.2.4
investment businesses 4.2.2
non-business assets 4.2.3
rates 4.2.1
replacement property 4.2.5
charge to 4.1.1
court orders for maintenance of children 4.1.8
death 4.1, 4.1.1, 4.1.6
domicile 4.1, 4.1.5, 9.1.3
entry charge 4.1.4
exit charge 4.1.4
family companies *see* family companies
family home
farmhouses 4.3.4
Mesher orders 4.1.5, 6.2.3
farmhouses 4.3.4
gifts with reservation of benefit (GROB) 4.4.1
pre-owned assets (POAT) 4.4.2
lifetime chargeable transfers 4.1.1, 4.1.4
lifetime exemptions
dispositions no intended to confer gratuitous benefit 4.1.5
family maintenance 4.1.5
general exemptions 4.1.5
lifetime transfers to minor children 4.1.5
Mesher orders 4.1.5
normal expenditure out of income 4.1.5
settlements created on family breakdown 4.1.5
lifetime trusts 4.1.4
maintenance payments 4.1.10, 4.1.5, 4.1.8, 4.4.2, 5.2.3
market value 10.3
Mesher orders 4.1.5, 6.2.3

nil rate band (NRB) 4.1.2, 4.1.5
death 4.1.7
transfer 4.1.2
offshore structures and anti-avoidance rules 9.5.3
overseas settlements 4.1.11
potentially exempt transfers (PETs) 4.1.1, 4.1.3, 4.1.5
death 4.1.6
pre-owned assets (POAT) 4.4.2
rate 4.1.1, 4.1.4, 4.1.5, 4.1.6
residence 4.1
secured maintenance orders 5.3.3
settlement, meaning 4.1.7
settlements made under Children Act 1989 4.1.10
taper relief 2.1.2, 4.1.1
territorial scope 9.1.3
transfer of assets between connected persons
couples married but separated 3.4.11
post decree absolute 3.5.1
transfer of value (ToV) 4.1, 4.1.1
meaning 4.1.1
trusts 4.1, 4.1.12
former spouse/civil partner 4.1.9
lifetime chargeable transfers 4.1.4
lifetime trusts 4.1.4
minor children 4.1.9
overseas trusts 4.1.11
interests in land and property *see* land and property
investment bonds
capital gains tax 8.2.1
income tax 8.2.2

land and property
buy-to-let investment property 6.5
exchange of interests in 6.6
land that is not a dwelling house 6.6.2
non-business interests 6.6.1
roll over relief on disposal of joint interest in land 6.6.2
trade use 6.6.3
family home *see* family home
holiday homes 6.5, 9.7.2

INDEX

life assurance policies
    capital gains tax 2.1.6, 8.2.1
    income tax 8.2.2
    life assurance premium relief 8.2.3
livestock
    capital gains tax 2.1.7
loan stock
    capital gains tax 2.1.6
lottery winnings
    capital gains tax 2.1.6
lump sum payments
    borrowing to fund, withdrawal of capital by sole traders/partnerships 8.3.1
    court orders for, capital gains tax and 2.1.11

maintenance payments 5.2
    borrowing to fund, withdrawal of capital by sole traders/partnerships 8.3.1
    capital gains tax 5.2.2
    income tax 5.2.1
    inheritance tax 4.1.10, 4.1.5, 4.1.8, 4.4.2, 5.2.3
    see also secured maintenance
market value 10.1
    buy-back of shares 8.4.5
    capital gains tax 2.2.5, 5.3.2, 6.1, 9.1.2, 10.2
        AIM shares 10.2.4
        assets generally 10.2.1
        HMRC agreement to market value 10.2.7
        hold over relief 2.2.8
        imputation 2.1.5
        listed securities 10.2.2
        Mesher orders 6.2.2
        offshore structures 9.7.1
        transactions between connected parties 10.2.5
        transactions between unconnected persons 10.2.6
        transfers below market price 2.1.5
        transfers at less than market value 2.1, 2.2.5
        unit trusts 10.2.3
        unquoted securities 10.2.4
    connected persons rule and 3.2.1, 3.2.2

    contingent corporation tax 10.10
    deemed market value rule 3.1
    family companies, valuation in court proceedings 10.7
    farmhouses 4.3.4
    HMRC agreement 10.1, 10.2.7
    inheritance tax 10.3
    more than one property 6.3.1
    options, grant of 8.4.5
    partnership interests 10.9
    private company shares
        agreed valuation binding on both parties for tax purposes 10.4
        valuation bases 10.5
    property subject to charge or mortgage 7.4
    quasi-partnership companies 10.6
    sales occurring between former spouses or civil partners after divorce or dissolution 6.2.5
    trading stock 3.3.3
    transfer or sale of shares 8.4.5
    transfers after decree absolute 3.5.1
    transfers between couples married but separated 3.4.1, 3.4.5
    transfers between couples married and living together 3.3.1, 3.3.4, 3.3.3
    undivided shares in jointly held land and property 10.7
    valuation bases for private company shares 10.5
        assets basis 10.5.2
        dividend yield basis 10.5.2
        earnings basis 10.5.1
        going concern basis 10.5.2
        going concern net asset basis 10.5.2
        influential shareholdings 10.5.1
        net asset basis 10.5.2, 10.10
        non-trading companies 10.5.2
        profitable trading companies 10.5.1
        shareholdings of less than 100 per cent 10.5.2
        trading companies 10.5.2
        uninfluential shareholdings 10.5.2
matrimonial home *see* family home

medals
    capital gains tax 2.1.6
mediation 1.2
Mesher **orders** *see* family home
motor cars
    capital gains tax 2.1.6, 2.1.7
    personalised number
        plate 2.1.7
offshore funds
    capital gains tax 2.4
offshore structures 9.7
    anti-avoidance rules *see* anti-
        avoidance rules
    offshore company owns foreign
        holiday property 9.7.2
    offshore trust owns offshore
        company owning UK property
        9.7.1

partnerships
    tax relief on borrowing to fund
        lump sum/maintenance
        payments 8.3.1
    valuation of interests 10.9
pensions 8.1
    annual allowance 8.1
    attachment orders 8.1.2
    cash equivalent 8.1.3
    lifetime allowance 8.1, 8.2.1
    pension credit 8.1.3
    pension debit 8.1.3
    pension sharing 8.1.3
    registered pensions 8.1
personal equity plan shares
    capital gains tax 2.1.6
personal injury winnings and
    damages
    capital gains tax 2.1.6
personalised number plate
    capital gains tax 2.1.7
pianos
    capital gains tax 2.1.6
polygamous marriages
    transfers of assets 3.3.2
        no gain, no loss 3.3.2
pre-owned assets (POAT)
    inheritance tax 4.4.2
premium bonds
    capital gains tax 2.1.6
principal private residence relief *see*
    family home
property *see* land and property

racehorses
    capital gains tax 2.1.6
remittance basis of taxation 9.3
    capital gains tax and 2.1.3, 2.1.8
    claims and associated
        costs 9.3.2
    divorce *see* remittance basis of
        taxation: divorce
    nominated income and
        gains 9.3.3
    remittance
        deemed 9.3.3, 9.4.2
        meaning 9.4
        relevant person 9.4.1
        'remitted to the United
            Kingdom', meaning
            9.4.2
remittance basis of taxation:
divorce 9.6
    professional fees 9.6.3
    transfer of funds for spouse 9.6.1
        payment constituting
            consideration 9.6.1
        settlement of relevant debt
            9.6.1
        structuring the
            payment 9.6.1
    transfers for children and
        grandchildren 9.6.2
    trust created for spouse 9.6.4
residence
    capital gains tax 2.1.1, 2.1.8
        companies resident in UK
            2.1.1
        individuals 2.1.1
        non-UK resident companies
            9.5.2
        non-UK resident individuals
            2.1.1, 2.1.8
        offshore structures and
            anti-avoidance legislation
            9.5.2
        temporary non-residents 2.1.1
        trusts 2.1.1, 9.5.2
        UK resident
            companies 2.1.1
        UK resident trusts 2.1.1
    inheritance tax 4.1
    intentions of taxpayer 9.2.1
    meaning 9.2
    ordinarily resident in UK 9.2.2
    physical presence test 9.2.1

INDEX

UK residence 9.2.1
  companies 2.1.1
  trusts 2.1.1
see also domicile

savings certificates
  capital gains tax 2.1.6
secured maintenance 5.1, 5.3
  capital gains tax 5.3.2
  income tax 5.3.1
  inheritance tax 5.3.3
  see also maintenance payments
settlement
  meaning 4.1.7
ships
  capital gains tax 2.1.7
shotguns
  capital gains tax 2.1.6, 2.1.7
sole traders
  tax relief on borrowing to fund lump sum/maintenance payments 8.3.1
stamp collection
  capital gains tax 2.1.7
stamp duty 7.1
stamp duty land tax 6.4, 7.1
  application 7.1
  exemptions 6.4, 7.1, 7.2, 7.4
  family home 6.4
  gifts 7.5
  loan from share owner 7.7
  property subject to charge or mortgage 7.4
  shares subject to a debt 7.3
  transfer of property on winding up 7.7
  transfers of shares/property to shareholder as part of liquidation of company 7.6

tax credits 1.1, 5.4
  child tax credit 5.4.1, 5.4.3
  permanent separation 5.4.2
  tax year of separation 5.4.3
  working tax credit 5.4.1
transfers of assets
  connected persons *see* transfers of assets between connected persons
  deemed market value rule 3.1
  general transfers 3.1
transfers of assets between connected persons 2.1.5, 2.1.8, 3.2

cohabitees 1.1, 2.1.5, 2.1.8, 3.5
couples married but separated 3.4
  assets transfers and deferred consideration 3.4.6
  date of transfer 3.4.3
  deferred charges 3.4.7
  establishing date of separation 3.4.2
  fixed deferred charge 3.4.9
  inheritance tax 3.4.11
  timing of transfer 3.4.1
  transfers after tax year of separation 3.4.5
  transfers in tax year of separation 3.4.4
  unascertainable future consideration 3.4.8
  valuation of unascertainable consideration 3.4.8, 3.4.10
couples married and living together
  meaning 3.3.4
  no gain, no loss 3.3.2
  polygamous marriages 3.3.2
  tax compliance issues 3.3.5
  trading stock 3.3.3
losses on disposals 3.2.3
market value 10.2.5
meaning of 'connected persons' 3.2.2
polygamous marriages 3.3.2
  no gain, no loss 3.3.2
post decree absolute 3.5.1
  inheritance tax 3.5.2
rule 3.2.1
Treasury gilts 2.4
trusts
  capital gains tax 4.1.12
    disposals 2
    former spouse/civil partner 4.1.9
    minor children 4.1.9
    non-UK resident trusts 9.5.2
    residence 2.1.1, 9.5.2
    UK resident trusts 2.1.1, 2.1.3
  former spouse/civil partner 4.1.9, 9.6.4
  income tax 4.1.12
    trusts for former spouse/civil partner 4.1.9, 9.6.4
    trusts for minor children 4.1.9

INDEX

inheritance tax 4.1, 4.1.12
    former spouse/civil partner 4.1.9
    lifetime chargeable transfers 4.1.4
    lifetime trusts 4.1.4
    minor children 4.1.9
    overseas trusts 4.1.11
minor children 4.1.9
offshore trust owns offshore company owning UK property 9.7.1
remittance basis: divorce 9.6.4

valuation *see* market value
venture capital trusts (VCTs)
    shares in 2.4

wasting assets
    capital gains tax 2.1.7
wines and spirits
    capital gains tax 2.1.6
working tax credit 5.4.1

yachts
    capital gains tax 2.1.7